What's

Cooking

BURT WOLF

Simon and Schuster
New York London Toronto Sydney Tokyo

SIMON AND SCHUSTER
Simon & Schuster Building
Rockefeller Center
1230 Avenue of the Americas
New York, New York 10020

Copyright © 1988 by Burton R. Wolf

SIMON AND SCHUSTER and colophon are registered trademarks
of Simon & Schuster Inc.

Designed by Irving Perkins Associates

Manufactured in the United States of America

10 9 8 7 6 5 4 3 2 1

Library of Congress Cataloging in Publication Data

Wolf, Burton.
  What's cooking? / Burt Wolf.
    p. cm.
  Includes index.
  1. Cookery. I. Title.
TX714.W64 1988   8-31675
641.5—dc19   CIP

ISBN 0-671-66584-7

Some of the recipes in this book appeared in *THE BEST
OF WHAT'S COOKING*, Copyright © 1985 by Burt Wolf.
Published by Acorn Associates, Ltd., 30 Lincoln Plaza,
New York, NY 10023

To Emily, Stephen, Andrew, and James.

Foreword

For over 20 years I have been writing, lecturing, and/or making television shows about eating and drinking. I have traveled around the world with my crew recording recipes, tips, and techniques from many skilled professionals. We have produced over 3,000 segments which are now being broadcast in all 50 of the United States, Canada, the Caribbean, Latin America, Europe, and the Far East. The material in this book was selected from my reports. All the original recipes were tested and in some cases modified for use in a home kitchen.

My objective was to produce a book that was informal and modest, containing a series of recipes that are worth their time, effort, and money.

None of this could have been achieved without the cooks, chefs, hotel and restaurant owners and managers, government and corporate communication personnel, authors, and editors who have shared their extensive knowledge with me. In addition I would like to acknowledge the substantial contributions of my researchers, producers, cameramen, sound and lighting technicians, and editors.

Burt Wolf

Contents

What's Cooking

Appetizers
and Dips

James Beard's Onion Cocktail Sandwiches

James Beard, the dean of twentieth-century American cooking, began his culinary career as a young man in the 1930s. An opera singer, he earned extra income as a caterer of cocktail parties. The kitchen in Beard's New York apartment was a converted closet, where he prepared hors d'oeuvres. Using the simplest ingredients—white bread, onions, mayonnaise, and parsley—he created his now classic onion cocktail sandwiches.

20 slices white bread
1 cup mayonnaise
2 large sweet mild onions, thinly sliced
1 cup finely minced fresh parsley

1 Using a 2-inch biscuit cutter or a glass with a 2-inch rim, cut out a circle from the center of each slice of bread.

2 Spread one side of each round with a thin coat of mayonnaise.

3 Arrange a slice of onion on a bread round and top with a second bread round, mayonnaise side down.

4 Lightly brush the edges of each sandwich with mayonnaise and roll the edges in the minced parsley.

MAKES 10 SANDWICHES

ABOUT MAYONNAISE

Mayonnaise has been made in the countries around the western Mediterranean Sea for hundreds of years. It's named after the town of Mahón, on the island of Minorca in the Spanish Balearic Islands. The Spanish say mayonnaise was invented there, but the French say they created the sauce and named it after a French naval victory near the port of Mahón.

Mayonnaise in its most basic form is a thick mixture of egg yolks and oil, which thickens as the oil is incorporated into the yolks. Technicallmayonnaise is an emulsification. The Spanish and French use olive oil, but any good vegetable oil or a blend of oils will do.

WHAT'S COOKING TIPS: HOW TO MAKE MAYONNAISE

1. The oldest method used to make mayonnaise is to pound the ingredients with a mortar and pestle. The classic French technique is to whisk the ingredients in a bowl. The modern cook can easily make mayonnaise in a blender or food processor.

2. Whether you use a blender or whisk the sauce by hand, there are a few tips you should know. First, choose the freshest eggs and the best quality vegetable oil, either corn, olive, peanut, soy, safflower, or sunflower. Always add the oil very slowly, drop by drop at first, then in a thin stream so that the eggs can incorporate the oil molecules.

3. Mayonnaise can curdle while you are making it if the oil is too cold or the eggs too warm, or if you pour the oil in too fast. You can correct this by stirring a fresh egg yolk in a separate bowl and slowly adding the curdled mayonnaise into the egg yolk, beating constantly.
Various ingredients can be added to mayonnaise to vary its flavor. Try fresh crushed garlic, fresh lemon juice, flavored vinegar, cayenne or roasted red peppers, fresh herbs, dry or prepared mustard. Mayonnaise can spoil quickly, but refrigerated will keep well for at least 1 week.

Eggplant Spread

2 tablespoons vegetable oil
3 large onions, coarsely
  chopped
3 garlic cloves, minced
2 large eggplants
2 green bell peppers
6 carrots
2 cups tomato ketchup
1 teaspoon salt
1 teaspoon freshly ground
  black pepper
1 tablespoon sugar
½ teaspoon cayenne pepper
½ cup minced fresh parsley
2 tablespoons chopped fresh
  dill
  Brown or black bread,
  toasted

1 In a large heavy pot heat the oil over medium heat. Sauté the onions until soft, about 5 minutes. Add the garlic and cook until pale gold, about 5 minutes more.

2 Meanwhile, prepare the vegetables. Remove the stem and blossom ends of the eggplants; cut the flesh into 1-inch cubes. Seed and core the peppers; cut into 1-inch squares. Scrape the carrots; cut into 1-inch lengths.

3 Add the green peppers and carrots to the onions, and sauté until lightly browned, adding more oil if necessary. Stir frequently and add a little water if necessary to prevent sticking.

4 Add the eggplant cubes. Cover and cook over very low heat for 1½ hours. Stir frequently and add oil and/or water as needed to prevent scorching.

5 When the vegetables are very soft, uncover and cook until any excess liquid evaporates. Mash coarsely. Stir in the ketchup.

6 Season with the salt, pepper, sugar, and cayenne. Stir in the parsley and dill and cook gently, stirring from time to time, for 10 minutes.

7 Let the spread come to room temperature before serving. Use on toasted brown or black bread.

MAKES 4 TO 6 CUPS

GARLIC AND THE VAMPIRES

During the 1300s, the Bubonic plague claimed the lives of one in three Europeans. Yet one group of people went largely untouched by the plague—the garlic vendors, who ate more garlic than anyone else and wore garlic bulbs around their necks. As the common belief was that the plague was spread by vampires, it was naturally assumed that vampires were afraid of garlic, and so avoided the vendors. In fact, garlic, in normal quantities, can act like a very mild antibiotic, but in the large quantities eaten by the vendors, apparently it was strong enough to protect many of them from the plague. But the myth persists that garlic can be used to ward off vampires.

ABOUT KETCHUP

Ketchup is believed to be Chinese in origin, and was first made with a base of mushrooms, rather than tomatoes. The Chinese word *Ke-tsiap* refers to the brine of pickled fish.

Today, ketchup usually has a spiced vinegar added to tomatoes. The grade of commercial ketchup is based on the percentage of tomato solids in the mix.

Guacamole

2 ripe avocados
2 tomatoes, cored, seeded, and chopped
1 medium onion, chopped
2 serrano chiles or green chiles, trimmed, seeded, and minced
2 sprigs cilantro, stems discarded, chopped
½ teaspoon salt
Tortilla chips

1 Cut the avocados in half and discard the pits. With a spoon, scoop the flesh into a bowl. Mash the pulp with a fork.

2 Stir in the tomatoes, onion, serrano chiles, cilantro, and salt.

3 Serve at room temperature with tortilla chips. If you refrigerate it, let it come to room temperature before serving.

MAKES ABOUT 2 CUPS

NOTE: If preparing guacamole ahead of time, place a sheet of plastic wrap directly on the surface to prevent the browning that occurs when avocado flesh comes in contact with air. A light coating of lemon juice on top of the finished guacamole will help hold its color.

ABOUT AVOCADOS

While the avocado is native to Central and South America, more avocados come from California than from any other part of the world. Their peak season is from January through April.

Avocados are highly digestible and provide vitamin A, several B vitamins, C, and E. There is a good amount of iron in avocados as well, and they are low in sodium. Avocados, however, are rich in fruit oil, which is a saturated fat. If you are on a low-saturated-fat diet (a good idea for most people), limit your intake of avocados.

Firm avocados can be ripened at home by leaving them in a sunny spot, or close them up in a paper bag and keep them in a warm spot. Check their progress daily. Avocados bruise easily, so store them carefully and avoid buying bruised ones because the quality of the flesh will be affected.

WHAT'S COOKING TIP: CANNED CHILES

When using canned chiles, buy whole ones rather than prechopped. By chopping them yourself, you'll get almost twice as much chile.

ABOUT CORIANDER

Both the leaves and seeds of the coriander herb are used. The leaves are called Chinese parsley or cilantro; the seeds are called coriander. The ancient Romans brought the herb back to Europe from the eastern Mediterranean. Its name comes from the Greek word for bedbug, because when the unripe seeds are bruised they give off a nauseating smell similar to that of the bug. Sugar-coated coriander seeds used to be served as candy in Scotland.

ABOUT CHILES

Chiles and sweet peppers belong to the same family. Both varieties start green and become red as they ripen. Sweet peppers become sweeter as they turn redder.

There are about 200 varieties of chiles, and they vary in flavor as well as hotness. Chiles can grow to over a foot long, and size is not necessarily a guide to hotness; very small chiles can be intensely hot.

The most common chile peppers are cayenne, jalapeño, poblano, Tobasco, yellow wax, and Hungarian paprika. The small, green serrano chile is the most common for sauces, or salsas.

Wash your hands well after handling chiles. They get their flavor from an oil called capsaicin, which can severely burn your eyes on contact. Capsaicin is the active ingredient in the military repellant called Mace. Dried chiles are not a substitute for fresh green chiles.

Chick-pea and Sesame Dip

4 cups cooked chick-peas
(garbanzo beans)
¼ cup cold water
¼ cup peanut oil
2 tablespoons sesame oil
1 cup tahini (sesame paste)
½ tablespoon ground cumin
Juice of 2 limes
2 dashes of Tabasco sauce
2 garlic cloves, crushed
1¼ teaspoons coarse salt
½–¾ cup red bell pepper strips
Pita or other bread, cut
into triangles, warmed or
toasted

1 In a food processor or blender combine the chick-peas, water, oils, tahini, cumin, lime juice, Tabasco, garlic, and salt. Puree until light and fluffy. If you are using a blender, the ingredients may be divided into 2 or 3 separate batches. Taste the dip and adjust the seasonings if necessary. If the mixture is too thick, add more lime juice or sesame oil.

2 Scrape into a decorative bowl and garnish with the pepper strips.

3 Serve with triangles of warm or toasted bread.

MAKES 6 CUPS

ABOUT CHICK-PEAS

The chick-pea is a member of the pea family, although it's not anything like a pea at all; it is more like a bean. Chick-peas are the hard seed found in the short, fat, hairy pods of the chick-pea plant. The seeds are large, almost round, and usually cream colored, beige, or yellow. The Spanish call them garbanzos, and the Italians call them ceci beans.

Chick-peas date back to ancient times. The Greek philosopher Plato thought that one of the reasons for the political problems of ancient Greece lay in the excessive luxury of Greek dining habits. He advised his fellow citizens to eat a more simple diet of figs, chick-peas, and broad beans.

Chick-peas are used extensively in the cuisines of Spanish and Latin countries, in North Africa, the Middle East, and Greece. They are an excellent source of low-fat protein, and they can be eaten whole in salads, soups, and stews, and ground in spreads and pastes.

ABOUT TAHINI

Tahini can be described as a roasted sesame seed butter, in the same way that peanut butter is a butter. Mature sesame seeds are harvested from the sesame plant, dried, roasted, and ground into a paste.

Tahini is a very common ingredient in Middle Eastern and North African cuisine. A dish of tahini mixed with ground chick-peas is called hummous bi tahini. An eggplant puree mixed with tahini is called baba ganouj.

Yogurt Cheese Spread with Scallions and Walnuts

8 cups plain yogurt
½ cup finely minced scallions
1½ cups coarsely chopped walnuts
Freshly ground black pepper
Pita bread triangles, crackers, celery, or endive

1 Line a colander with several large layers of dampened cheesecloth.

2 Place the yogurt in the cheesecloth. Set the colander in a bowl and refrigerate overnight. The moisture in the yogurt will drain out and the volume of the yogurt will reduce by half.

3 If you discover that the yogurt has become overly thick, beat in a little of the liquid that drained into the bowl. Stir in the scallions, walnuts, and pepper to taste.

4 Mound the mixture in a dish or bowl. Serve with triangles of pita bread or crackers, or use the mixture to stuff celery or endive spears.

MAKES ABOUT 4 CUPS

The ancient Romans believed that the walnut was a physical model of the brain. The hard shell was the skull, the papery partition was the membrane, and the nut itself represented the brain's two hemispheres.

The ancient Greeks, Persians, and Phoenicians traded walnuts throughout the Mediterranean. The feast of the goddess Diana was held under the branches of walnut trees. Walnuts, symbols of fertility, were often given as gifts at wedding parties. King Solomon grew walnut trees in his garden.

WHAT'S COOKING TIP: HOW TO STORE SOFT CHEESE

Soft cheeses such as yogurt cheese, cream cheese, Limburger, Liederkranz, Neufchâtel, and Boursin need to be handled correctly or they will dry out and go bad. When keeping the cheese overnight, place it in an airtight container and turn the cheese over every night so that one side does not get overexposed, causing the cheese to deteriorate. All soft cheeses should be held in the refrigerator and eaten as quickly as possible because they are not aged or cured to extend their longevity.

ABOUT WALNUTS

The walnut, a native of Persia, Europe, and North America, is second only to the almond in popularity and consumption. The major American species, the black walnut, is native to the Appalachians. The English walnut, which was brought to Europe by the Romans, is now grown mainly in California and is preferred by producers because it is easier to shell and is not quite so bitter.

The Franciscan fathers brought walnut trees to the first missions in California. Today, the California walnut industry produces 95 percent of the walnuts eaten in the United States.

The walnut is an excellent food for vegetarians, because its protein is closer to animal protein than any vegetable other than the soybean.

Fried Fontina Cheese Strips

1½ pounds Fontina cheese, cut
   into finger-sized strips (see
   Note)
   Freshly ground black pepper
1 cup all-purpose flour
4 eggs, well beaten
1½ cups fine dry bread crumbs
   About 1 quart vegetable oil
   for deep-frying

1 Sprinkle the cheese with pepper. Dip each strip into the flour to thoroughly coat it, then into the beaten eggs, and then into the bread crumbs. Coat each strip a second time, using only the beaten eggs and bread crumbs.

2 Pour 1 inch of the vegetable oil into a heavy, deep saucepan. Place a deep-frying thermometer into the oil and heat to 375° F.

3 When the oil is hot, add 4 or 5 strips of the coated cheese to the oil. Deep-fry, turning gently with tongs, until golden brown, about 1 minute.

4 Carefully remove the cheese strips from the oil with a slotted spoon or wire skimmer. Pat dry with paper towels. Continue frying until all of the cheese has been cooked. Serve immediately.

MAKES 4 SERVINGS

NOTE: Mozzarella cheese may be substituted for Fontina cheese in this recipe.

ABOUT BLACK PEPPER

Black pepper was first domesticated from its wild ancestor on the Malabar coast of India. Pepper was the first Oriental spice brought to the West, and was a major foreign trade item for ancient Rome. At the time, pepper was worth more than its weight in gold.

When Christopher Columbus arrived in the West Indies, he thought he was in India. So, when he tasted a spicy dish that had been seasoned with chili, he wrongly jumped to the conclusion that it had been seasoned with pepper. The locals asserted the flavor was "chili" and Columbus said it was "pepper." The compromise name "chili pepper" stuck.

Pepper is actually a berry (called a peppercorn), that turns black when dried in the sun. The strongest flavor is concentrated in the black skin. At the moment you break the kernel the flavor is at its peak, which is why freshly ground pepper is preferred. White pepper is black pepper with the outer skin removed; it is milder than black pepper and preferred by many chefs for dishes that are light in color because black pepper on a white sauce, for instance, can make it look dusty.

Cheese Straws

½ pound sharp Cheddar
   cheese, finely shredded, at
   room temperature
½ cup unsalted butter, at room
   temperature
1¾ cups sifted all-purpose flour
¼ teaspoon salt
¼ teaspoon cayenne pepper
½ teaspoon Tabasco sauce

1 In a bowl beat together the cheese and butter until well blended.

2 Sift the flour, salt, and cayenne directly onto the cheese-butter mixture. Add the Tabasco sauce and mix until thoroughly blended. Form the dough into 2 discs. Cover with plastic or foil and refrigerate for 1 hour.

3 Preheat the oven to 425° F.

4 Using a rolling pin on a lightly floured surface, roll out each portion of dough to a thickness of about ⅛ inch. Cut the dough into 3- × ½-inch rectangular strips and carefully place the strips on an ungreased baking sheet.

5 Bake the cheese straws for 8 minutes. Remove to a rack and let cool. If you are not serving the cheese straws immediately, store in an airtight container.

MAKES 2 DOZEN

NOTE: This dough can be kept on hand in the freezer for up to 3 months and rolled out as needed.

HOW CHEDDAR CHANGED ITS NAME

Cheddar cheese gets its name from the English town where it was made originally. During the Revolutionary War, Americans did not want to eat a cheese named after a city in enemy territory. So they renamed it American cheese. Since then the name has switched back and forth, but today in the former colonies American cheese and Cheddar are distinctly different.

TABASCO

In 1868, Edmund McIlhenny planted a small crop of red peppers on a little island off the coast of Louisiana. When he harvested the peppers, he cut them up, mixed them with vinegar and salt from a salt dome under the island, and aged the mix in wooden barrels. Once aged, he stored the mixture in some old cologne bottles. A year later, he shared some of this blend with his neighbors, who encouraged him to market the spicy sauce. He called it Tabasco, after a small river in Mexico. Today, Edmund's grandchildren manufacture and sell over 100,000 bottles of Tabasco sauce each day.

Corn Sticks

2 cups water
1½ cups yellow cornmeal
1 cup grated Edam, Gouda, or
    Fontina cheese
    About 1 quart vegetable oil
    for deep-frying
    Russian Dressing (page 240)

1 In a saucepan bring the water to a boil. Add the salt.

2 Remove the pan from the heat and stir in the cornmeal.

3 Return the pan to medium heat and cook, stirring, for 3 to 5 minutes, or until the mixture thickens into a paste and separates from the bottom of the pan.

4 Remove from the heat and stir in the cheese until melted throughout.

5 Form tablespoon-size portions of the mixture into small balls. Press the balls into cigar-shape tubes, about 3 inches long.

6 Pour 1 inch of the oil into a heavy skillet and heat to 375° F.

7 Working in batches, without overcrowding, deep-fry the corn sticks until golden brown.

8 Drain on paper towels and serve hot, with Russian dressing.

MAKES ABOUT 3 DOZEN

ABOUT CORNMEAL

Cornmeal is available in two colors: yellow and white. The former is ground from yellow corn kernels, the latter from white corn. In cooking, they are interchangeable. If a recipe calls for yellow cornmeal, you can use white; the color is the only difference. Generally, yellow cornmeal is used in down-home-style foods and white cornmeal is used when a more refined presentation is desired.

Buffalo Chicken Wings

Buffalo chicken wings were invented at the Anchor Bar in Buffalo, New York, by its proprietor, Mama Bellissimo. One evening a group of hungry friends came into the bar at closing time and asked her to cook something. The only ingredients available to her were some chicken wings that she was saving for a spaghetti sauce. She fried them and doused them with barbecue sauce. Today they are the most popular food in Buffalo. They have become an extremely common party food, because they are not only delicious but inexpensive.

In Buffalo, July 29 is official Chicken Wing Day.

1 Separate the chicken wings at the joint. Trim off and discard the tips.

2 In a wide saucepan or a high-sided skillet heat 2 inches of the oil to 375° F.

3 Deep-fry the chicken wings for 8 minutes, or until golden brown.

4 In a medium skillet melt the butter and stir in the hot sauce. Set aside.

5 When the chicken is cooled, drain on paper towels and add to the hot butter mixture. Toss until very well coated. Serve with blue cheese dressing on the side as a dipping sauce.

MAKES ABOUT 6 SERVINGS

30 chicken wings
Vegetable oil for deep-frying
½ cup unsalted butter
½ cup hot pepper sauce (such as Trappey's, Durkee's, or Goya)
Blue Cheese Dressing (page 243)

Lemon-Glazed Spareribs

3–4 pounds pork spareribs, cut into 2-inch pieces

Glaze:

¾ cup fresh lemon juice
¼ cup soy sauce
¾ cup sugar
1 tablespoon cornstarch
½ teaspoon salt
¾ teaspoon grated lemon zest
½ teaspoon ground ginger
¼ teaspoon freshly ground black pepper
2 garlic cloves, crushed
½ teaspoon lemon extract
¾ cup water

1 Preheat the oven to 350° F.

2 Line 1 or 2 shallow baking pans with heavy-duty aluminum foil and arrange the ribs in a single layer in the pan(s). Bake for 1 hour, turning occasionally, and draining off the fat.

3 While the ribs are baking, make the glaze. Combine all the remaining ingredients in a small saucepan. Bring to a boil, stirring often. Reduce the heat and simmer for 3 minutes.

4 Pour about half of the sauce over the ribs. Bake for 20 minutes longer.

5 Turn the ribs and baste with the remaining sauce. Return the ribs to the oven and bake until they are well browned and glazed.

MAKES 8 TO 10 SERVINGS

ABOUT PORK RIBS

Buying and using the right kind of spareribs can be confusing. There are spareribs, baby back ribs, St. Louis ribs, country-style ribs, barbecue ribs, and even rib tips.

Spareribs, St. Louis ribs, barbecue ribs, and rib tips all come from the rib cage of the pig. A slab of spareribs is an entire half of the pig's rib cage. Cut off the hard sternum area on one side and you have barbecue ribs. Cut off the rib tips on the other side and you have St. Louis ribs, the leanest and most tender part of the sparerib. The sternum side is chewy and flavorful. The rib tips are fatty and tender. All of them need long, slow cooking to be at their best.

Baby back ribs are cut from the center part of the pork loin. They are two inches long and very meaty. Country-style ribs are really pork chops cut from the forward blade end of the loin. They are very meaty and flavorful, but they can be tough if not cooked properly.

When buying ribs look for meat that is pale pink with pure white fat. Fresh ribs will last only 1 or 2 days in the refrigerator.

ABOUT GINGER

Fresh ginger is the root of the Zingiber officinale plant that is native to the United States, Asia, and China. Most of the ginger we get in the United States is grown in Jamaica and the West Indies. Ginger beer, a nonalcoholic drink made with grated fresh ginger, is popular throughout the Caribbean.

Ginger comes fresh and ground, where the root has first been cracked and dried. Good-quality fresh ginger is generally available and gives more flavor than the ground variety, though ground is usually preferred in baking. When buying fresh ginger look for roots that are fresh and firm, not shriveled—the roots look like the finger and palm of your hand. It can be stored tightly wrapped for a few days in the refrigerator. Peeled and submerged in a jar of sherry wine, fresh ginger will last for up to 6 months. In cooking, slice the ginger very thinly or grate it.

Candied or crystallized ginger has been cooked and preserved in sugar syrup. It is best to use candied ginger in making desserts, but in a pinch, it can be washed of its sugar coating and used like regular fresh ginger.

Honey-Spiced Hazelnuts

These flavored nuts are ideal as a snack with drinks or as a garnish for soups or salads.

2 tablespoons olive oil
2 garlic cloves, minced
1½ tablespoons ground cumin
½ tablespoon Chinese chili
   sauce, or ¼ teaspoon
   Tabasco sauce
½ cup honey
1½ pounds shelled hazelnuts
   (about 4 cups), roasted and
   peeled (see Tip)

1 Preheat the oven to 400° F. Line a baking sheet with wax paper or foil.

2 In a large skillet warm the olive oil over medium heat. Stir in the garlic, cumin, chili sauce, and honey. Reduce the heat to low and simmer, stirring often, for 10 minutes. Do not allow to burn.

3 Add the hazelnuts and stir to coat well.

4 As soon as the nuts are coated, remove them from the pan and spread them in a single layer on the prepared baking sheet. Bake for 10 minutes.

5 Place the baking sheet on a wire rack and allow the hazelnuts to cool completely.

6 When completely cool, separate the nuts.

MAKES 1½ POUND

The hazel tree has long been known for its mystical properties. A Y-shaped hazel branch is used as a divining rod for finding water in the ground. Moses used a hazel branch to smite rocks and produce water. Merlin the magician carried a hazel rod.

The ancient Greeks thought hazelnuts were good for your health. Consequently, the serpents of the medical profession's symbol are entwined around a hazel-tree branch. Greek medicine men recommended eating chopped hazelnuts with honey as a cure for nagging coughs. And mashed hazelnut shells, mixed with fat and smeared on the head, was an ancient Greek recipe for curing baldness.

WHAT'S COOKING TIP: HOW TO ROAST AND PEEL HAZELNUTS

Preheat the oven to 350° F. Place the shelled hazelnuts in a roasting pan or heavy skillet with a heat-resistant handle. Place the nuts in the oven and roast for 20 minutes. Remove the pan from the oven and allow the nuts to cool to the point where you can handle them. Take a handful of the nuts and rub them together in your hands or in a kitchen towel. The skins will start to rub off. Continue until all or most of the skins are removed.

ABOUT HAZEL TREES

The hazel tree is a low-growing shrub that dates back at least to 4500 B.C. The filbert tree is the domesticated hazel tree, but the nuts are the same for cooking purposes. The nuts of the filbert tree become ripe in late August, on or about the 20th, which is St. Philbert's Day, hence the name.

Soups

Minestrone Soup

Soup in Italy is served and enjoyed as often as pasta, and minestrone is the most popular. It is made in more ways than there are parts of Italy, but it is always a thick, hearty vegetable soup, with cooked dried beans. Often pasta, rice, or crusty country bread is added. Freshly grated Parmesan or Romano cheese is sometimes sprinkled on top, which greatly enhances the nutritional value of the beans.

¼ cup olive oil
1 large onion, chopped
2 celery ribs, diced
2 large carrots, peeled and diced
1 garlic clove, minced
2 medium potatoes, peeled and diced
1 cup Italian plum tomatoes, peeled, seeded, and chopped
7 cups water
1 large zucchini, diced
½ cup cooked chick-peas
½ cup cooked cannellini (white beans)
½ cup cooked red kidney beans
Salt and freshly ground black pepper
1 tablespoon chopped fresh parsley
½ teaspoon dried oregano
½ teaspoon dried basil

1 In a large stockpot or saucepan heat the oil over moderate heat. Add the onion, celery, and carrots and sauté until the onion is translucent, 3 to 5 minutes. Stir in the garlic, potatoes, tomatoes, and water. Bring to a boil. Reduce the heat and simmer for 45 minutes.
2 Add the zucchini and simmer for 30 minutes.
3 Add the chick-peas and beans; season with salt and pepper to taste. Crush the herbs and add to the soup. Bring to a boil and reduce the heat. Simmer for 15 minutes.

MAKES 6 TO 8 SERVINGS

NOTE: Cut the vegetables into similar sizes so they will cook evenly.

WHAT'S COOKING TIP: BUYING A STOCKPOT

Stockpots, however large, should be tall and narrow. The narrowness of the pot reduces the surface of the stock that is exposed to the air, which reduces the amount of liquid that boils away into steam. In addition, the height of the stockpot forces the liquid to bubble up through the layers of meat, bones, vegetables, wine, and seasonings, blending and enriching the flavors. Heavy-duty anodized aluminum or stainless steel with an aluminum slab sandwiched to the bottom are good materials for stockpots. Make sure that the handles are big enough so you can get a good grip when you are wearing cooking mitts.

Bermuda Vegetable Soup

2 tablespoons unsalted butter
1 cup chopped celery
1 cup finely chopped onion
1 cup chopped green bell
   pepper
1 cup chopped carrots
1 cup chopped zucchini
1 cup finely chopped turnips
1 cup chopped potatoes
½ cup tomato puree
¼ teaspoon dried thyme
¼ teaspoon dried marjoram
   Freshly ground black pepper
2 tablespoons Worcestershire
   sauce
3 cups V-8 juice
2 cups water
   Minced fresh parsley as
   garnish

1 In a large saucepan that is big enough to hold all the ingredients melt the butter. Add the vegetables and cook, stirring from time to time, for 5 minutes.

2 Pour in the tomato puree and add the thyme, marjoram, and pepper. Stir in the Worcestershire sauce, V-8 juice, and water. Cook for 5 minutes.

3 Ladle into soup bowls and garnish with parsley before serving.

MAKES 10 SERVINGS

ABOUT WORCESTERSHIRE SAUCE

The Romans were fond of a salted fish sauce called garum. Worcestershire sauce is an anchovy-based meaty-tasting condiment that has its roots in this ancient Roman condiment. The modern version was developed by two English druggists, John Lea and William Perrins, who were given a recipe for a sauce by the British governor general of Bengal. They hated the sauce and poured it into a wooden barrel in their basement. Several years later they rediscovered the sauce, tasted it, and found they now liked it; they named it Worcestershire because it was made in the English district of Worcester.

Lea & Perrins Worcestershire sauce is still made the same way. Anchovies, soybeans, tamarind, vinegar, garlic, shallots, molasses, and spices are mixed and aged for 2 years in wooden vats. The sauce is pressed out, strained, and put in bottles.

ABOUT V-8 JUICE

V-8 is a popular beverage made from blending juices from eight vegetables: tomatoes, carrots, celery, beets, parsley, lettuce, watercress, and spinach. It was originally named Veg-min when it was developed as a health drink in 1933 by W. G. Peacock, Sr. in Evanston, Illinois. The manager of a specialty food store that was selling Veg-min advised Mr. Peacock to change the name to V-8.

In the 1930s only twenty-five cases of V-8 were made each day. All the juices were extracted with a small cider press and all the canning was done by hand. The Campbell Soup Company bought V-8 in 1948 and last year produced over three million gallons of V-8 juice—enough to fill eighteen Olympic-size swimming pools.

ABOUT MARJORAM

Marjoram is an aromatic, mild-flavored herb that is native to the countries around the Mediterranean Sea. It is often used to flavor soups and stews and, like oregano and basil, is a regular addition to pasta sauce.

Fresh marjoram can be chopped and added to lettuce salads or sprinkled on pot roast. Whole stems of marjoram are sometimes tied into a bouquet and added to soups.

People once believed that marjoram could keep milk from becoming sour. On the island of Crete it was a symbol of honor, and in Sicily it was used to keep sadness away from a household.

Gazpacho

6 large fresh ripe tomatoes,
  peeled, seeded, and diced
2 green bell peppers, halved,
  seeded, and diced
2 cucumbers, peeled, seeded,
  and diced
2 onions, minced
2 garlic cloves, minced
1 cup tomato puree
1 cup tomato juice
½ cup red wine vinegar
10 drops Tabasco sauce
½ teaspoon cayenne pepper
  Chopped red or green bell
  pepper and chopped onion
  as garnish

1 Working in batches if necessary, combine all of the ingredients except garnish in a blender or food processor and blend until smooth.

2 Chill for at least 6 hours or overnight. Garnish with chopped green or red bell pepper and onions.

MAKES 8 TO 10 SERVINGS

ABOUT GARLIC

Garlic has lived up to age-old claims of its benefits as a cardiac drug. Researchers have shown that eating garlic increases the amount of time your blood takes to coagulate, and reduces the blood levels of bad low-density lipid cholesterols, while boosting levels of the good high-density lipid cholesterols.

FRED WARING AND THE BLENDER

Fred Waring, the popular band leader of the 1930s, did not invent the Waring Blendor, but he did make it happen. He and his Pennsylvanians had just finished a radio broadcast in New York when he was approached by the inventor Fred Osius. Osius was looking for backers for his new concept of the electric mixer. Waring invested his time and money in the project and after several months of trial and error, the new Miracle Mixer was debuted at the National Housewares Show in Chicago in 1937.

Fred Waring began promoting his mixer on the radio and through a singing group, The Waring Blendors. A campaign with the Ronrico Rum Company made Waring Blendors a must-have tool for mixing drinks in bars. The mixer soon made the jump from saloon to home kitchen and became an institution in American cooking. Today, the Waring Professional products represent the state of the art in quality kitchen equipment.

Carrot and Walnut Soup

2 tablespoons unsalted butter
1 pound carrots, peeled and
   cut into ½-inch lengths
¼ cup chopped onion
½ cup chopped walnuts, plus
   extra as garnish
3½ cups chicken stock
   Salt and freshly ground
   black pepper
   Pinch of grated nutmeg
1 cup heavy cream or
   buttermilk

1 In a large saucepan melt the butter over moderate heat. Add the carrots and onion and sauté for 2 minutes. Stir in the walnuts and sauté for 1 minute.

2 Add 2 cups chicken stock and bring to a boil. Add a pinch of salt, pepper, and nutmeg; reduce the heat and simmer for 45 minutes, until the carrots are very tender.

3 Puree the soup until smooth in a processor or blender.

4 Return the soup to the pan and stir in the remaining 1½ cups chicken stock and the heavy cream or buttermilk. Cook, stirring, until heated through. Season with salt and pepper to taste.

5 Garnish with chopped walnuts.

MAKES 6 SERVINGS

WHAT'S COOKING TIP: FAT-FREE STOCK

How you store cans of beef or chicken stock can help you cut calories and lose weight. There is a small amount of fat in every can of stock. Place the cans of stock in the refrigerator overnight. The fat will congeal and you can spoon it off the top. You can save as much as 150 calories per can.

WHAT'S COOKING TIP: HOW TO STORE NUTS

1. English walnuts, black walnuts, almonds, hazelnuts/filberts, and pecans can be stored in their shells in a cool, dry place for several months, even as long as a year. Once these nuts are shelled, or if you buy them already shelled, they should be kept in an airtight container in the refrigerator where they will keep for several weeks.
2. Cashew nuts, which always come out of the shell, along with chestnuts, macadamia nuts, and pistachio nuts, should always be kept in an airtight container in the refrigerator. It is best to use these nuts as quickly as possible in order to enjoy their best flavor and texture.
3. Peanuts, which are not really nuts but tubers, have a very high fat content. To prevent spoiling, put the peanuts in an airtight jar and store them in the refrigerator. They will keep this way up to three months.

Curried Corn Soup

1 tablespoon unsalted butter
1 large onion, finely chopped
1 tablespoon finely chopped
    garlic
2 tablespoons curry powder
3 tablespoons all-purpose flour
2 large ripe tomatoes, cored,
    cut into bite-sized pieces
4 cups chicken stock or broth
¼ teaspoon Tabasco sauce
2 cups cooked fresh, canned, or
    frozen corn
1 cup plain or low-fat yogurt

1 In a saucepan melt the butter over moderate heat. Add the onion and sauté for 2 minutes. Add the garlic and cook for 1 minute more.
2 Stir in the curry powder and flour. Mix in the tomatoes, chicken stock, and Tabasco. Simmer for 20 minutes.
3 Puree the soup in a food processor or blender. Return the soup to the pot and bring to a simmer. Add the corn and cook for 1 minute.
4 Off the heat, blend in the yogurt and serve.

MAKES 6 SERVINGS

HOMEMADE YOGURT

2 cups milk
2 tablespoons plain low-fat
    yogurt

1 In a very clean saucepan heat milk to 180° F. Then allow it to cool to 110° F.
2 Meanwhile, wash a glass jar with a tight-fitting lid in very hot soapy water. Rinse well with boiling water.
3 Stir the store-bought yogurt into the milk. Pour the mixture into the glass jar and seal tight.
4 Put the jar into a preheated 100° F oven or insulated picnic cooler for 7 hours. The longer the incubation, the more tangy the yogurt. (Once you refrigerate, the process stops.)
5 Refrigerate the yogurt for 2 hours before using. It will hold in the refrigerator for about 1 week. Save some of the yogurt from this batch to use as a starter for your next batch of yogurt.

MAKES 2 CUPS

ABOUT CURRY

The term *curry* describes a blend of spices commonly used in Indian cooking. In India, curry is usually not bought, but blended at home from curry leaves, garlic, ginger, pepper, yellow turmeric, and other spices. Because of the freedom in the amounts and types of spices used, there is no standard definition of what makes up a curry seasoning.

ABOUT CORN

There are more than 200 varieties of sweet corn grown in the United States, most of them from Florida. Corn originated as a gigantic grass growing on the slopes of the Andes mountains of South America. The cultivation of corn, which dates back over 3,000 years, marked the end of the nomadic life-style for many Indian tribes.

Corn is a good source of carbohydrates and fiber. Yellow corn is rich in vitamin A. An average corn ear has about 90 calories.

As soon as a corn cob is picked, the sugar in the kernels begins to turn into starch, so the sooner you eat it after picking, the sweeter it will taste. It is best stored refrigerated.

Look for fresh green husks, and tight rows of kernels. Avoid corn with dry or discolored stems, or very large (overripe) kernels.

Bouillabaisse

Bouillabaisse is a fisherman's soup or stew that originated in Marseilles, France, and is now popular throughout the coastal regions of southern France. No two Frenchmen make bouillabaisse the same way, because it is always made with whatever fish the fishermen fail to sell in the market when they return to port. The anise-flavored liqueur pastis or Pernod is often added to the pot, along with tomatoes, fresh herbs, and vegetables.

This dish is traditionally topped with slices of toasted French bread rubbed with garlic.

4 cups fish stock
½ cup scallops
8 shrimp, shelled and deveined
2 lobster tails, halved lengthwise
1 pound fish fillets (striped bass, flounder, and/or whiting), cut into 2-inch squares
1 carrot, scraped and thinly sliced
1 celery rib, thinly sliced
1 red bell pepper, seeded and minced
1 small zucchini, seeded and thinly sliced
¼ teaspoon dried dill
¼ teaspoon dried chervil
¼ teaspoon dried tarragon
1 tablespoon minced fresh parsley
Salt and freshly ground black pepper

1 In a stockpot or large saucepan bring the fish stock to a simmer over moderate heat. Add the scallops, shrimp, and lobster and cook for 2 to 3 minutes.

2 Add the fish fillets, vegetables, and herbs. Cover and cook for 10 minutes. Season with salt and pepper to taste.

MAKES 4 SERVINGS

FISH STOCK

Some people now make their own fish stock because canned fish stock and its substitute, clam juice, are often too high in salt. Also, when you make your own fish stock, you have more control over the flavor and quality of the stock.

1 Place the fish heads, tails, and bones in an 8- to 10-quart stockpot.

2 Add the leeks, onions, carrots, parsley, and celery.

3 Add the herbs.

4 Fill the pot with 8 quarts of water, bring to a boil, reduce the heat to low, and simmer for 2 to 4 hours.

5 Strain the stock through a colander lined with cheesecloth.

6 Pour what stock you aren't using into containers, cover, and freeze.

MAKES 8 QUARTS

About 5 pounds fish heads, tails, and bones
1 cup chopped leeks
1 cup chopped onions
1 cup chopped carrots
1 cup chopped fresh parsley
1 cup chopped celery
3 bay leaves, crushed
1 tablespoon dried thyme
1 tablespoon dried tarragon
1 tablespoon dried marjoram

ABOUT LOBSTER

Lobster has become one of America's true luxury foods. But it wasn't always that way. When European settlers first came to Maine and Massachusetts, lobsters were plentiful and easy to capture. It was not until after high-speed transportation spread the lobsters' fame across the country that demand forced prices higher.

The Maine lobster is fished from Maine to New Jersey. The smaller spiny, or rock lobsters, are caught in the waters around Florida. South Africa is a major producer of lobster tails.

Nutritionally, lobsters are a good source of low-fat protein. They also contain amounts of calcium, and are not as high in cholesterol as previously thought.

It is important that lobsters be alive when cooked. They should be moving their tails and flailing their claws. As soon as a lobster dies, its uncooked flesh attracts dangerous bacteria that can cause food poisoning, to say nothing of the loss of flavor.

Continued . . .

ABOUT FISH STEW

Other cultures and parts of the world have their own hearty fish stews. Manhattan clam chowder is a tomato-based soup made exclusively with clams. Cioppino was made popular by Italian fishermen in San Francisco and like bouillabaisse combines several types of seafood. Conch chowder is made in the Florida Keys, and Spanish cooks make a sopa de pescadores and a shellfish stew called zarzuela, both of which are seasoned with saffron.

ABOUT CHERVIL

Chervil is a delicately flavored herb with a taste that is a cross between parsley and anise. It is little used by Americans but is a great favorite with the French, who use it in their herb blends and for flavoring omelettes, soups, and salads.

Chervil is native to the Balkans and the Middle East. The Romans introduced it into France and Britain. One important thing to remember about chervil is that when boiled or overcooked it loses much of its flavor. It should be added at the very last minute to soups, and sprinkled fresh on leaf salads and potato salad.

ABOUT SCALLOPS

Scallops are delicate sweet shellfish that are found in four varieties in the coastal waters of the United States. The largest is the sea scallop, about the size of a walnut, which is found in deep water. Bay scallops, especially Peconic Bay scallops fished on Long Island, are very sweet and succulent and are about the size of a small finger joint. They are extremely rare. Small bay scallops or calico scallops are the size of lima beans and are fished off the Carolina coast. One of the only varieties of scallop served in the shell is the pink scallop found near Seattle. These are about the same size as Peconic Bay scallops.

Scallops are called *coquilles St. Jacques* in French. Legend has it that Saint James the Apostle (Saint Jacques) saved a bridegroom from the sea. The bridegroom was covered with scallop shells and the scallop became a symbol for Saint James.

Nutritionally, scallops contain 100 calories per ½-pound serving. They are low in fat, and high in protein and calcium.

Onion Soup Lyonnaise Style

Lyon is in an area of France known for its delicious food. A food prepared in a Lyonnaise style will typically be made with a sauce of onions cooked in butter.

1 Preheat the oven to 400° F.

2 In a large saucepan melt the butter. Add the onions and sauté over moderate heat for 10 to 15 minutes, or until nicely browned.

3 Add the stock and salt and pepper to taste. Bring to a boil, reduce the heat to moderately low, and simmer, covered, for 15 minutes.

4 Slice the bread into ¼-inch-thick slices, allowing 2 to 3 slices per serving, depending on the width of the bread. Place the bread slices on a baking sheet and toast in the oven for 3 to 5 minutes, or until golden brown. Do not turn off the oven.

5 Place one-third of the toast in the bottom of an ovenproof soup tureen or casserole. Sprinkle with ⅔ cup cheese. Add half of the remaining toast and cheese. Top with the remaining toast.

6 Pour the soup into the tureen. Sprinkle the remaining cheese on top and bake for about 25 minutes, or until the cheese is golden brown and bubbling. Serve immediately.

2 tablespoons unsalted butter
4 cups thinly sliced onions
8 cups chicken stock or broth
Salt and freshly ground black pepper
1 loaf French or Italian bread, 3-inch diameter if available
2 cups shredded Gruyère or Swiss cheese

MAKES 6 TO 8 SERVINGS

ABOUT GRUYÈRE AND SWISS CHEESE

Gruyère cheese has superb melting qualities that make it the best choice for many cooked dishes as well as fondues and soup toppings. The best gruyère comes from Switzerland, and is sold by the piece. Avoid the tiny foil-wrapped triangles—they will not work well in most recipes.

Swiss cheese is a generic name for all imitations of the original Swiss Emmenthaler. The words *Imported Swiss* do not mean that the cheese is from Switzerland, or even that it is imported. They just refer to this type of cheese.

Spinach Soup with Pears

6 cups chicken stock
1 cup chopped carrots
1 cup chopped celery
10 ounces fresh spinach,
    cleaned and stemmed, or one
    10-ounce package frozen
    spinach, thawed and drained
    Freshly ground black pepper,
    to taste
1 cup plain yogurt
1 pear, peeled, cored, and cut
    into matchstick-size pieces,
    as garnish

1 In a large pot combine the chicken stock, carrots, and celery over moderately low heat. Simmer for about 30 minutes.

2 Add the spinach and pepper, cover, and cook for 5 minutes.

3 Puree the mixture in a food processor or blender until smooth. Stir in the yogurt.

4 Return the soup to low heat and cook until just warmed through. Garnish each serving with the pear pieces.

MAKES 8 SERVINGS

NOTE: Do not bring the soup back to a boil after the yogurt has been added or it may separate.

ABOUT PEARS

The pear is a member of the rose family that originated in southeastern Europe and western Asia, and has a history that dates back to Homer, the ancient Greek storyteller. The Romans were great pear lovers and growers and they spread the pear tree throughout their empire.

The French have been using pears since the Middle Ages; as a result most of our popular pear varieties have French names, such as Anjou, Bosc, Comice, and Forelle.

Except for Bartletts, which turn yellow when ripe, it is hard to judge a pear by its color. If the pears are still firm at your market, bring them home and place them under a bowl at room temperature. That will bring them to a point of ripeness within a day or two. The pear is ripe and ready when it yields to gentle thumb pressure at the stem end.

ABOUT SPINACH

Spinach originated in Persia, now Iran. It was unknown in Europe until the Moors planted it during their invasion of Spain in the Middle Ages. A green leafy vegetable that is most closely associated with Popeye the Sailor and with little children who don't want to eat it, spinach is delicious when eaten raw or lightly cooked and horrible when it is overcooked. It is an excellent source of vitamin A.

Folacin, or folic acid, as it's sometimes called, is a vitamin that is found in green leafy vegetables such as spinach and is important to good health. Folic acid takes part in two of our essential body processes: It makes up genes and it helps form hemoglobin, the protein that carries oxygen throughout the body. Sufficient folic acid is also essential to a safe pregnancy. (Other good food sources of folic acid include wheat germ, dried beans and peas, and liver.)

There are two main types of spinach—smooth leaf, which usually ends up frozen, and crumpled leaf, which is usually sold fresh. Fresh spinach, whether sold in a bag or loose in bunches, should be thoroughly washed before you use it. The crumpled leaves hide sand and dirt, and it is important to wash the leaves in several changes of water before cooking.

Cold Yogurt and Cucumber Soup

2 cups plain yogurt
1 cucumber, peeled, seeded, and grated
1 tablespoon white wine vinegar
2 teaspoons chopped fresh mint
1 teaspoon chopped fresh dill, plus 2–3 sprigs as garnish (optional)

1 In a blender or in a bowl combine the yogurt, cucumber, vinegar, mint, and chopped dill with a whisk.
2 Cover and refrigerate for 2 hours.
3 Ladle into bowls and garnish with dill sprigs.

MAKES 2 TO 3 SERVINGS

YOGURT AND LONG LIFE

The active cultures that turn milk into yogurt were first isolated by the Russian doctor Elie Metchnikoff of the Pasteur Institute in Paris. He was obsessed with research that might lead him to a longer life. While many claims have been made about yogurt's health benefits, it has not been proven to increase longevity.

DILL

Dill is most widely known as the seed that gives dill pickles their flavor. Though native to Asia, dill is now grown the world over. Medicinally, small amounts of dill have been used as a mild tranquilizer to help infants sleep.

CUCUMBERS

Cucumbers date back about 12,000 years in Thailand. They thrive in most places where there is hot weather. The emperors Augustus and Tiberius loved them so much that they asked their imperial gardeners to grow them year-round. Toward this end the gardeners invented the first hothouse.

Cucumbers are refreshing, but are not nutritional storehouses. The phrase "cool as a cucumber" comes from the fact that cucumbers maintain an internal temperature several degrees below their surroundings.

Pea Soup

2 tablespoons unsalted butter
1 medium onion, chopped
1 celery rib, diced
1 medium carrot, scraped and finely chopped
1 cup dried yellow peas, soaked overnight in cold water
8 cups chicken broth
¼ pound slab bacon
Salt and freshly ground black pepper

1 In a large stockpot or saucepan melt the butter over moderate heat. Add the onion, celery, and carrot and sauté for 2 minutes.

2 Drain the peas and add them to the vegetables. Add the chicken broth and bring the soup to a boil. Skim off any foam that rises to the surface.

3 Add the bacon and simmer for 1 hour, or until the peas are tender.

4 Remove the bacon and cut into ½-inch cubes. Return the bacon to the soup. Season with salt and pepper to taste.

MAKES 8 SERVINGS

ABOUT YELLOW SPLIT PEAS

Yellow split peas are one of more than two dozen types of dried peas and beans commonly sold in supermarkets. They are a good source of protein and are low in fat, as are other peas and beans. The yellow split peas are very popular in the cooking of French Canadians, East and West Indians, and Germans and Czechs.

Yellow split peas are usually packed in one-pound plastic bags. They will keep indefinitely, but should be stored in a cool, dry place.

ABOUT BACON

When news reports quote prices for fresh pork bellies on the
commodities exchange, they're talking about the raw product from
which bacon is made. American bacon is the cured belly muscle and fat
of the pig. In its natural state, bacon is attached to the rib bones, which
are cut away to make spareribs. Some Polish and Hungarian butcher
shops have bacon with the rib bones still attached.

There are several methods of making bacon. It may be smoked over
apple wood, hickory, or corn-cob chips for distinctive flavors; sometimes
it is marinated in apple juice or maple syrup to impart flavor before it is
smoked. Most commercial supermarket bacon is injected with a brine
cure and then lightly smoked before it is sliced and packaged.
Country-style bacon is rubbed with salt and brown sugar and then
smoked. It is possible to make bacon with beef (a favorite in Cleveland),
veal, or lamb bellies, but pork is by far the most common. Canadian
bacon is not bacon at all. It is the cured and smoked tenderloin of pork
that runs down the pig's back.

Tuscan Bean Soup

The cannellini bean used in this soup is popular in many parts of Italy, but particularly in Tuscany. It is a small white bean similar to a navy or pea bean, which may be substituted.

2 19-ounce cans cannellini beans
3 tablespoons olive oil
2 garlic cloves, crushed
1 medium onion, chopped
1 cup sliced carrots
1 cup chopped chard or green cabbage
3 tablespoons tomato concentrate or tomato paste
3 cups chicken stock or water
Salt and freshly ground black pepper
6 slices Italian bread, toasted

1 Drain the beans and puree them in a food mill, food processor, or blender.

2 In a deep saucepan heat the olive oil over moderate heat. Add the garlic and onion and sauté for 2 minutes. Add the carrots, chard, or cabbage, and the tomato concentrate and stir. Simmer for 3 minutes.

3 Stir in the pureed beans and the chicken stock or water and cook for 35 minutes. Season with salt and pepper to taste.

4 Place 1 slice of the toast in the bottom of each bowl and ladle the soup over it.

MAKES 6 SERVINGS

ABOUT BEANS

Beans are the seeds of plants in the legume family. About a dozen major varieties have been grown for thousands of years in countries around the world. Beans are a rich source of iron and B vitamins and they are filled with valuable dietary fiber. One cup of beans supplies more fiber than equal amounts of celery, carrots, or rice. Four ounces of cooked dried beans have only about 115 calories.

When shopping for beans, remember that dried beans are much more nutritious, firm, and flavorful than canned or frozen beans.

TUSCANY

Tuscany is a hilly agricultural province in northern Italy. The ancient Etruscans were early inhabitants of Tuscany and became the first military and cultural rivals of the ancient Romans. The Tuscan countryside is dotted with rustic villas, medieval villages, small farms, olive groves, and vineyards. Florence, the main city of Tuscany, was the birthplace of the Renaissance; Michelangelo worked here and the city is filled with art museums and historic buildings.

Chianti wine is made in the hills of Tuscany near Florence. Tuscany is also famous for the quality of its pure and virgin olive oils. Most of the food served in Tuscany is hearty country fare—stick-to-the-ribs bean and vegetable soups, thick steaks drizzled with olive oil, and juicy pork sausages are favorite foods.

Black Bean Soup

1 pound dried black beans
10 cups chicken stock
¼ cup unsalted butter
2 celery ribs, finely chopped
2 medium onions, finely chopped
1 garlic clove, crushed
1½ tablespoons all-purpose flour
1 bay leaf
Salt and freshly ground black pepper
½ cup Madeira wine (optional)
Lemon slices or chopped onion, chopped tomato, and cooked rice as garnish

1 Wash the beans. Place in a large pot and add cold water to cover. Let soak overnight, or boil the beans in 6 to 8 cups of hot water for 2 minutes, then set aside for 1 hour.

2 Drain the beans and place them in a large pot. Add the chicken stock and bring to a boil. Reduce the heat to low and simmer for 1½ hours, adding water if necessary.

3 In another pot melt the butter over moderate heat. Add the celery, onions, and garlic and sauté until softened, but not browned.

4 Stir in the flour and cook, stirring constantly, for 1 minute.

5 Stir the vegetable mixture into the beans. Add the bay leaf and pepper to taste. Cover and simmer, stirring occasionally, over low heat for 2 to 3 hours. Check occasionally and add water if the beans are not completely covered with liquid.

6 Remove and discard the bay leaf. Add salt to taste. Puree the soup through a food mill, food processor, or blender until smooth.

7 Return the soup to the pot and add the Madeira, if desired. Reheat the soup and correct the seasoning. Garnish each portion with a lemon slice or serve with chopped onion, chopped tomato, and cooked rice.

MAKES 6 TO 8 SERVINGS

WHAT'S COOKING TIP: THE IMPORTANCE OF REMOVING BAY LEAVES BEFORE SERVING

Bay leaves, which are also called laurel or bay laurel leaves, add a fragrant and delicate aroma and taste to a dish. They have a sharp central spine which if eaten whole could become stuck in the digestive tract. They are great for seasoning but not for eating. Remove bay leaves from all recipes before serving.

ABOUT MADEIRA

In Shakespeare's *Henry IV, Part 1,* Falstaff sells his soul for "a cup of Madeira and a cold capon's leg." A sweet wine from the Madeira islands in the Atlantic Ocean off the coast of Morocco, Madeira is a blend made from black and white grapes, which is left in the sun to caramelize. Madeira travels very well, and it is often agitated to simulate the conditions of the bumpy sea voyages that once carried it around the world.

Mild Cheddar Soup

10½ tablespoons unsalted
    butter
  3 medium carrots, peeled
    and finely chopped
  1 celery rib, diced
  1 medium onion, minced
  1 medium turnip, peeled and
    grated
  3 cups beef broth
  ⅓ cup all-purpose flour
10 ounces mild Cheddar
    cheese, grated
  1 cup cold milk
    Salt and freshly ground
    black pepper

1 In a large stockpot or saucepan melt 8 table-spoons butter over moderate heat. Add the vegetables and sauté for 15 minutes.

2 Add the beef broth and bring to a simmer. Simmer for 10 minutes, skimming off any fat that rises to the surface.

3 Blend the remaining 2½ tablespoons butter into the flour, making a thick paste (this is called a beurre manie). In teaspoon-sized pieces, stir the paste into the soup until completely blended. Simmer, stirring frequently, for 20 minutes.

4 Blend in the cheese and simmer, stirring frequently, for 5 minutes.

5 Blend in the milk and simmer, stirring, for 5 minutes. Season to taste with salt and pepper.

MAKES 6 SERVINGS

WHAT'S COOKING TIP: HOW TO BUY AND STORE ONIONS

1. Pick onions that are firm and dry. The outside should have a crunchy, crackly texture and should feel papery. There should be no soft spots or wetness, and the flatter the stem end the better.
2. Moisture is the enemy of stored onions. Keep them in a dark, dry place, away from potatoes, which give off moisture.

ABOUT BEURRE MANIE

A beurre manie is a butter and flour mixture used as a thickener for soups and sauces. Work together equal amounts of butter and flour with a fork or your fingers until it forms a thick paste, with the flour completely absorbed by the butter. Roll the paste into tiny balls, which you can use to thicken a liquid at the end of its cooking time. The mixture, called beurre manie because the butter (*beurre* in French) is manipulated or kneaded with the flour, can be made ahead of time and stored under refrigeration for 2 to 3 weeks.

If you have a stew that is too thin, remove the meat and vegetables, bring the liquid to a boil, and drop in one or two beurre manie balls, cooking and stirring constantly until the liquid is thickened. Once the liquid has thickened, taste it. If there is a floury taste, let it simmer gently for a few more minutes. Then return the meat and vegetables to the pot and let them reheat.

Shrimp Bisque

A Bisque is a shellfish-based cream soup developed by French cooks, who use crawfish, lobster, shrimp, and crab in their bisques. The Cajuns of southwest Louisiana make a delicious crawfish bisque that includes cayenne pepper and whole crawfish floating in the broth. Modern cooks have stretched the meaning of bisque and now make tomato and vegetable bisques, using the name whenever they thicken a soup with fresh heavy cream.

¼ cup unsalted butter
1 carrot, chopped
1 leek, chopped
¼ cup chopped shallots
1 celery rib, chopped
¾ pound medium shrimp, peeled and deveined
¼ cup brandy (optional)
3 cups Fish Stock (page 47) or 1½ cups bottled clam juice mixed with 1½ cups water
1 cup dry white wine
2 tablespoons tomato puree
4 sprigs fresh parsley
1 cup water
⅛ teaspoon dried basil
⅛ teaspoon dried oregano
⅛ teaspoon dried thyme
⅛ teaspoon dried tarragon
3 tablespoons long-grain white rice
½ cup heavy cream
Salt and freshly ground white pepper

1 In a large stockpot or saucepan melt the butter over moderate heat. Add the carrot, leek, shallots, and celery; cook, covered, until softened, about 5 minutes. Stir in the shrimp and cook for about 2 minutes, just until the shrimp turn pink.

2 Add the brandy, if desired. Add the fish stock or clam juice, wine, tomato puree, parsley, and water. Crush the dried herbs in the palm of your hand and add them to the pot. Bring to a simmer. Add the rice and simmer, uncovered, for about 20 minutes, until the rice is very tender.

3 Puree the soup in a processor or blender until smooth.

4 Return the soup to the pot and stir in the heavy cream. Season to taste with salt and white pepper. (If using clam juice, season carefully as it is quite salty.) If the soup is too thick, thin with a little white wine, fish stock, or water.

MAKES 6 SERVINGS

ABOUT TARRAGON

Tarragon is a relative newcomer to the herb scene. It is native to
southern Russia and has only been cultivated for about 500 years.
Tarragon is a feathery perennial that is impossible to grow from seed.
That is one reason why it is not very popular in herb gardens. The long
slender stems can be immersed in white wine vinegar to make tarragon
vinegar. Both fresh and dried tarragon have a soft, near-sweet flavor.

ABOUT BRANDY

Brandy is an alcoholic liquor distilled from grape wine or the fermented
juice of apples, cherries, pears, or other fruits. The distillation process
consists of heating the wine or fruit juice to vapor, passing the vapor
through metal tubing, and then cooling it back to a liquid state. The
"spirit" of the wine is captured in the brandy, which is placed in oak
barrels and left to age for several years. The aging process gives brandy
a distinctive color, taste, and smell.

   Brandy is a large generic term that encompasses many different
types. Cognac and Armagnac, which are made from wine, and Calvados,
made from apple cider, are the most famous brandies of France.
California is a major producer of wine and fruit-based brandies. Outside
of California the leading brandy-consuming state in the United States is
Wisconsin, where it is drunk almost to the exclusion of Bourbon and
Scotch.

Continued . . .

ABOUT LEEKS AND PHOENICIAN SAILORS

Leeks are mild-flavored members of the onion family. They have thick
white roots and light green stems. The entire leek can be used in
cooking. Leeks are at their best in the autumn months.

When buying leeks, look for ones that are medium-size. Avoid ones
that look wilted or brown on the edges. Leeks will keep in a plastic bag
in the refrigerator for about a week. They must be washed thoroughly
because the broad leaves are a nesting ground for sand and dirt.

Phoenician sailors took leeks to England, where they became the
national symbol of Wales. The Welsh pinned leeks to their hats to
distinguish their soldiers in a battle with the Saxons in A.D. 640. The
Welsh won the battle and it is still traditional to wear a leek on St.
David's Day (March 1st) to honor the patron saint of Wales.

ABOUT THYME

After parsley and sage, thyme is the most commonly used herb in the
world. Thyme is native to the rocky slopes around the Mediterranean
and was first used for its medicinal value. The Greeks and the Romans
cooked with thyme and extracted its aromatic oil to use in perfumes.

Fresh thyme has a wonderful bitter tang and the whole branches are
often used in a marinade for meats to be grilled outdoors. Lamb rubbed
with fresh thyme and olive oil is a classic Mediterranean barbecue.
Dried thyme is a good substitute for fresh. It adds flavor to soups, stews,
and roasted meats.

Chicken Egg-Drop Soup with Corn

1 In a large saucepan bring the chicken stock to a boil.

2 Add the water chestnuts and simmer for 1 minute.

3 In a small bowl mix the cornstarch and water until smooth. Stir this mixture into the soup and cook, stirring, until the soup thickens.

4 Add the scallions.

5 Turn off the heat. Slowly pour in the beaten egg, stirring gently with chopsticks or a fork to spread the egg throughout the soup.

6 Add the corn, stir, and serve at once.

MAKES 6 SERVINGS

4 cups chicken stock or broth
½ cup finely minced water chestnuts
2½ tablespoons cornstarch
2½ tablespoons cold water
¼ cup green part of scallions, cut into ¼-inch pieces
1 egg, lightly beaten
2 cups cooked fresh, canned, or frozen corn

WATER CHESTNUTS

Water chestnuts grow so thickly in some areas of the Potomac River that they sometimes hamper navigation.

The water chestnut was once called the "Jesuit nut" because its seeds were often used to make rosary beads.

ABOUT SCALLIONS

Scallions, also called green or spring onions, are actually adolescent onions, harvested before the bulb has a chance to develop. To buy the best scallions, look for those with crisp, green unwithered tops and clean white bottoms. At home, cut off any brown tops or edges and store the scallions in a plastic bag in the refrigerator for not more than 5 days.

Many people find it difficult to chop scallions with a knife. Line up 2 or 3 scallions and place them on a cutting board. Holding them in a row with one hand, chop them into tiny rounds, going all the way into the dark green portion. Another technique is to take the bunch of scallions in one hand, and with a clean, dry scissors, snip them into small pieces.

Manhattan Clam Chowder

¼ cup unsalted butter
1 cup diced potatoes
½ cup diced celery
½ cup chopped onions
¼ cup all-purpose flour
6 cups homemade clam broth
   or bottled clam juice
2 tablespoons tomato paste
1 cup chopped canned
   tomatoes, drained
2 cups chopped cooked fresh
   or canned clams (see Note)
1 teaspoon dried thyme
   Salt and freshly ground black
   pepper
   Crackers

1 In a large pot melt the butter over moderate heat. Add the diced potatoes, celery, and onion and sauté for 2 minutes. Stir in the flour. Cook for 1 minute, stirring, until thoroughly mixed.

2 Add the clam broth or juice, tomato paste, and tomatoes. Mix well. Simmer for 1 hour, stirring occasionally. Add more clam broth or water if necessary.

3 Add the cooked clams and thyme and simmer for 3 minutes. Season with salt and pepper to taste.

4 Serve the chowder with large plain white crackers.

MAKES 6 SERVINGS

NOTE: If using canned clams, reserve the juice and include in step 2 of the recipe.

ABOUT CLAMS

There are two major types of clams, hard-shell and soft-shell. Hard-shell, also known as quahogs, are named on the East Coast by size. The smallest are littlenecks, then top necks, then cherrystones, and then chowder or surf clams. Littlenecks, top necks, and cherrystones can all be eaten fresh on the half-shell. The larger ones are better for chowder. The 8-inch-wide geoduck clam of the Pacific Northwest is shelled, pounded, and served as geoduck steak.

Soft-shell clams are not good on the half-shell. They can be used in chowder, but they are best steamed; hence their popular name steamer clams. They can also be pulled from their shell, battered, and deep-fried.

All clams are a good source of iron, low-fat protein, and dietary fiber.

ABOUT CRACKERS

Crackers get their name from the cracking sound they make when they are broken. What Americans call crackers, the English call biscuits. Nineteenth- and early twentieth-century American grocery stores displayed barrels full of crackers for sale to customers and as a center for small talk. That is the origin of the expression "heard around the cracker barrel."

In their most primitive form, crackers are simply wheat or rye flour mixed with water, rolled thin, and baked until crisp. All sorts of flavorings, butter, salt, sugar, and spices have been added over the years to create dozens of different crackers.

Fish and
Shellfish

Baked Fish Fillets in Orange Butter

2 pounds white-fleshed fish
  fillets (such as halibut or
  flounder), each about ½ inch
  thick
  Freshly ground black pepper
1 tablespoon grated lemon zest
1 tablespoon grated orange zest
2 tablespoons minced scallions
2 tablespoons chopped fresh
  parsley
2 tablespoons unsalted butter
2 tablespoons fresh lemon juice
2 tablespoons white wine,
  chicken broth, or water

1 Preheat the oven to 350° F.
2 Sprinkle the fish fillets with black pepper.
3 Butter a large baking dish and place the fish fillets in a single layer. Sprinkle with the lemon and orange zest. Add the scallions and parsley, and dot with the butter. Pour on the lemon juice and wine, broth, or water.
4 Bake for about 10 minutes, until the fish is opaque and flaky but not dry.
5 Serve the fish with the pan juices poured on top.

MAKES 4 TO 6 SERVINGS

WHAT'S COOKING TIPS: FISH

1. Measure the fish at its thickest point.
2. Allow 10 minutes of cooking time per inch of thickness.
3. Double the cooking time for frozen fish.
4. Add an extra 5 minutes for fish cooking in foil or sauce.

ABOUT ORANGES

The orange is a 20-million-year-old berry, and one of the most important fruits in world economics. Oranges are native to China, and were first planted in Europe by the Moors in the twelfth century. Christopher Columbus brought oranges from the Canary Islands to the West Indies. Later they were planted in Panama, where the Aztec priests took excellent care of them. Oranges have been grown in Florida since the mid 1500s, and in California since 1769, when oranges were first planted by missionaries.

Oranges do not continue to ripen once they have been picked, and their orange color is not a sign of ripeness, but rather a reaction to cold weather.

Look for oranges that are firm, heavy for their size, and smooth-skinned. Store them in a cool place. They are an excellent source of vitamins A and C, potassium, and folic acid.

Oranges grew well in the south of France, but it took such care and expense to raise them in northern France (they had to be raised under glass) that only the nobility could afford to do so. The orange thus became a symbol of royalty and civility. In *Much Ado About Nothing,* Shakespeare described a count as being "civil as an orange." The five golden balls on the coat of arms of the Medici family are believed to represent oranges.

Herbed Fish Fillets

Juice of ½ lemon
1 teaspoon chopped garlic
1 teaspoon chopped fresh
  parsley
1 teaspoon chopped fresh thyme
1 teaspoon chopped fresh basil
2 tablespoons butter, melted
5 tablespoons olive oil
  Salt and freshly ground black
  pepper
2 pounds fish fillets

1 In a saucepan combine the lemon juice, garlic, parsley, thyme, and basil. Blend in the butter and 2 tablespoons olive oil.

2 Salt and pepper the fish fillets to taste. Paint both sides of the fish fillets with the herb butter and let them marinate at room temperature for 10 minutes.

3 Put the 3 remaining tablespoons olive oil into a heavy skillet and place over high heat. Add the fish fillets and cook for 2 minutes on one side. Turn them over and paint the fish fillets again with the herb butter mixture; cook for 3 minutes more.

4 Serve immediately.

MAKES 4 SERVINGS

ABOUT MARINADE

A marinade is usually a liquid that contains a mild acid and a flavoring. Marinades may contain an oil as well, to keep food from drying out when it is cooked. The acid tenderizes the food that is placed in the marinade by beginning to break down tissue. For this reason, some foods, such as some poultry or fish, should not be left too long in a marinade or the flesh will get mushy. A very simple and good marinade for meat or chicken is made by mixing equal parts of dry vermouth and olive oil flavored with tarragon, rosemary, or thyme.

ABOUT OLIVE OIL

Olive oil comes in three grades: extra virgin, which comes from the first pressing of the best olives; virgin, which comes from the second pressing; and pure, which is the lowest-quality olive oil. High in monounsaturated fats, olive oil may actually help lower cholesterol levels in the blood.

The oil should be stored refrigerated in an airtight container. To keep air out of the container, you can add water to displace the oil you use. This will keep the bottle full and air free. The oil will float above the water. If the oil gets cloudy or solid, just let it come back to room temperature and it will be fine.

Fish Fillets with Mustard Sauce

½ cup mayonnaise, store-bought or homemade (see page 15)

2 tablespoons Dijon-style mustard

2 pounds white-fleshed fish fillets (such as halibut or flounder), each about ½ inch thick

1 Preheat the broiler.

2 In a small bowl mix together the mayonnaise and mustard.

3 Arrange the fish in a single layer in a lightly buttered heatproof baking dish. Coat the fish on the top side with a ¼-inch-thick layer of the mustard sauce.

4 Broil for 7 minutes; the fillets do not need turning.

MAKES 6 SERVINGS

WHAT'S COOKING TIP: MUSTARD

When cooking with mustard, remember this: Heat reduces its sharpness, and time allows it to blend with other flavors. So if you add it early it will be milder and blended throughout the dish. If you add it later it will be sharper but will not dominate the other flavors.

ABOUT MUSTARD

People have been making mustard for over 5,000 years, and the early methods still produce the best-tasting mustards. Freshly ground mustard seeds are tasteless, but when they are mixed with water, vinegar, or wine, they release their intense flavor.

As eighteenth-century Spanish missionaries made their way north along the coast of California, they sprinkled mustard seeds that took root and served to mark their path to other missionaries following them. The bright yellow bushes made an easy-to-see trail called the Mission Trail, parts of which are still visible.

Mustards do not spoil, but they lose their flavor over time. They keep best if refrigerated after they are opened.

Blackened Fish

The trick to this dish is to get the cast-iron skillet so hot that the surface of the fish is seared by its first contact with the pan. The heat can be generated on top of a normal stove or it can be prepared by placing the pan directly on top of ash-covered coals in an outdoor barbecue grill. With either system, an enormous amount of smoke will be generated when the fish hits the hot pan.
Louisiana-born Paul Prudhomme spent 12 years apprenticing with chefs across the country before becoming the chef and owner of his own top-rated restaurant, K-Paul's Louisiana Kitchen in New Orleans. He has written several best-selling cookbooks, and appeared on television nationwide. He is an enormously talented cook and is credited with single-handedly starting the nationwide craze for blackened fish dishes.

1 Place a cast-iron skillet over high heat and preheat until the surface of the pan is as hot as possible, about 10 minutes.

2 In a second skillet or sauté pan melt the butter. Spread the spice mixture on a flat dish. Dip both sides of the fish fillet into the melted butter and then into the mixed spices.

3 Pan-fry the fish for 2 minutes on each side.

¼ cup unsalted butter

2 tablespoons (total) mixed spices: salt, freshly ground black pepper, cayenne pepper, dried oregano, and dried thyme

1 6-ounce boneless, skinless fillet of redfish, tile fish, or salmon

MAKES 1 SERVING

ABOUT CAST IRON

Iron was the first metal used commercially for making pots. It is heavy and heats slowly, but it conducts heat evenly and retains it well. When you cook on cast iron, valuable traces of iron are absorbed by the food. In fact, iron deficiency was virtually unknown in the United States until we began to cover cast-iron pots with enamel, and use other cooking materials.

Charred Tuna with Mango Sauce

Mango Sauce:

¼ **cup chopped mango**
¼ **cup chopped tomato**
¼ **cup minced scallions**
   Salt and freshly ground black pepper
2 **tablespoons olive oil**
2 **tablespoons rice wine vinegar**

Tuna:

6 **tablespoons clarified butter (see sidebar, page 333) or olive oil, or a combination of both**
¼ **teaspoon minced garlic**
¼ **teaspoon dried red pepper flakes**
¼ **teaspoon minced fresh ginger**
1 **teaspoon minced scallions**
   Salt and freshly ground black pepper
2 **5-ounce tuna fillets, skinned (or other meaty fish fillets, such as swordfish or shark)**

1 Heat the sauté pan or griddle until the surface is quite hot.

2 Prepare the sauce by combining the mango, tomato, scallions, salt, and pepper. Stir in the olive oil and vinegar.

3 In a dish combine the clarified butter or olive oil, garlic, red pepper flakes, ginger, scallions, and salt and pepper to taste. Dip the tuna into the seasoned butter and then place in the hot pan. Char for 1 minute on each side; remove to a serving plate.

4 Cut the tuna into slices as you would a steak. Fan them out on the plate and serve the sauce on the side.

MAKES 2 SERVINGS

ABOUT RICE WINE VINEGAR

Rice wine vinegar is as tangy as regular vinegar, only it is made from rice wine rather than apple cider or grape wine. Rice wine, also known as sake in Japan, is a popular drink in Asian countries where rice is the main grain.

Rice wine vinegar is preferred in Asian dishes because of its unique flavor. Substitute a light cider vinegar if absolutely necessary, but avoid wine vinegars for recipes that call for rice wine vinegar.

LOOKOUT FOR TUNA

Seamen in the Mediterranean hunted tuna for thousands of years before the birth of Jesus. Tuna travel in schools and swim close to the surface when migrating, so ancient fishermen would post scouts on steep cliffs or in cedar trees on high cliffs along the coastal waters. The lookouts would signal the fisherman, who would capture the tuna. Fishing tournaments off the coast of Long Island still post a tuna scout in a crow's nest high above the power boat's decks.

ABOUT TUNA

Tuna is a firm-fleshed, oily member of the mackerel family. Six different varieties of tuna come to the market fresh, frozen, and canned. Canned is by far the most popular. Light meat tuna comes from yellowfin, skipjack, and small bluefin tuna. White meat tuna comes only from albacore. Generally speaking, darker fleshed tuna tends to be less delicately flavored than lighter fleshed tuna.

To people in the eastern United States, bluefin tuna has always been a sporting fish and not an eating fish, but the Japanese love bluefin for sushi and sashimi and are now buying all the bluefin tuna that is caught at New York fishing tournaments. They pack the freshly caught tuna in ice and ship them straight out of Kennedy Airport to Japan.

Tuna is a low-fat source of protein. It also contains high amounts of Omega 3 fish oil, which has been found to fight heart disease.

Sautéed Flounder with Shrimp

2 pounds flounder fillets, cut into a total of 6 pieces, each about ½ inch thick
¾ cup all-purpose flour
2 eggs, beaten
¼ cup dry bread crumbs
5 tablespoons unsalted butter
2 tablespoons vegetable oil
2 tablespoons (total) mixed herbs and spices such as black pepper, cayenne, dried basil, oregano, and thyme
12 large shrimps, shelled and deveined

1 Lightly coat the flounder with the flour (shaking off any excess), then dip the fish into the eggs and finally into the bread crumbs.

2 In a sauté pan, melt 2 tablespoons butter with the vegetable oil over moderate heat. When almost smoking, add the flounder and sauté for 2 to 3 minutes on each side, until nicely browned. Remove the fillets to a serving dish.

3 In the same pan heat the remaining 3 tablespoons butter and the herbs and spices until the butter begins to brown. Add the shrimp and sauté for 2 minutes. Place 2 of the cooked shrimp on top of each fillet. Pour the flavored butter sauce over the shrimp and fish and serve.

MAKES 6 SERVINGS

WHAT'S COOKING TIPS: EGGS

1. Extra large eggs are usually the best value. Brown and white eggs are virtually identical inside.
2. To check for damaged eggs in the supermarket, run your fingers down each row of eggs. Unbroken eggs will move slightly, while damaged eggs usually stick in place. Don't eat eggs with even slight damage. They pick up bacteria very quickly.
3. Keep eggs in the carton they come in—it keeps them much fresher than storing them openly in the refrigerator.
4. Fresh eggs hold their shape best for frying. Older eggs are runnier.
5. Eggs can be frozen for extended storage. They should first be separated, however. Seal the whites in a moistureproof container. Add a half teaspoon of sugar per yolk before freezing to retard thickening.
6. To stop eggs from cracking when you boil them, punch a small hole in the large end with a pin before boiling. This allows the tiny amount of air in the large end of the egg to escape before it expands and cracks the shell. Then place the egg in a saucepan and cover with cold water. Turn the heat to high and bring the contents to a boil. Reduce the heat to medium-low immediately so the water is just below the boiling. Soft-cooked eggs should be removed from the water 2 to 3 minutes after you reduce the heat, depending on the runniness that you prefer. Hard-cooked eggs should be removed from the heat 12 minutes after you reduce the heat. Immediately plunge the hard-cooked eggs into cold water. This stops the cooking process and keeps the yolks a bright yellow color.
7. When eggs that are a week or so old are hard-boiled, they peel more easily than fresher eggs. They also peel more easily while they are still hot. Peeling them under cold running water will help your fingers deal with the hot surface.
8. To check if an egg has been hard-boiled, try spinning it like a top. If it spins it is boiled, if it flops over it is raw.

Pepper-Broiled Salmon with Sour Cream Sauce

Fiery Szechuan cooking comes from the subtropical southwestern part of China. Located at the headwaters of the Yangtze river, Szechuan has always been a frontier area of China. The food is essentially hearty peasant cooking and it is not only hot, but heavily seasoned with scallions, ginger, and garlic. Hot and sour soup, steamed dumplings, chicken, squash, and cucumbers cooked in red and green chiles and crushed Szechuan peppercorns are some of the region's popular dishes.

Szechuan peppercorns, grown in the Szechuan province of China, are more fragrant and spicy than hot. Szechuan peppercorns leave a slight numbing feeling in your mouth that the Chinese call ma.

Basting butter:
- 1 cup unsalted butter, at room temperature
- ¼ cup minced shallots or onions
- 1½ tablespoons cracked Szechuan peppercorns (see Note)
- 4 garlic cloves, minced
- ½ teaspoon salt
- 1 cup bread crumbs

- 4 4-ounce salmon steaks or fillets

Sauce:
- 1 cup white wine
- ¼ cup fresh lime juice
- ½ cup cooked tiny shrimp or minced larger shrimp
- 1 cup sour cream
- 1 small bunch cilantro or parsley, washed and chopped

1 Preheat the broiler.

2 To make the basting butter combine the butter, shallots or onions, peppercorns, garlic, and salt in a medium bowl. Stir in the bread crumbs.

3 Arrange salmon on a broiling pan lined with foil. Spread 1 tablespoon basting butter on each piece of salmon.

4 Broil the salmon about 8 inches from the heat, until the bread crumbs are golden. Turn the fish over and spread again with the basting butter. Continue broiling, adding more basting butter if desired, or transfer the pan to a 400° F oven and bake until the salmon flakes easily. Total cooking time should be about 10 minutes.

5 Combine the wine and lime juice in a small saucepan. Bring to a moderate boil and simmer until the wine is reduced in volume by about half. Add the shrimp and remove from the heat. Stir in the sour cream and cilantro or parsley.

6 Place the fish on serving plates and cover with the sauce.

MAKES 4 SERVINGS

NOTE: If Szechuan peppercorns are unavailable, substitute cracked black peppercorns.

ABOUT SOUR CREAM

Sour cream as we know it today is cultured, and not sour tasting at all.
It is made in commercial dairies by blending cream and whole milk
with a bacteria culture. It is then warmed and left to incubate and
thicken in a process similar to that used to make yogurt. You can make
your own sour cream by mixing 2 cups heavy cream with 1½
tablespoons buttermilk. Let the mixture stand at room temperature,
covered, for 24 hours, then refrigerate.

Sour cream will curdle if allowed to boil or even if heated too much,
so when using sour cream in a cooked dish, add it over very low heat, or
after taking the pot off the heat.

Planked Salmon

Planked salmon is salmon that is baked on a wooden board called a plank. The American Indians, especially those in the Pacific Northwest, cooked salmon on planks propped up around and facing an open-wood fire.

Planked salmon is a festive and delicious dish that can be fun to try. First, select a good-quality plank. It should be 1½ to 2 inches thick with a groove running around the edge to catch the juices and made from untreated oak, hickory, or ash. It should be large enough to hold the salmon steaks or fillet that you are going to cook.

1 *untreated* cedar or oak plank, 12 × 6 × ½ inch thick
2 tablespoons olive oil
1 teaspoon salt
½ teaspoon freshly ground black pepper
½ teaspoon dry mustard
1 2–2½-pound salmon fillet, skinned

1 Preheat the oven to 250° F.

2 Rub one side of a cedar or oak plank with a small amount of the olive oil. Place the plank in the oven, oiled side up, for about 30 minutes, until it starts to brown slightly.

3 In a mixing bowl combine the salt, pepper, and dry mustard. Brush both sides of the salmon fillet with the remaining oil and sprinkle each side evenly with the seasoning mixture.

4 Remove the plank from the oven and increase the oven temperature to 350° F.

5 Put the fillet on the plank with the skinned side down. Put the plank into the oven and bake the salmon for 15 to 20 minutes, depending on the thickness of the fish.

MAKES 6 SERVINGS

DRY MUSTARD

Powdered mustard was invented by Mrs. Clements of Durham, England, in 1729. She sold the mix riding by horseback from town to town, but made her fortune when King George I became a loyal customer.

ABOUT OMEGA 3 OIL

Eating more fish may be the best thing you can do to help lower your chances of stroke or heart attack. Researchers noted that heart disease was almost nonexistent in Alaskan Eskimos, and pinpointed the reason for their low rate of cardiovascular disease as being their diet, which is high in fatty fish such as salmon.

Omega 3, a particular fat found in fish, can lower cholesterol levels and help prevent heart attacks. Omega 3 is a monounsatured fat, which means it lowers LDL (low density lipid), the "bad" form of cholesterol, and raises HDL (high density lipid), the "good" form of cholesterol.

All fish contain Omega 3, but fatty fish—salmon, mackerel, tuna, bluefish, and sardines—are among the best sources. A study at the Massachusetts Institute of Technology especially recommended solid white tuna packed in water. The tests indicate that the solid variety of white tuna contained twice as much Omega 3 as chunk tuna and that when tuna was packed in oil the Omega 3 leeched out of the tuna and into the oil. When you drain out the packing oil, you drain out up to 25 percent of the Omega 3.

There is no scientific evidence to prove that taking fish oil supplements will be at all effective in fighting heart disease. At this point, all existing research on the effect of Omega 3 deals with the oil within the fish and not the extracted oil alone.

Salmon Loaf

1 cup cooked whole-grain (brown) rice
1 15-ounce can salmon, drained
1 cup plain dry bread crumbs
½ cup skim milk
2 eggs
1 tablespoon chopped fresh parsley
1 tablespoon unsalted butter
2 tablespoons fresh lemon juice
1 tablespoon chopped fresh dill (optional)
Salt and freshly ground black pepper, to taste
Cucumber slices as garnish

1 Preheat the oven to 375° F.
2 In a bowl combine all of the ingredients except for the sliced cucumbers and shape into a loaf. Butter a 9- × 5- × 3-inch loaf pan and place the salmon mixture in it. Bake for 45 minutes.
3 Unmold and serve, garnished with sliced cucumbers.

MAKES 6 SERVINGS

ABOUT WHOLE-GRAIN (OR BROWN) RICE

White rice is made by milling off the bran layer of whole-grain rice. Whole-grain or brown rice has the bran layer intact, which results in a rice with more protein, calcium, phosphorus, potassium, niacin, vitamin E, and fiber.s

ABOUT SALMON

Almost all the salmon we eat comes from Oregon, Washington, and Alaska. Some salmon is caught in the Great Lakes and the north Atlantic and some of it is imported from Norway.

Fresh salmon comes whole, split, and boned, in fillets and in steaks. The dark red–fleshed salmon is from the chinook or king salmon and the red or sockeye salmon. The lighter-fleshed salmon is from the pink salmon, and the pale-fleshed salmon is usually the coho. All salmon is firm fleshed, meaty, and oily.

Canned salmon almost always comes from the red or sockeye salmon of the Pacific Northwest. It is a good source of calcium and low-fat protein, but it can contain as much as four to five times as much sodium as fresh salmon.

Swordfish with Mustard Sauce

1 Preheat the oven to 450° F.

2 In a sauté pan boil the shallot in the wine for 5 minutes, or until the wine is reduced to about 2 tablespoons.

3 Add the cream and simmer until reduced by one-third, about 10 minutes. Stir occasionally during the cooking time.

4 Add the mustards and season with salt and pepper to taste. Simmer for 2 minutes.

5 In a skillet heat the oil.

6 Sprinkle salt and pepper on the swordfish. Sauté the fish steaks for 2½ minutes on each side. Remove the fish from the skillet and place on a rack in a roasting pan. Bake in the oven for 5 minutes.

7 Pour some of the sauce onto each serving dish and place the swordfish steaks on top of the sauce.

MAKES 4 SERVINGS

1 tablespoon minced shallot
6 tablespoons dry white wine
2 cups heavy cream
¼ cup coarse-grained mustard
2 tablespoons smooth mustard
   Salt and freshly ground black pepper
2 tablespoons vegetable oil
4 4-ounce swordfish steaks, trimmed of all skin and any discolored areas

ABOUT SWORDFISH

The swordfish is named for its long, pointed bill that looks like a sword. It is very aggressive, and therefore popular as a gamefish.

Swordfish can reach 600 pounds in size. It is usually cut and sold in steaks. The flesh is white and delicate and it is often served grilled or broiled. Be careful not to overcook swordfish, which will leave it dry and chewy.

Swordfish Steaks with Fennel Seeds

1 garlic clove, halved
2 4-ounce swordfish steaks
1 teaspoon plus ½ cup dry
   vermouth
2 teaspoons olive oil
1 teaspoon dried rosemary
1 teaspoon fennel seeds
1 tablespoon unsalted butter
   Lemon slices and Italian
   parsley as garnish

1 Rub the cut side of the garlic over both sides of the fish and sprinkle with 1 teaspoon vermouth, the olive oil, rosemary, and fennel seeds. Cover and refrigerate for 2 hours.

2 Preheat the broiler.

3 Scrape the rosemary and fennel seeds off the fish. Broil for about 4 minutes on each side. Remove the fish from the broiler and place on a warm serving plate.

4 Pour the remaining ½ cup vermouth into a sauté pan and place on high heat. Cook and reduce the liquid to about 3 tablespoons. Add the butter to the pan and stir together.

5 Pour the sauce over the swordfish and garnish with lemon slices and Italian parsley.

MAKES 2 SERVINGS

ABOUT VERMOUTH

Vermouth is known to most Americans as something that is mixed with gin or vodka to make a martini. Europeans drink vermouth in a variety of cocktails and use it extensively in cooking. The name comes from the German word *Wermut* (*wein*), wormwood (wine), from the herb wormwood which is still added, along with nutmeg, cloves, coriander, marjoram, angelica root, and camomile.

The French and the Italians are the major producers of vermouth. Wine is first blended with a mixture of herbs and spices; eventually the wine is drawn off, fortified with brandy, and bottled. Vermouths come in sweet and dry styles. A dry white vermouth can sometimes be used as a flavorful substitute for white wine in cooking.

ABOUT FENNEL

Fennel is native to southern Europe and grows widely in countries around the Mediterranean Sea. The fennel seeds we use in cooking are the dried seeds of a tall, feathery-topped green plant that is a member of the carrot family. The fully mature fennel plant looks like the wildflower Queen Anne's lace that grows in the eastern United States.

Fennel seeds have a delightful anise or licorice flavor. They should be pounded in a mortar to release their essence. People from India often chew whole fennel seeds after a meal as a breath refresher.

A number of Provençal dishes call for dried fennel stalks to be tossed onto an outdoor barbecue fire to season fish or meat as it cooks.

Crabmeat Imperial

1½ pounds cooked lump
   crabmeat
½ cup diced green bell pepper
2 tablespoons diced pimiento
¼ cup diced scallions
1 egg yolk
1 tablespoon Worcestershire
   sauce
   Dash of Tabasco sauce
1 tablespoon Dijon-style
   mustard
6 tablespoons mayonnaise

1 Preheat the oven to 350° F.

2 In a mixing bowl gently stir together all the ingredients except 3 tablespoons mayonnaise.

3 Divide the mixture among 6 small ramekins or custard cups or place in 1 large shallow baking dish. Spread the remaining 3 tablespoons mayonnaise on top and bake for 12 minutes, or until the top is nicely browned.

MAKES 6 SERVINGS

NOTE: You can do all the preparation for this dish in advance and keep the mixture in a covered bowl for 24 hours in the refrigerator. Cook it just before serving.

ABOUT PIMIENTOS

The word *pimiento* is Spanish for sweet peppers, but pimientos are not the same as the sweet red bell peppers we know. In fact, fresh pimientos are rarely available in the United States. These peppers are typically used to garnish and flavor other foods. Pimientos are generally roasted, peeled, and stored in oil.

WHAT'S COOKING TIPS: CRABS

1. In choosing live crab, go for the active ones, rather than the listless ones that are already half-dead. Choose the heavier ones, and give them a shake. If you feel water swishing around, the crab will not be firm inside. They should also smell fresh and their joints should be intact.

2. If you plan to serve crabs in the shells, they should be scrubbed well, and rubbed with a little oil to bring out their shine.

3. Never hold a crab where it can reach you with its claws, which should be bound if possible.

4. Crabs are cannibals, and will eat each other, so don't leave two together.

5. It is commonly believed that crabs can be humanely killed by piercing them with a needle between the base of the eyes and the thoracic ganglion. To do this properly, the crab must be on its back, and the operator must have considerable practice. A much simpler method is to put the crabs into a pot with cold water, then heat the water until it is boiling. As the water heats up, the crabs will fall unconscious.

Shrimp Creole

Creole Sauce:

2 tablespoons vegetable oil
1 onion, chopped
2 bell peppers (red or green), chopped
3 cups diced tomatoes
3 celery ribs, chopped
2 cups tomato puree
1 teaspoon cayenne pepper
2 tablespoons chopped garlic
1 tablespoon chopped fresh parsley
1 cup chicken stock
    Salt and freshly ground black pepper, to taste
4 drops Tabasco sauce

Shrimp:

¼ cup unsalted butter
24 large shrimp, shelled and deveined
    A few sprigs fresh parsley

Cooked rice

1 To make the Creole sauce, heat the vegetable oil in a large saucepan. Add the onion, bell peppers, and tomatoes. Cook and stir for 1 minute. Add the celery. Stir and add the tomato puree. Simmer for 5 minutes.

2 Stir in the remaining sauce ingredients. Reduce the heat and simmer for 7 minutes.

3 To make the shrimp, melt the butter in a large sauté pan over moderate heat. Add the shrimp and parsley and sauté for 4 minutes.

4 Stir in the Creole sauce and serve over the rice.

MAKES 4 SERVINGS

ABOUT CELERY

At 8 calories per stalk, celery is an excellent diet food, except for those on a no-sodium diet because celery is rather high in natural sodium.

The two color groups of celery are gold and green. The major gold variety is Golden Self Blanching, and the main green types are Utah, a stringless nutty celery, and Summer Pascal.

When buying celery, avoid woody-looking, soft, or wilted stalks. Celery is quite perishable, and should be kept moist and refrigerated until you use it.

ABOUT SHRIMP

Shrimp is America's favorite shellfish. There are hundreds of different varieties of this tiny crustacean, but brown shrimp and white shrimp make up the bulk of the catch. Shrimp are fished primarily off the Atlantic Coast waters of the Carolinas, Florida, and in the Gulf of Mexico. Demand is so great for shrimp that we import hundreds of tons from Mexican and South American fishermen. We have even begun to get shrimp from aquaculture shrimp farms.

Prawns and scampi are incorrect names for shrimp. Both prawns and scampi are members of the tiny lobster or langoustino family. In this country, however, large shrimp are sometimes referred to as prawns, and shrimp cooked in an Italian sauce of oil, lemon, and bread crumbs are called scampi.

Shrimp are an excellent source of low-fat protein. They do not contain high levels of cholesterol, as was once thought.

Fried Noodles with Shrimp

½ pound thin egg noodles, cooked

2 cups plus 3 tablespoons vegetable oil

½ pound shrimp, shelled and cleaned

½ cup sliced mushrooms

½ cup thinly sliced carrots

½ cup cleaned chard or spinach

1 teaspoon minced fresh ginger

3 scallions, thinly sliced

1 teaspoon soy sauce

1 teaspoon dry sherry

1 teaspoon sugar

2 tablespoons cornstarch dissolved in 1 cup chicken stock

1 Place the noodles in a colander and run cold water over them to remove the starch.

2 Shape the noodles into 4 patties, each about 1 inch thick.

3 In a wok or deep-frying pan heat 2 cups oil to 325° F. Fry the noodle patties on both sides until golden brown, about 2 minutes.

4 With a slotted spoon or spatula, remove the noodle patties. Drain them on paper towels.

5 Remove the oil from the wok or pan. Add the remaining 3 tablespoons oil to the wok, toss in the shrimp, and stir-fry for 30 seconds. Add the mushrooms, carrots, chard, ginger, and scallions. Stir in the soy sauce, sherry, and sugar. Continue to stir-fry for 1 minute. Pour in the cornstarch and chicken stock mixture and cook for 30 seconds more.

6 Place each noodle patty on a plate and serve with the shrimp and vegetables on top.

MAKES 4 SERVINGS

ABOUT THE WOK

A heavy round-bottomed skillet used in Chinese cooking, woks are usually made from iron, carbon steel, stainless steel, or aluminum. The most durable ones are made from iron or carbon steel because they can better handle the intense heat needed for best results. A wok is designed to fit over a brazier with an open flame, but it can be used effectively at home directly over a gas flame, if it's supported by a metal ring. Iron woks need to be seasoned with oil before their first use. Wash the wok with soap and water and dry it. Rub it with a very light coating of vegetable oil. Heat it in a 250° F oven for 30 minutes. Always clean a wok with warm water and a nonabrasive sponge. Wipe it dry and use it often to keep it seasoned.

NOODLE NOTES

The Chinese have been eating noodles for 7,000 years. It may well be that pasta was first brought to Italy by the Ostrogoths, a Teutonic tribe that invaded Italy in the year A.D. 405. It is from their word *nudel* that we get ours. Noodles were noted in Italy by a Roman soldier named Ponzio Bastone 13 years before Marco Polo returned from the Orient, but Marco Polo generated a renewed interest in the food.

Pasta has been eaten with oil and grated cheese for at least 600 years, and the recipe for Fettucini Alfredo dates back to the 1300s. There is a record of pasta being exported from Italy in 1772. The shipment went from Genoa to London.

ABOUT SHERRY

Sherries are aged wines that have been fortified with brandy. They come from the province of Cadiz, Spain, and are divided into three major types: fino, oloroso, and dulces. The fino variety is light, dry, and straw colored, with alcohol contents from 15.5 to 17 percent. The oloroso sherries are darker, stronger, and heavier than the finos, with alcohol contents of up to 18 percent. Cream sherry is a blend of dry oloroso and Pedro Ximenez wine, which is one of the deeply colored sweet wines. Muscatel is another sweet sherry.

The earliest sherries were made in the town of Jerez, and were labeled VINO DE JEREZ, SACA, which means wines of Jerez, for export. The word *Jerez* was changed to sherry, and the word *saca* became sack. Shakespeare's Falstaff often roared for "a cup of sack."

Deep-Fried Shrimp

2 eggs
¼ cup heavy cream
   Salt and freshly ground black
   pepper
15 shrimp, shelled and deveined
   Flour
   Breadcrumbs
   Vegetable oil
   Cocktail Sauce (page 258)

1 In a mixing bowl combine the eggs, cream, and salt and pepper to taste.

2 Butterfly the shrimp by cutting each one three-quarters of the way down the center.

3 Lightly flour each shrimp. Dip them into the egg mixture and then coat with bread crumbs.

4 In a deep-sided frying pan preheat about 1 inch of vegetable oil to 375° F.

5 Deep-fry the shrimp for 3 to 5 minutes, until golden brown. Serve with cocktail sauce.

MAKES 3 SERVINGS

WHAT'S COOKING TIPS: DEEP FRYING

Deep-frying is a cooking technique that should leave your food light and crispy, not soggy and greasy. There are several tips to successful deep-frying:

1. Use vegetable oil rather than lard or beef tallow. Vegetable oil is unsaturated and better for your heart.

2. Choose a vegetable oil that has a high smoking point. Many chefs prefer peanut oil, but safflower, sunflower, soy, and corn oil are good substitutes. Pure olive oil is also very good for deep-frying, but the flavor is not suitable to all dishes or tastes.

3. Make sure the oil is at the proper temperature before you put the food in: 375° F is an effective temperature. Drop a piece of food in the hot oil. If it snaps and sizzles briskly, the oil is hot enough. If the oil is too cool, the food just sinks to the bottom and gets soggy.

4. Have the food at room temperature. Food that is too cold will cause the oil temperature to drop and the food will not cook properly.

5. Be sure the foods you are frying are fully submerged in deep oil or fat. This will allow the entire surface of the food to be quickly sealed by the fat, and the natural moisture and juices held in.

6. It is possible to use oil more than once. Simply let it cool and drain it through a strainer lined with a piece of paper toweling or a coffee filter in order to remove any burned food particles. Keep the oil in the refrigerator between uses.

Louisiana Shrimp and Crabmeat Sauté

2 tablespoons unsalted butter
¼ cup chopped scallions
1 garlic clove, minced
12 medium shrimp, shelled and deveined
½ teaspoon freshly ground black pepper
¼ teaspoon cayenne pepper
½ teaspoon dried oregano
½ teaspoon dried thyme
2 tablespoons Dijon-style mustard
½ cup sliced mushrooms
1 cup cooked lump crabmeat
⅓ cup Fish Stock (page 47), white wine, or water
4 cups cooked rice

1 In a sauté pan melt the butter over moderate heat. Add the scallions and garlic and cook for 1 minute. Add the shrimp and cook until they start to curl and turn pink, about 2 minutes.

2 Add the spices and herbs and sauté for 30 seconds. Stir in the mustard and sauté for 30 seconds. In the same way, add the mushrooms and then the crabmeat. Stir in the stock, wine, or water and cook for 1 minute.

3 Serve over the cooked rice.

MAKES 4 SERVINGS

ABOUT RICE

Rice has been grown and eaten in India and Asia for thousands of years. Alexander the Great introduced rice to Europe in 300 B.C., and the Moors were the first to cultivate rice in Spain, in the eighth century. In 1635, a trading ship carrying rice was wrecked off the coast of South Carolina. The washed up seeds were planted, and an American industry began.

Asian people eat as much as 400 pounds of rice per person per year. Americans average only 9 pounds of rice per person.

There are two main types of rice, long grain and short grain. Long grain is generally better in savory dishes, while short grain rice works better in sweet dishes. Brown rice can be either long or short grain. Italian rice, also called Valencian and Arborio, is round and perfect for making risotto and paella, two rice dishes that soak up a lot of liquid.

WHAT'S COOKING TIP: MUSHROOMS

1. Don't pick your own mushrooms unless you know exactly what you're doing. There are many extremely poisonous mushrooms that closely resemble the edible varieties.
2. Large mushrooms with the stems removed can be used as stuffing mushrooms. For most dishes, however, you are better off with small short-stemmed mushrooms.
3. In shopping for mushrooms, look for tightly closed caps that are curled down over the gills on the bottom of the cap, surrounding the stem. Mushrooms are highly perishable and should be refrigerated in a plastic bag with a damp paper towel to keep them from drying out.

Poultry

Pecan Breaded Chicken

4 whole boneless, skinless
  chicken breasts, split in half
  Freshly ground black pepper
6 tablespoons unsalted butter
¼ cup plus 2 tablespoons
  Dijon-style mustard
2 cups finely ground pecans
2 cups sour cream

1 Preheat the oven to 400° F. Lightly butter a baking pan.

2 Flatten the chicken breasts with a meat pounder and lightly pepper them.

3 In a saucepan melt the butter and then remove the pan from the heat. Whisk in ¼ cup mustard.

4 Dip the chicken into the butter-and-mustard mixture and then into the ground pecans.

5 Place the chicken breasts in the baking pan. (At this point you may refrigerate the chicken breasts for up to 24 hours.)

6 Place the pan in the oven and bake for about 15 minutes, until golden. Remove the chicken from the pan.

7 Pour the pan drippings into a bowl, add the sour cream and the remaining 2 tablespoons mustard, and mix thoroughly.

8 Place 2 tablespoons of the sour cream-and-mustard mixture on each dinner plate and cover with a chicken breast.

MAKES 8 SERVINGS

ABOUT PECANS

The pecan, a member of the hickory nut family, is America's native nut, grown mainly in the southern states. George Washington planted pecan trees at Mount Vernon and is said to have carried pecan nuts in his pockets throughout the Revolutionary War. Thomas Jefferson grew pecans in his gardens at Monticello.

Pecans, like all nuts, are good sources of protein. The oil in pecans is high in polyunsaturates and the nut is very low in sodium.

You can buy pecans in the shell, shelled in halves, and shelled crushed. Shelled pecan nuts can easily be ground in a food blender or smashed with a rolling pin. Shelled, especially ground pecans, are very perishable. They keep best tightly covered in the refrigerator or freezer.

WHAT'S COOKING TIPS: POULTRY

1. When storing raw poultry in the refrigerator, be sure that it is tightly wrapped, to prevent the meat or its juices from coming into contact with any other surfaces. Assume that all raw chicken has some salmonella bacteria that could cause food poisoning.
2. Wash raw chicken surfaces inside and out with cold water. Wash any surface that the raw poultry comes in contact with before it touches anything else. After you have touched raw poultry, wash your hands before you touch any other foods.
3. Make sure that the internal temperature of cooked poultry reaches at least 180° F before serving. Never partially cook poultry.
4. Don't store poultry—cooked or raw—with stuffing inside. The densely packed stuffing stays warm and promotes bacterial growth. If you are going to hold stuffed chicken or other fowl for more than a few minutes, remove the stuffing after the bird is cooked and refrigerate it separately.

Chicken Gruyère

Batter:
2½ cups finely shredded
   Gruyère cheese
 2 eggs
 ⅓ cup milk
 ⅓ cup light cream
 1 tablespoon all-purpose flour
   Salt and freshly ground
   black pepper
   Pinch of nutmeg

Chicken:
3 whole boneless, skinless
   chicken breasts, split in half
   and flattened
1 cup all-purpose flour
1 teaspoon vegetable oil

1 Preheat the oven to 350° F.

2 In a bowl combine all of the batter ingredients and mix well.

3 Lightly dredge the chicken breasts in the flour. Dip the floured chicken in the batter and coat evenly.

4 Using a nonstick skillet with a heatproof handle, lightly coat the bottom with the oil.

5 Add the chicken breasts and sauté until nicely browned on one side. Turn the chicken breasts and bake in the oven for 10 minutes, until browned and cooked through.

MAKES 6 SERVINGS

ABOUT NUTMEG

Nutmeg is the inner kernel of the fruit from the nutmeg tree. Freshly ground nutmeg is more potent than powdered, but isn't always worth the effort.

There is a lattice-patterned skin on the surface of a nutmeg. When removed and ground it is used as a seasoning called mace.

ABOUT CREAM

Normally pasteurized cream has a supermarket shelf life of 66 hours. Ultra-pasteurized cream is heated to a much higher temperature, and has a shelf life of 30 days. There is a slight difference in taste, but it is not noticeable in most cooked dishes.

There are four types of cream commonly sold, which differ in the percentage of milk fats they contain:

Type of Cream	Fat Content
Half and half	10.5–18%
Light cream	18–30%
Light whipping cream*	30–36%
Heavy cream*	36% or more

* Light whipping and heavy cream can both be used to make whipped cream.

Grilled Chicken with Mustard Sauce

1 teaspoon unsalted butter
4 skinless, boneless chicken breasts, split in half, fat removed, pounded lightly
2 tablespoons Dijon-style mustard
2 tablespoons mayonnaise
1 tablespoon plain yogurt

1 Preheat the broiler.
2 Butter the bottom of a heatproof baking dish that will hold the chicken breasts in a single layer.
3 Place the chicken breasts, skinned side up, in the pan.
4 Blend together the mustard, mayonnaise, and yogurt. Spread the mixture over the chicken breasts.
5 Place the baking dish about 6 inches below your heating element and cook for 15 minutes.

MAKES 8 SERVINGS

ABOUT CHICKEN TYPES

There are different types of chicken, each of which is superior for specific methods of cooking.

For roasting, the top choices are roasters, which range from 3 to 5 months old and weigh from 4 to 7 pounds, and capons, which are castrated male birds 4 to 5 months old, and weigh from 6 to 9 pounds. The Rock Cornish game hen, a special hybrid weighing 1 to 2 pounds, is also a good roaster. It is usually 5 weeks old.

The broiler, or fryer, is 7 to 9 weeks old and weighs 2 to 4 pounds. If you're not sure which bird to use, tell your butcher how you plan to cook it.

The best-tasting birds are fresh-killed and young. Freezing affects both the taste and texture of chicken.

Yogurt-Baked Chicken

1 Preheat the oven to 350° F. Line a shallow baking pan with heavy-duty aluminum foil and grease the foil lightly.

2 Rinse the chicken pieces and pat them dry.

3 In a shallow plate combine the bread crumbs and seasonings.

4 Place the yogurt in a shallow dish and lightly coat the chicken pieces in it. Dredge the pieces in the seasoned crumbs.

5 Arrange the chicken in the prepared pan and bake for 45 minutes, until cooked through.

6 Serve hot, or, if made ahead of time, serve cold. It's perfect for a picnic, eaten out of hand, like fried chicken.

MAKES 4 SERVINGS

1 2½–3-pound frying chicken, cut into 6 to 8 pieces, skin removed and trimmed of all fat
½ cup dry bread crumbs
¼ teaspoon salt (optional)
1 teaspoon finely minced garlic
½ teaspoon paprika
¼ teaspoon curry powder
¼ teaspoon freshly ground black pepper
1 cup plain yogurt

ABOUT PAPRIKA

Paprika is a dark red powdery seasoning that is made from dried sweet red peppers. Like all members of the Capsicum pepper plant, paprika was first grown in Central America and brought to Europe after Columbus. Paprika took hold in Hungary, where it is an essential ingredient in goulash and paprikash. Paprika is sweet, not hot, and it adds color as well as taste to food. Like wine, this seasoning has different styles and flavors. The best have a true essence of sweet red pepper and a hint of smokiness.

In Spain, paprika is known as *pimentón*. It is used extensively in paella and in chorizo, a Spanish pork sausage. The best Spanish paprika is grown on the Mediterranean coast in the province of Murcia.

Tandoori-Style Chicken

2 broiling chickens, skin
  removed, cut into pieces
⅓ cup fresh lemon juice

Marinade:
2 large garlic cloves
1 tablespoon chopped fresh
  ginger
1 teaspoon ground roasted
  cumin seed
½ teaspoon ground cardamom
½ teaspoon cayenne pepper
1 tablespoon paprika
⅓ cup plain yogurt

Vegetable oil for basting

1 Prick the pieces of chicken all over with a fork or thin skewer. Make diagonal slashes, ½ inch deep, 1 inch apart, on the meat. Put the chicken in a large bowl.

2 Add the lemon juice to the chicken and rub the juice into the slashes and all over the chicken. Cover and marinate in the refrigerator for 30 minutes.

3 Put all the ingredients for the marinade except the oil into the container of a blender or food processor and blend until reduced to a smooth sauce.

4 Pour the marinade over the chicken pieces and mix, turning and tossing, to coat well. Cover and marinate for 4 hours, or refrigerate overnight, turning several times.

5 Take the chicken from the refrigerator at least 1 hour before cooking to bring it to room temperature. The chicken is now ready to be either roasted in the oven or broiled over an electric or charcoal grill.

6 To roast in the oven, preheat the oven to 500° F. Take the chickens out of the marinade. Brush with oil and place them on an extra-large shallow roasting pan; preferably the chicken should be sitting on a wire rack above the pan. Set the pan in the middle level of the oven, and roast for 20 to 25 minutes, or until the meat is cooked through.

MAKES 6 SERVINGS

ABOUT CARDAMOM

The aromatic spice cardamom is the dried seeds of a fruit that is a member of the ginger family. Cardamom is native to India and Ceylon, and is widely used in Arab countries and by northern Germans and Scandinavians, especially in cookies and cakes.

Cardamom is also called "grains of paradise." Both Indians and Arabs chew cardamom seeds as a breath freshener. Arabs like to put cardamom seeds in their strong black coffee.

ABOUT TANDOORI COOKING

Tandoori is an Indian way to bake, roast, and grill meats and breads and sometimes fish and seafood. A tandoor is a deep clay oven that is a rectangular or rounded pit with a narrow opening at the top. A wood or charcoal fire is built in the bottom of the tandoor and pancake-shape flatbreads are smacked up against the inside walls. When they are baked, they are removed with specially designed sticks. Meat that is mounted on a skewer like a shish kebab is also lowered down into the tandoor. Juices dripping on the coals give off a delicious smoke that helps flavor the meat.

Because of the dry smoky cooking process, all meats that are cooked in a tandoor are first marinated to keep them moist, usually in a yogurt-based sauce. Chicken is always scored so that the marinade and the heat can penetrate into the meat. The tandoor was first used in ancient Persia. Today it is used all over Central Asia, India, Pakistan, and in parts of the Soviet Union.

Chicken with Forty Cloves of Garlic

As the garlic in this dish is slowly baked with the chicken, the flavor mellows and the natural sugar in the cloves caramelizes, making the final product quite sweet.

40 garlic cloves
⅔ cup olive oil
4 celery ribs, thinly sliced
6 sprigs parsley
1 tablespoon dried tarragon
2 frying chickens, quartered
1 teaspoon salt
¼ teaspoon freshly ground black pepper
Dash of nutmeg

1 Preheat the oven to 375° F.

2 Peel the garlic, leaving the cloves whole.

3 Put the oil into a large, heavy baking pan that will hold the chicken pieces in one layer. Add the celery, parsley, and tarragon. Arrange the chicken pieces on top and sprinkle with the salt, pepper, and nutmeg. Turn the chicken several times so all surfaces are coated with oil. Toss in the garlic. Cover with heavy-duty aluminum foil, making sure that the edges are tightly sealed.

4 Bake for 1½ hours, without removing the foil.

5 Remove the foil and bake for an additional 15 minutes, or until browned. Serve the chicken with the garlic.

MAKES 6 SERVINGS

WHAT'S COOKING TIPS: HOW TO STORE GARLIC

1. Do not store garlic in the refrigerator or in a plastic bag. The moisture will shorten its life.
2. Good fresh bulbs will keep nicely at room temperature for a couple of weeks. Or, store garlic by taking the skin off the cloves and popping them into a jar of vegetable oil. Cover with a tight lid. The oil acts as a natural preservative, and the garlic will last for months in the refrigerator. Also, the oil will pick up the flavor of the garlic and you can use it to flavor your cooking and dressings.
3. The easiest way to get the skin off a garlic clove is to trim the tips off and gently hit the clove with the flat side of a knife. That will loosen the skin and it should come away easily.

ABOUT CHICKEN

The chicken as we know it today is a descendent of the red jungle bird of Southeast Asia. It was domesticated in India as early as 2500 B.C.

Although chicken is inexpensive and plentiful today, it wasn't always so. From the late 1500s when King Francis IV of France hoped for a "chicken in every pot," chicken was confined to Sunday dinner. The advent of modern poultry-raising technology in the twentieth century made chicken popular and available.

Fresh chicken is very perishable. For best results, buy and cook chicken the same day, especially if it is cut up or split. Nutritionally, chicken can be a very good source of lean protein. Light meat is lower in fat and calories than dark meat and most of the fat and calories are in the skin. Take the skin off your chicken, even before you cook it, and you reduce the fat by more than half. Smaller broilers and fryers have less fat and calories than older birds such as roasters or stewing hens.

The mild taste of chicken meat can be greatly enhanced by the use of a marinade. There are two types of marinades—wet and dry. A wet marinade, originally developed as a brine for pickling, contains an acid such as lemon juice to tenderize the bird, and an oil to lubricate it. In India, chicken is marinated in yogurt and cardamom; Greeks use lemon juice, olive oil, garlic, and oregano. Dry marinades are combinations of herbs and spices that are rubbed into the chicken skin with a little oil.

Chicken and Vegetable Rice

4 teaspoons olive oil
1 medium onion, finely chopped
2 green bell peppers, finely chopped
4 garlic cloves, finely chopped
1 2½–3-pound chicken, skin and fat removed, cut into pieces
3 cups long-grain rice
1 cup tomato sauce
6 cups hot chicken broth with a pinch of saffron (the saffron is optional)
Salt and freshly ground black pepper
1 cup shelled green peas
1 cup green beans, cut into 2–3-inch pieces
½ cup chopped red bell pepper

1 Preheat the oven to 400° F.

2 In a deep sauté pan heat the oil and sauté the onion, green bell peppers, and garlic for 5 to 7 minutes.

3 Wash the chicken with cold water and pat dry with paper towels. Add the chicken pieces to the vegetables in the pan and continue to sauté until the chicken is lightly browned on both sides, about 10 minutes.

4 Add the rice to the pan and stir until completely coated with oil. Stir in the tomato sauce.

5 Pour in the hot chicken broth and season with salt and pepper to taste.

6 Add the peas, green beans, and red bell pepper. Bring to a boil. Reduce the heat and simmer for 5 minutes. Place the pan in the preheated oven and bake for 15 minutes, or until most of the liquid is absorbed and the rice is tender.

MAKES 4 SERVINGS

ONE OF THE OLDEST VEGETABLES

The ancient Egyptians believed that the onion was the symbol of the universe and would place their hand on an onion when they took an oath. Greek and Roman soldiers were fed onions to make them brave. The onion gets its name from the Latin word unio, *which means the uniting of many things in one, a reference to onions' many layers.*

ABOUT ONIONS

Botanically, onions are members of the same family as lilies and daffodils. They were first grown for food in the Middle East. The Spaniards brought them to the Americas and now billions of pounds are grown in the United States each year.

There are dozens of types of onions. But the most common are the yellow or white Globe onions which have a strong aroma and a firm crisp texture. These are the best all-purpose onions for cooking, stewing, and frying. The large sweet red onion, Bermuda, Vidalia, and Maui onions are better for salads and sandwiches.

Onions not only taste good but they are good for you. Doctors in ancient Greece and in the Far East used onions to treat a variety of ills. Now, modern science is discovering that onions may help prevent high blood pressure, heart attacks, and stroke. There is a chemical in onions that helps raise your body's high density lipids, or "good" cholesterol level. This keeps your blood flowing freely, reducing the chance of fat buildup in the veins and hardening of the arteries. Perhaps the tradition of cooking high-cholesterol meats such as liver with onions is in response to body knowledge. A doctor at Tufts University in Boston has used onions to treat patients with high cholesterol levels.

The hotter the onion the better for your health. Tangy yellow and white onions are more beneficial than mild red onions. So next time you're teary-eyed from peeling an onion, you can consider them tears of joy.

Buy onions as you need them and store them in a cool, dry place. Look for onions that are hard and firm, with no soft spots or green sprouting tips; the flatter the base the better the taste.

Chicken with Pineapple

2 tablespoons vegetable oil
8 ounces skinless, boneless
chicken breast, trimmed of all
fat and sliced into 1½-inch
strips
2 slices canned pineapple, cut
into chunks, or ½ cup
pineapple chunks (save the
liquid)
½ cup diced green or red bell
pepper
½ cup sliced canned bamboo
shoots
½ cup sliced bok choy or
Chinese cabbage
½ cup sliced celery
6 canned water chestnuts,
sliced
½ cup pineapple juice
2 tablespoons rice or white
wine vinegar
2 tablespoons sugar
½ teaspoon salt (optional)
2 tablespoons ketchup
1 tablespoon cornstarch
2 tablespoons water
Cooked rice

1 In a large sauté pan over high flame heat the
oil until hot. Add the chicken strips and cook,
stirring, until the meat is opaque, about 1
minute. Add the pineapple and vegetables
and cook, stirring, for 30 seconds.
2 Stir in the pineapple juice, vinegar, sugar,
and salt. Cover and cook for 2 minutes.
3 Dissolve the ketchup and cornstarch in the
water. Stir into the chicken mixture and cook
until thickened, about 30 seconds.
4 Serve over the cooked rice.

**MAKES 2 MAIN-DISH SERVINGS OR 4 SERVINGS IF PART
OF A CHINESE-STYLE MEAL**

The term "below the salt," used to connote low social status, dates back to medieval times when salt was placed at the center of the table. Royalty sat at the head of the table, and common folk sat further down, "below the salt."

In the past, salt was extremely important in preserving food and was very valuable. The Romans named the god of health Salus, after the Latin sal, from which are derived the words salutary, salvation, salary, and salute. The town of Salzburg, Austria, gets its name from its huge salt-mining industry that was started there during the Bronze Age, about 5,500 years ago.

ABOUT THICKENING AGENTS

Cornstarch is a common thickening powder that is made from highly refined dried corn. Oriental cooks use cornstarch to thicken sauces and as a batter coating for deep-frying. American bakers use cornstarch as a thickener for fruit pies.

A frequent substitute for cornstarch is arrowroot, which is the dried and powdered root of the arrow plant. The American Indians used arrowroot to heal wounds caused by poison arrows.

When making the substitution, use 1 tablespoon arrowroot for every 2½ tablespoons cornstarch. Tapioca flour is another thickening substitute for cornstarch. Tapioca flour is the powder made from the dried and ground root of the Brazilian cassava plant.

Cornstarch, arrowroot, and tapioca flour will break down and lose their thickening properties if they are cooked too long. When using cornstarch in puddings, custards, and pie fillings, use a double boiler and follow the recipe instructions carefully to avoid overcooking.

Continued . . .

SALT STORIES

Common table salt is known chemically as sodium chloride. Sodium is a major offender in high blood pressure, and most people would do well to lower their sodium intake. Another type of salt, however, called potassium chloride, has been shown to reduce blood pressure.

There are no nutritive or flavor advantages to sea salt, bay salt, rock salt, or kosher salt over regular table salt—they are all basically sodium chloride.

ABOUT PINEAPPLE

Pineapples originally grew wild in the jungles of South America. The Europeans first learned of them after Christopher Columbus discovered the island of Jamaica. Hawaii, thought of as a pineapple-growing area, actually got its first pineapple from Jamaica. Jamaica's national coat of arms has a pineapple on it, and the watermark on Jamaican money is a pineapple. When Columbus took pineapples back to Spain, they were called *pina de los Indies* (pine cone of the Indies). Portuguese traders took pineapples to Africa, India, and on to Hawaii. Today Hawaii produces over 60 percent of the world's pineapples, most of which are canned or made into juice.

Pineapple is naturally sweet, so skip the heavy syrup in canned pineapple if you are watching your calories. When you buy fresh pineapple look for a yellow-gold color around the eyes and at the base. The old test of pulling a leaf out easily to prove ripeness is not valid. The best test is to smell the bottom. If you get the smell of pineapple, it is ripe. Pineapple should be firm but tender. Avoid pineapples that are soft or discolored. Nutritionally, pineapples have 75 calories per cup. They're low in sodium and high in vitamin C.

Moroccan-Style Broiled Chicken

Morocco sits right across from Gibraltar, on the northwestern corner of Africa. Olive trees, citrus fruits, and grapes are grown there in vast plains supported by deep artesian wells.

1 In a bowl mix together the scallions, garlic, herbs, salt, and spices. Blend with the butter to make a paste.

2 Rub the paste over the chicken pieces, inside and out, reserving any extra paste for basting. Let stand for 1 hour.

3 Burn the charcoal in an outdoor grill or preheat the broiler.

4 If using a grill, arrange the chicken pieces skin side up over the coals. If broiling, arrange chicken skin side down in a baking pan and place under the broiler. Cook for 5 minutes, turn, and baste with any extra paste or the juices in the roasting pan. Continue turning and basting every 5 minutes, until the chicken is cooked through, about 20 minutes.

MAKES 4 SERVINGS

Paste:

3 scallions, white part only, chopped
1 garlic clove, chopped
1 tablespoon coarsely chopped fresh coriander
1 tablespoon coarsely chopped fresh parsley
1 teaspoon salt
1½ teaspoons paprika (sweet variety, if available)
Pinch of cayenne pepper
1½ teaspoons ground cumin
¼ cup unsalted butter, at room temperature
1 4-pound broiling-frying chicken, quartered

ABOUT CUMIN

Cumin is a tall feathery plant that is a member of the carrot family. The part used as a seasoning is the seeds, which are harvested, dried, roasted, and ground.

The Romans began using cumin as a seasoning in their food and it remained popular throughout the Middle Ages. Cumin is used extensively in Indian curries and chutneys, and in Mexican dishes such as enchiladas and chili. The biblical Hebrews believed cumin had the power to keep lovers from being fickle.

Chinese Chicken with Peanuts

3 pounds boneless, skinless
   chicken breasts, trimmed of
   all fat and cut into ½-inch
   cubes
1 egg white
1 tablespoon cornstarch
1 teaspoon salt
6 tablespoons vegetable oil
1 green bell pepper, seeded
   and cut into bite-size
   pieces
1 red bell pepper, seeded
   and cut into bite-size
   pieces
¼ cup Chinese bean sauce
   (optional)
½ cup chicken stock
¼ cup sugar
½–1 cup unsalted peanuts
   Cooked rice

1 Mix the chicken cubes with the egg white, cornstarch, and salt.

2 In a wok or deep saucepan heat 3 tablespoons oil until hot. Stir-fry the chicken in small batches for about 3 minutes. Drain on paper towels.

3 In the same wok or pan heat 1 tablespoon oil. Add the bell peppers and stir-fry for 1 minute. Remove from the pan.

4 Add the remaining 2 tablespoons oil to the wok. Add the bean sauce, if used, and cook, stirring, over very low heat for 3 minutes. Stir in the stock and sugar and cook for 1 minute.

5 Add the chicken and peppers and heat through.

6 Top with the peanuts and serve over cooked rice.

MAKES 6 TO 8 SERVINGS

ABOUT BELL PEPPERS

Most bell peppers begin green and become red, sweeter, and more nutritious as they ripen. Bell peppers are very high in vitamins A and C.

For stuffing, large "fancy-style" bell peppers are best, but for cooking and salads the "choice" grade is fine. Peppers should be firm and dark. Peppers that have been picked too early are pale, soft, and thin skinned; overripe ones are dull. Avoid shriveled or wilted peppers. Take a good look at the stem side of the pepper—that's where decay usually starts.S

ABOUT PEANUTS

The peanut is native to South America, but has been found around the world for over 500 years. The ancient Inca Indians of Peru had jars in the shape of peanuts.

Peanuts have been grown in the South since the 1800s, and were used as a staple food by troops from the North and South during the Civil War. The United States produces only about 3 percent of the world's peanut crop. The largest producers are in India and China.

Peanut butter was invented in 1890 by a St. Louis doctor who was looking for a high-protein food that could be easily digested by his patients. Soon hospitals were serving it to undernourished patients, and in the 1920s it emerged as a popular spread, becoming a mainstay food in four out of five homes.

Sesame Chicken

2 eggs
2 tablespoons milk
1 cup all-purpose flour
½ cup sesame seeds
½ teaspoon salt
¼ teaspoon freshly ground
   black pepper
3 whole boneless, skinless
   chicken breasts, cut into
   1-inch strips
   Vegetable oil for deep-frying

1 In a small bowl whisk together the eggs and milk. On a large plate combine the flour, sesame seeds, salt, and pepper. Dip the chicken in the egg mixture, then coat with the flour mixture.

2 Pour 3 inches of vegetable oil into a large saucepan. Heat the oil to 375° F.

3 Working in batches, fry the chicken strips in the hot oil for 5 to 7 minutes, until golden brown. Adjust the heat to maintain a temperature of 350° to 375° F.

4 Remove the chicken from the oil and drain on paper towels before serving.

MAKES 4 SERVINGS

ABOUT SESAME SEEDS

Sesame seeds are the dried seeds of an herb plant native to Indonesia and east Africa. The Chinese were using sesame seeds 5,000 years ago. The Egyptians used ground sesame for flour and sesame seeds were found at the excavation site on Mount Ararat.

Sesame seeds are small, white, and somewhat flat. They are full of oil, which is extracted and used in Chinese cooking. As the raw seeds are fairly bland, it is important to toast them on a flat pan for 10 minutes at 350° F to release their nutty flavor.

Ground sesame paste is called tahini and it is used in Middle Eastern dishes that are eaten with pita bread. Ground sesame seeds are also the basis of many candies, baked goods, and confections, including halvah.

Chicken or Turkey Chili

1 In a saucepan heat the vegetable oil over moderate heat. Add the onions and cook until translucent. Add the garlic and cook for about 2 minutes, without browning the garlic or onions.

2 Add the tomatoes, cayenne, Tabasco, and chili powder and cook for 3 minutes, until heated through.

3 Mix in the cooked chicken or turkey, corn, and kidney beans and heat thoroughly.

4 Serve over rice.

MAKES 6 SERVINGS

1 teaspoon vegetable oil
2 medium onions, diced
2 garlic cloves, minced
1 32-ounce can Italian plum tomatoes, drained
Pinch of cayenne pepper
3–5 drops Tabasco sauce
3 tablespoons chili powder
3 cups diced cooked chicken or turkey
1 cup cooked fresh, canned, or frozen corn
1 15-ounce can red kidney beans, drained and rinsed
Cooked rice (optional)

ABOUT CHILI POWDER

Chili powder is a blend of chili, red pepper, cayenne, paprika, cumin, cloves, marjoram, and garlic. If you add sugar, you've got a barbecue spice mixture.

ABOUT RED KIDNEY BEANS

While many red beans look alike, any red bean should not be substituted for red kidney beans. Kidney beans hold their shape and color best, both in salads and in cooked dishes.

Calcutta Chicken Curry

Sauce:
2 tablespoons unsalted butter
1 onion, chopped
1 large garlic clove, minced
3 tablespoons curry powder
1 large green apple, cored,
  seeded, and diced
1 small cucumber, peeled and
  diced
2 tablespoons chopped
  pimiento
2 large carrots, chopped
2 cups chicken stock
½ cup coconut cream

2 cooked chicken breasts, cut
  in half

1 In a large saucepan melt the butter over
moderate heat. Add the onion and garlic and
sauté until the onion is limp, about 3 minutes. Stir in the curry powder and cook for 2
more minutes.

2 Add the apple and stir. Add the cucumber,
pimiento, and carrots and cook for 1 minute.
Add the chicken stock and bring to a boil.
Cook for 5 minutes.

3 Puree the curry sauce in a food mill, food
processor, or blender and return the sauce to
the pan.

4 Stir in the coconut cream and reheat over low
heat.

5 Serve over cooked chicken.

MAKES 4 SERVINGS

WHAT'S COOKING TIPS: HOW TO MAKE COCONUT MILK OR CREAM

1. The liquid that comes out of a fresh whole coconut is called coconut milk, but there is another version that is used in cooking. This variety—culinary coconut milk or cream—is made by pouring hot water on grated fresh coconut. The mixture is left to steep for 10 minutes and then is poured through a double layer of cheesecloth and squeezed. The liquid that comes out is coconut milk or cream.
   Another method is to place the coconut meat in an electric blender with water and blend for 10 seconds. Again strain through cheesecloth.
2. Coconut milk is as perishable as fresh cow's milk. It should be kept in a closed container in the refrigerator and used within 3 to 4 days.
3. It is possible to use coconut milk as a drink, but it is not a real substitute for cow's milk since it doesn't have the same protein or nutritional benefits.
4. Coconut milk will curdle if cooked at a high heat. It is best to add it to dishes at the very last minute, or use a double boiler.

Meat

Veal Saltimbocca

Saltimbocca is the name of an Italian dish. It means "jump into the mouth," because the dish is so delicious it seems to leap off the plate and into your mouth. Saltimbocca originated in the town of Brescia, but is now a specialty of Rome.

There are many variations of saltimbocca, but it's basically a combination of thin veal scaloppine flavored with sage and topped with a slice of prosciutto ham. Sometimes the scaloppine is rolled into little bundles with the ham inside and other times it is left flat. Saltimbocca is often served on a bed of spinach. It's always sautéed in butter and served with a pan sauce made with Marsala or white wine.

1½ pounds boneless veal scaloppine, cut into thin slices (or boneless, skinless chicken breasts)
½ cup all-purpose flour
2 10-ounce packages frozen leaf spinach, or 2 pounds fresh spinach
2 tablespoons unsalted butter
½ cup vegetable oil
½ pound prosciutto (see sidebar), thinly sliced
½ teaspoon dried sage
2 teaspoons finely chopped fresh parsley
Freshly ground black pepper
2 eggs, hard-boiled, peeled, and sliced crosswise into rounds (optional)

1 Place the sliced veal between 2 sheets of wax paper and pound them into thin scallops with a mallet or the flat side of a cleaver. Lightly dust the veal scallops with flour.

2 Cook the frozen spinach according to package directions. Drain and toss with the butter. (If fresh spinach is used, wash very well in cold running water and remove the stems. Cook in a covered pan in just the water that clings to the leaves after washing. Cook for about 5 minutes, or until just tender. Drain the spinach and stir in the butter.) Make a bed of the hot spinach on a large platter.

3 In a large skillet heat half the oil. Place as many veal scallops in the pan as will fit without crowding. Cook until lightly golden on both sides, about 2 minutes per side. Remove the veal from the pan and drain on paper towels. Repeat with the remaining veal, adding more oil as needed.

4 Cut the prosciutto slices to approximately the size of the veal scallops.

5 Sprinkle each veal scallop with the sage, parsley, and 2 turns of the pepper mill. Lay slices of prosciutto on each veal slice.

6 Arrange the veal on top of the spinach. Place a slice of egg, if used, on each scallop and spoon the pan juices over all.

MAKES 6 SERVINGS

ABOUT SAGE

Sage is a flavorful leafy perennial herb that comes primarily from the Mediterranean. The sage plant grows to a height of 2 feet and has 2-inch silvery-green leaves that are used fresh or dried.

British cooking is partial to sage, which is used to flavor pork sausages called bangers and as the color and subtle flavor in green Lancashire cheese.

The Chinese drink sage tea, and many people believe that sage helps build a long and healthy life.

ABOUT PROSCIUTTO

Prosciutto is an Italian air-dried ham, and the best prosciutto is thought to come from the town of Parma because the pigs there are fed on the discarded rinds and curds of Parmesan cheese.

Prosciutto is made by rubbing ham with salt and hanging it in a cool, dry place for several months. The salt kills off the bacteria, and preserves the meat. Prosciutto is usually eaten sliced very thinly and wrapped around melons or figs, chopped and added to pasta dishes, or layered on veal for saltimbocca.

The United States Department of Agriculture does not allow the importation of Italian hams to America, but there are other sources. Switzerland provides us with many of our prosciuttos, as do American companies like Hormel and John Volpi in St. Louis. Virginia or Smithfield hams have a slightly different flavor, but can be used as substitutes for prosciutto.

Veal Marsala

2 tablespoons unsalted butter
2 tablespoons vegetable oil
¼ cup all-purpose flour for
    dredging
6 pieces veal cutlet or veal
    scaloppine
½ cup Marsala

1 In a large skillet melt the butter with the vegetable oil over medium-high heat.

2 Lightly dredge each piece of veal cutlet on both sides with flour. Add to the pan and cook for 1 minute. Turn and cook for 1 minute more. Remove the veal to a warm dish.

3 Add the Marsala to the pan, turn up the heat, and continue to cook until the sauce thickens, about 3 minutes.

4 Return the veal to the pan. Cook for 30 seconds, coating the veal with the sauce.

5 Serve at once, spooning some of the sauce over each portion.

MAKES 3 SERVINGS

ABOUT MARSALA

Marsala is a brownish red sweet wine that tastes of caramelized sugar. Made in the northwestern part of Sicily near the town of Marsala, it is blended from aromatic white wine, ground dried grapes, and brandy, then matured in oak casks for 2 to 5 years.

ABOUT VEAL

Veal is baby beef. It is more common in Europe than in America, but in cities with large Italian populations veal is readily available. European farmers do not have as much pasture and crop land as American farmers do, so they often slaughter young beef animals when they are 2 to 5 months old. They have been milk-fed their entire lives and have not had a chance to start exercising their muscles, which makes the meat creamy white and very tender. Some American veal is allowed to become a few months older and feed on grass. This veal is called calf.

Veal cutlets are thin, boneless pieces of meat cut from the rump or round portion of the animal. The best cutlets, called scaloppine, are cut across the grain from the single muscle of the top round. You may also come across cutlets that are cut from the whole hind leg that contain a small round bone in the center. This is a less successful cut.

The scaloppine must be cut slightly larger than ¼ inch thick and pounded to slightly less than ¼ inch thin. When pounding meat, use a pendulumlike motion, rather than coming straight down from the top. The best tool to use is a brass or stainless-steel pounder that is flat and smooth on the bottom, about 3 inches in diameter, with a vertical handle on top.

Sliced Veal in Cream Sauce with Mushrooms and Avocados

9 tablespoons unsalted butter
1¼ pounds top round leg of
    veal or veal scaloppine,
    trimmed of fat, thinly sliced
    Salt and freshly ground
    black pepper
2 tablespoons finely chopped
    shallots or onion
½ pound mushrooms
¼ cup white wine or chicken
    stock
¾ cup heavy cream
1 avocado, peeled, pitted,
    sliced, and cubed
2 tablespoons chopped fresh
    chives

1 In a large sauté pan melt 6 tablespoons butter. Add the veal, sprinkle with salt and pepper, and cook for 2 minutes. Remove the veal and set aside on a warm plate.

2 Pour the veal juices from the plate back into the sauté pan. Add the remaining 3 tablespoons butter and cook for 1 minute. Add the shallots or onions, mushrooms, and white wine or stock. Sauté, stirring, for 1 minute.

3 Add the heavy cream and cook for 3 minutes, or until the cream thickens enough to coat the back of a spoon.

4 Remove the pan from the heat. Add the veal, avocado, and chives. Stir together and serve.

MAKES 4 SERVINGS

ABOUT CHIVES

Chives are the most delicate member of the onion family. They are best cut with scissors to avoid bruising the stalks.

ABOUT SHALLOTS

Shallots are the high-class European cousin of the onion; they are shaped like garlic cloves and grow in clusters like garlic. Their flavor is distinctive—tangier than red onions but not as sharp as garlic.

Shallots are used extensively in French cooking. They are native to the Middle East and were brought to Europe by returning Crusaders. French explorers brought them to America. When buying shallots, look for bulbs that are about ¾ inch in diameter. The skin should be smooth and dry.

Soy Sauce Ginger Beef

1 In a large skillet heat 2 tablespoons oil over high flame. Add half of the beef cubes and stir-fry until seared on all sides. Remove the meat cubes and repeat with the remaining tablespoon of oil and the beef.

2 Return the beef to the skillet. Add the scallions, sherry, soy sauce, sugar, and ginger. Cook, stirring, over high heat.

3 Add the water and bring to a boil. Cover, reduce the heat to moderately low, and cook, stirring occasionally, for 1 hour, or until the meat is tender. There should be about ½ cup of liquid left. If there is more, increase the heat to high, uncover the pan, and cook for 5 minutes more.

MAKES 6 TO 8 SERVINGS

3 tablespoons peanut oil
2 pounds boneless beef shank, shin, or chuck, trimmed of all fat, cut into 1-inch cubes
2 scallions, white and green parts, cut into 1-inch lengths
½ cup dry sherry
3 tablespoons soy sauce
1 tablespoon sugar
2 slices fresh ginger, each about ¼ inch thick
1 cup cold water

ABOUT SOY SAUCE

Soy sauce is made by fermenting boiled and ground soybeans, roasted barley, or cracked wheat and salt. The Japanese use light soy sauce, the Chinese use soy sauce that is darker and stronger tasting, and Indonesian soy sauce is sweetened with molasses. In general, the high salt content of soy sauce keeps it from spoiling at room temperature, but refrigeration does not hurt the flavor.

From a nutritional standpoint, soy sauce should be used carefully by people on a low-sodium diet. One tablespoon of soy sauce can contain 1,479 milligrams of sodium. Some manufacturers make low-sodium soy sauce that contains only 605 milligrams of sodium per tablespoon. Bear in mind, however, that many doctors believe that a low-sodium diet should not exceed 1,000 milligrams of sodium per day.

Pepper Steak

⅓ cup vegetable oil
2 pounds top round steak, trimmed of all fat, cut into ½-inch strips
Salt and freshly ground black pepper
1 medium onion, chopped
2 large garlic cloves, chopped
3 medium red bell peppers, cored, seeded, and cut into strips
3 medium green bell peppers, cored, seeded, and cut into strips
2 cups sliced fresh mushrooms
2 cups beef stock
1 tablespoon Worcestershire sauce
3 tablespoons cornstarch dissolved in ½ cup water
¼ cup soy sauce
8 cups cooked rice

1 In a skillet warm the oil over moderate heat. Add the steak strips, and cook until lightly browned.

2 Season with salt and pepper to taste. Stir in the onion, garlic, peppers, and mushrooms. Sauté, stirring often, for 5 minutes, or until the vegetables are tender. Add the beef stock and Worcestershire sauce and cook for 2 minutes more.

3 Add the cornstarch mixture and soy sauce to the steak and cook for 2 minutes, stirring constantly, until thickened.

4 Serve with rice.

MAKES 8 SERVINGS

ABOUT MUSHROOMS

Most edible fungi are called mushrooms. There are close to 2,000 varieties. Mushrooms are of little nutritional value, providing only a few minerals and B vitamins. The word *mushroom* stems from the Teutonic word for moss, *mousse.* After the Norman invasion, the English began calling them mushrooms. In France they are called *champignons,* after the French word for field, *champs.* The Italians simply call them *funghi.*

Most of the mushrooms we buy as white button mushrooms are grown in underground caves in Pennsylvania and near St. Louis. In the last few years a number of companies have started cultivating wild mushrooms, including shiitake, chanterelle, boletus, and oyster mushrooms.

ABOUT STEAK

Steak is a common word for a slice of meat; it almost always refers to beef and is usually cut against the grain.

The tenderest cuts of steak—rib eye, T-bone, porterhouse, Delmonico, and others—can be broiled or pan-fried. Chuck, arm, and round steaks all need to be either marinated or cooked in liquid to be tender. The flank is just under the tenderloin, and contains one of the most versatile cuts, the flank steak. The most common flank steak dish is London broil.

USDA prime, choice, and select are the three main gradings for steak. The gradings are based on the quality of fat or "marbling" in the meat. Ninety percent of the steak we eat is choice. Prime is very expensive and hard to come by and nearly all of it is bought by and served in restaurants. Select is the leanest grade of steak and is now being upgraded by the beef industry. Steak, like all beef, is a good source of protein, iron, and B vitamins. It is also a source of saturated fat, which has been linked to heart disease. However, nutritionists say that beef can be a part of a healthy diet if portions are restricted.

Tangerine Beef

1 egg
2 cups plus 3 tablespoons vegetable oil
¼ teaspoon cornstarch
¼ teaspoon salt
¼ teaspoon baking soda
1 pound flank steak, cut into ½-inch cubes
¼ teaspoon minced garlic
¼ teaspoon dried red pepper flakes
¼ cup grated orange or tangerine zest
4 scallions, minced
2 teaspoons soy sauce
2 teaspoons dry sherry
2 teaspoons rice wine vinegar
2 teaspoons ketchup
Cooked rice

1 In a large mixing bowl whisk together the egg, 1 tablespoon vegetable oil, the cornstarch, salt, and baking soda.

2 Place the beef in the bowl and stir to coat well. Set aside to marinate for 1 hour.

3 In a wok or large skillet heat 2 cups vegetable oil to 375° F. Working in batches, add the flank steak to the oil and cook for 45 seconds. Remove with a slotted spoon.

4 Drain the oil from the wok and heat the remaining 2 tablespoons oil over medium-high heat. Add the garlic, pepper flakes, and zest; stir-fry for about 10 seconds. Add the flank steak, scallions, soy sauce, sherry, vinegar, and ketchup and stir-fry for 1 minute longer.

5 Serve at once, with rice.

MAKES 4 SERVINGS

ABOUT DRIED RED PEPPER FLAKES

Commercially prepared dried red pepper flakes are a common condiment in pizza parlors in the United States. The peppers that are used to make these hot little flakes are usually long red cayenne, short Thai, or serrano peppers. The peppers turn red on the compact bushy plants, are harvested, and dried. They are crushed and put in bottles. Whole dried red peppers can be kept in a jar and crushed by hand whenever they are needed.

Steak with Mustard Cream Sauce

1 Preheat the oven to 180° F.

2 Sprinkle both sides of each steak with pepper.

3 In a large heavy skillet that will hold all the steaks in a single layer melt the butter over moderately high heat. Sauté the steaks for 4 minutes on each side. Using tongs, remove the steaks to a heatproof serving platter and keep them warm in the oven.

4 Add the red wine to the skillet and cook over high heat, scraping up the browned bits that cling to the bottom of the pan.

5 Add the mustard and cook, stirring for about 1 minute. Add the cream and reduce the heat to low. Simmer for 4 minutes, until the sauce is thick enough to coat the back of a spoon.

6 Remove the steaks from the oven and pour the sauce over them. Serve immediately.

MAKES 4 SERVINGS

- 4 6-ounce boneless shell steaks (New York strip), trimmed of all fat
- 1 teaspoon freshly ground black pepper
- 3 tablespoons unsalted butter
- ½ cup red wine
- 4 tablespoons coarse-grained mustard
- 1½ cups heavy cream

Tofu Tomato Beef

2 tablespoons vegetable oil
8 ounces sirloin steak, sliced ½ inch thick on the diagonal, across the grain
8 ounces fresh soft tofu, diced
1 medium tomato, cut into 8 wedges
¼ cup sliced celery
4 water chestnuts, sliced
1 cup chicken stock or broth
1 tablespoon cornstarch
2 tablespoons ketchup
1 teaspoon sugar
½ teaspoon salt
3 tablespoons water

1 In a large sauté pan over a high flame heat the oil until hot. Add the steak, and stir-fry until the meat is seared on all sides. Add the tofu and vegetables and cook, stirring, for 30 seconds. Add the stock or broth, cover, and cook for 1½ minutes.

2 Dissolve the cornstarch, ketchup, sugar, and salt in the water. Stir into the beef mixture and cook until thickened, about 30 seconds. Serve immediately.

MAKES 2 MAIN-DISH SERVINGS OR 4 SERVINGS IF PART OF A CHINESE-STYLE MEAL

ABOUT TOFU

Tofu is Oriental soybean curd.

Keep tofu refrigerated, but do not let it freeze. Drain and replace the water you store it in daily.

To firm up tofu before using it, let it drain for several hours or overnight. Old tofu can be refreshed by quickly boiling or deep-frying it.

WHAT'S COOKING TIPS: STIR-FRYING

Stir-frying is the Oriental method of quickly sautéing foods. The method is basically an open-fire technique of cooking because the pan, usually a wok in China, is placed over a direct flame on a brazierlike stove. The heat is very intense and the food is stirred quickly.

The keys to successful stir-fry cooking are simple:

1. Use a heavy iron, steel, or aluminum alloy skillet with deep sides. The Chinese wok is the best tool.
2. Prepare all the ingredients in advance and chop them into bite-size pieces so they can cook quickly.
3. Warm your wok or pan over medium heat for several minutes before turning it to high. Always add the oil *just before you add your first ingredient.*
4. Follow your recipe carefully. Adding the foods in the proper order is essential. The ingredients are put into a wok in order of the amount of time they need to cook, so that they are all done at the same moment.
5. Do not get distracted while stir-frying. You need to stay right over the wok and pay attention. Overcooking toughens meat and causes vegetables like broccoli to lose their bright color and crunchy texture.

Oriental Imperial Steak

½ cup safflower oil
6–8 ounces fillet of beef,
   trimmed of all fat, cut into
   cubes
   Dash of sherry wine
8 whole dried Chinese
   mushrooms, soaked and
   sliced lengthwise
8 snow peas, cut into ½-inch
   pieces
½ cup drained and sliced
   bamboo shoots
½ cup sliced water chestnuts
1 small head bok choy
   (Chinese cabbage),
   shredded
1 cup chicken stock
1 tablespoon oyster sauce
   (optional) (see sidebar)
1 tablespoon cornstarch
   dissolved in 2 tablespoons
   cold water

1 In a wok or deep skillet heat ¼ cup oil until almost smoking. Add the beef cubes and cook, stirring, for 2 minutes, until browned. Add the sherry and cook, stirring for 2 minutes more. Remove the beef and set aside.

2 Add the remaining ¼ cup oil and all of the vegetables. Stir-fry for 2 minutes.

3 Add the chicken stock, cover, and cook for 2 minutes.

4 Add the oyster sauce and cornstarch and water mixture and cook for 2 minutes more.

5 Return the steak to the pan and cook until just heated through. Serve immediately.

MAKES 4 SERVINGS

OYSTER SAUCE

Oyster sauce is a common ingredient in Chinese grocery stores. But here is how to make your own.

12 oysters, shelled and chopped,
   liquid reserved
3 tablespoons soy sauce

1 In a pot bring the oysters and their liquid to a boil, and simmer for 20 minutes.

2 Strain the mix through a sieve and discard the solids.

3 Add the soy sauce.

4 Store refrigerated in a tightly sealed jar.

ABOUT BAMBOO SHOOTS

Bamboo shoots come in winter and spring varieties. The winter type is smaller and more tender. When buying canned shoots, look for those packed in water, which are usually better than those packed in brine.

Alamo Burgers

1 pound ground beef chuck
¼ cup taco sauce
4 pita breads
Refried beans, warmed
½ head iceberg lettuce, finely sliced
1 cup shredded Cheddar or Monterey Jack cheese

1 Burn charcoals in an outdoor grill or preheat the broiler.

2 In a bowl mix the beef with the taco sauce.

3 Shape the meat into 4 patties and grill or broil to the desired point of doneness.

4 Slice 1 inch off one side of each pita bread and open the pocket. Coat one side of the inside of the pita with some of the warm refried beans.

5 Put the cooked burgers into the pita pockets and stuff with lettuce and cheese.

MAKES 4 SERVINGS

ABOUT PITA BREAD

Pita bread, also known as pocket bread, is made from white or whole-wheat flour and is the staple food of Middle Eastern countries. It is round, flat, only lightly leavened, and hollow inside. It is a good source of dietary fiber and B vitamins.

People in the Middle East believe that pita bread is a gift from God. They eat it with every meal, often tearing it into finger-size pieces to scoop food from platters to their mouths. Fresh pita bread warmed in an oven or over a flame swells up like a pouch.

ABOUT MONTEREY JACK

Monterey Jack is a firm cow's milk cheese that originated in Monterey County, California. The "Jack" comes from a Scottish immigrant named David Jacks who made cheese and shipped it out of Monterey, with his name on the shipping crate. Eventually, customers in northern California began asking for Monterey Jack cheese.

Monterey Jack is a modern version of a Queso Blanco or white cheese that was made by Spanish missionaries in California. Monterey Jack works very well in Mexican cooking. Less commonly known than the mass-produced Monterey Jack cheese are some very fine types made on a small scale in northern California.

Danish Meatballs

1 In a mixing bowl combine the veal, pork, onion, bread crumbs, and eggs.

2 Slowly add the club soda or seltzer, and mix until thoroughly combined.

3 Shape the meat into small 1-inch balls.

4 In a skillet or sauté pan melt the butter with the oil over moderate heat. Fry the meatballs until lightly crusted on all sides.

MAKES 4 SERVINGS

½ pound ground veal, ground twice

½ pound ground pork, ground twice

1 onion, finely chopped

1 cup dry bread crumbs

4 eggs

1½ cups club soda or seltzer

¼ cup unsalted butter

¼ cup vegetable oil

WHAT'S COOKING TIP: UN-SALTED BUTTER

When buying butter, get the unsalted variety. Salt masks the flavor of butter, making it hard to tell if it has gone bad. In addition, most of us would do well to reduce our salt intake. If you need to have salt in something, you can put it in yourself.

ABOUT SELTZER

Seltzer was brought to the United States by Jewish immigrants in the early 1900s. It consists of nothing but carbonated filtered water. The basic spritzer consists of "shpritzing" seltzer into a quarter of a glass of sweet wine.

Blackened Burgers

1½ teaspoons freshly ground
    black pepper
1½ teaspoons cayenne pepper
½ teaspoon salt
1½ teaspoons fennel seed
1½ teaspoons garlic powder
1½ teaspoons dried thyme
1½ teaspoons dried oregano
1 pound ground beef, divided
    into 2 patties
4 tablespoons vegetable oil
½ cup chopped scallions
1 garlic clove, chopped
½ cup sour cream

1 In a mixing bowl combine the seasonings. Dip the hamburgers into the spices and coat thoroughly on both sides.

2 In a frying pan heat 2 tablespoons vegetable oil. Place the hamburgers in the pan and cook to the desired point of doneness.

3 In another frying pan heat 2 tablespoons vegetable oil. Add the scallions and garlic and sauté for about 1 minute. Stir in the sour cream and heat for 1 minute.

4 Place the hamburgers on a plate and pour the sauce on top.

MAKES 4 SERVINGS

ABOUT HAMBURGERS

Along with hot dogs, hamburgers are the most American of all foods. The name hamburger is derived from the German port city of Hamburg, but that's not where hamburgers were born. Through the latter half of the nineteenth century, some form of hammered beef steak was served in restaurants there. But the first time the name hamburger was used was at the Louisiana Purchase Exposition and World's Fair in St. Louis in 1904.

The advent of the White Castle hamburger chain in the 1920s and the McDonald's chain in the 1950s spread hamburger culture deep into America.

Hamburgers should be called beef burgers because it is rare that hamburgers are made of veal, lamb, or pork. Hamburger meat bought at the supermarket cannot contain more than 30 percent fat. A hamburger should contain 20 to 25 percent fat, although it is possible to buy meat that is as lean as 10 percent fat. Ground chuck has the proper fat content, and the beefiest flavor.

WHAT'S COOKING TIPS: MAKING HAMBURGERS

1. An important rule for preparing hamburgers at home is to handle the meat as little as possible. The more you handle it, the more juice is lost. As the meat loses its moisture it loses its tenderness. Quickly form it into a patty and leave it alone. Uneven edges don't matter.

2. If you're pan-frying a hamburger, do not press the meat down with a spatula. That presses out the natural juices.

3. The best way to tell if a burger is done is to press it gently with your finger. Well-done meat is firm and resistant to the touch. Rare meat is softer. Do not cut the burger open to test for doneness; the most flavorful juices will drain out.

4. Don't keep uncooked ground meat in the refrigerator for more than 24 hours.

New York Firehouse Chili

Chili con carne is Spanish-American for chile peppers with meat. The chili powder now commonly used to season chili dishes was invented in 1902 by a German immigrant in New Braunfels, Texas. In Texas, a bowl of chili is commonly called a bowl of red.

5 tablespoons vegetable oil
2 pounds ground round beef
1 pound Italian sausage, skinned and crumbled
4 cups beef stock
1 teaspoon saffron threads
2 cups coarsely chopped shallots
2 tablespoons minced garlic
1 10-ounce can green chiles, chopped to form a rough puree
1 teaspoon crushed dried oregano
1 teaspoon ground cumin
½ teaspoon cayenne pepper
2 tablespoons chili powder
1 teaspoon salt
Freshly ground black pepper
1 6-ounce can tomato paste
1 30-ounce can red kidney beans, drained

1 In a large heavy skillet heat 2 tablespoons oil over medium-high flame. Add the ground meat and sausage and sauté until browned.

2 Transfer the meat to a 4-quart pot. Add the beef stock to the skillet, and bring to a boil. Remove the stock from the heat. Crumble the saffron into the stock. Set aside.

3 In another large skillet heat the remaining 3 tablespoons oil over medium-high flame. Add the shallots and garlic and sauté for 5 minutes, until lightly browned. Remove from the heat.

4 Stir in the chiles and seasonings, plus a few grinds of black pepper to taste. Stir in the tomato paste and mix thoroughly.

5 Pour the contents of the skillet into the large pot of meat and mix well. Place over medium-high heat and bring to a boil. Reduce the heat to low and simmer, half-covered, for 1½ hours.

6 Add the beans and cook for 10 minutes before serving.

MAKES 8 SERVINGS

ABOUT SAFFRON

Saffron comes from the stigma of the crocus, and 75,000 must be hand picked to get a pound. That explains why it is one of the most expensive food products on the planet—about $2,000 a pound. Fortunately, the flavor is very powerful and only a pinch is needed for a whole pot of food. Saffron is sold in long, thin "threads" and crushing them in a little hot water will bring out all of the flavor.

Lamb Chops with Blue Cheese Sauce

1 In a small saucepan bring the heavy cream almost to a boil.

2 Remove from the heat and whisk in the cheese until smooth. Return to low heat and cook for 10 minutes. Preheat the broiler.

3 Season with salt and pepper to taste.

4 Broil the lamb chops to the desired doneness.

5 Serve the cheese sauce over the broiled lamb chops.

MAKES 2 SERVINGS

⅓ cup heavy cream
6 ounces blue cheese, crumbled, at room temperature
Salt and freshly ground black pepper
4 rib or loin lamb chops

ABOUT BLUE-VEINED CHEESES

Blue cheese, or *bleu* in France, is a firm but crumbly cheese that gets its blue streaks from injections of perfectly edible bacteria. Roquefort is a particular type of blue cheese made of sheep's milk in the caves near the French town of Roquefort. Legend has it that Roquefort cheese was made accidentally when a sheep herder left his lunch of hard cheese and bread on a ledge in a cave. He discovered his lunch a few weeks later and found a delicious blue mold had grown in the cheese.

There are dozens of different places in France that make forms of bleu cheese besides Roquefort. Bleu de Bresse and Bleu d'Auvergne are two of the most famous.

Gorgonzola is the Italian version of blue cheese, but there are important differences. Gorgonzola is made from cow's milk and the green mold occurs naturally when the cheese is aged. The caves for this cheese surround the town of Gorgonzola in northern Italy.

The British also make several blue cheeses. Stilton is a white cow's milk cheese with blue veins running throughout. There is also Dorset Blue, Blue Cheshire, and Blue Wensleydale. British blue cheeses tend to be firmer textured than French or Italian.

Denmark makes two types of blue cheese: firm and dry Danablu, and creamy Saga, which is now also made in the United States.

The American Midwest produces delicious cow's milk blue cheeses. Maytag Blue, Treasure Cave, and Nauvoo blue are three of the most well-known.

Brisket with Apples and Caraway

The brisket is to the cow what the breast is to the chicken. It is one of the most flavorful cuts of meat, and is excellent for stews and pot roasts.

4 cups tart apples sliced, cored, but not peeled
3 cups sliced onions
1 slice bread, preferably rye
2 tablespoons caraway seeds
3 pounds beef brisket, very well trimmed of fat, lightly dusted with flour
½ teaspoon salt
¼ teaspoon black pepper
1 cup apple juice or water
1 tablespoon red wine vinegar

1 Preheat the oven to 350° F.

2 In a large heavy casserole arrange half of the apples, half the onions, the bread, and 1 tablespoon caraway. Place the meat on top, sprinkle it with salt and pepper, and spread the remaining apples, onions, and caraway seeds over it. Pour in the apple juice or water and cover.

3 Place the casserole in the oven and bake the meat for 2 hours, or until very tender.

4 Remove the brisket from the pot and skim off any fat. Pour the apple-onion mixture into a food mill, processor, or blender and puree. Pour the puree into a saucepan. Add the vinegar, and additional salt and pepper to taste. Thin the puree, if necessary, with apple juice.

5 Slice the meat and arrange it on a heated platter. Heat the sauce through and pour it over the meat.

MAKES 4 TO 5 SERVINGS

WHAT'S COOKING TIPS: HOW TO USE A MEAT THERMOMETER

1. Sticking a meat thermometer into a roast and leaving it there until it registers the desired temperature is a bad idea. First, it can damage the meat by conducting heat to the interior, and second, it creates a big hole through which juices escape.
2. The best way to test for doneness is to use a tiny instant thermometer. It reads internal temperature in seconds. Just poke the meat with the thermometer, judge the doneness, and pull it out.
3. To calibrate your thermometer, bring a pot of water to boil, place the thermometer in the water, and adjust the little screw near the dial so that it reads 212° F. If you are making this test in a kitchen that is much above sea level, you must adjust the 212° F to the temperature at which water boils in your location.

ABOUT APPLE JUICE

When apple juice is pressed out of apples, the vitamins and nutrients come out intact, making apple juice a rather healthy drink. If it is allowed to ferment until some of the sugar is used, you get sweet cider. If all the sugar is used, you have hard cider. Applejack, or Calvados, is made by distilling hard cider.

ABOUT CARAWAY

Caraway seeds are most famous for the role they play as the seeds in rye bread. They are also used to flavor aquavit liquor. Caraway roots resemble parsnips, and can be cooked the same way.

ABOUT RYE

Rye's main uses are in rye bread and rye whiskey. Rye flour is brown-gray, and if used alone makes a very dark bread, like pumpernickel. Rye bread is usually a mixture of rye, wheat, barley, and pea flours.

Lamb Chops with Honey-Mustard Crust

¼ cup honey
¼ cup coarse-ground mustard
¼ cup smooth Dijon-style
mustard
1½ cups fresh bread crumbs
4 lamb chops, cut about ¾
inch thick, with fat removed
from the last inch of each
bone (Frenched)
3 tablespoons vegetable oil

Sauce:
1 1-pound can apricots in syrup
2 tablespoons honey
2 tablespoons chopped fresh
mint

1 Preheat the oven to 350° F.
2 In a shallow bowl blend together the honey and the mustards.
3 Place the bread crumbs in a shallow dish.
4 Dip both sides of the lamb chops into the honey-mustard mixture until lightly coated overall. Coat the chops with the bread crumbs.
5 In a large ovenproof skillet heat the oil over medium-high flame.
6 Add the chops and sauté for 3 minutes on each side. Place the skillet into the oven for 15 to 20 minutes to complete the cooking.
7 To make the sauce, puree the apricots and their juices together with the honey and the mint. Heat the puree in a saucepan until warm and serve with the lamb.

MAKES 4 SERVINGS

ABOUT APRICOTS

Apricots are a member of the plum family and have a hard stone pit inside. They originated in northern China and were brought to Europe around 400 B.C. King Henry VIII's gardener brought apricots to England from Italy in 1542.

If you can't get apricots that are perfectly ripe and juicy, dried apricots are a good substitute. They are an excellent source of vitamin A and iron, and can be soaked and pureed for use in puddings, and as a topping for ice cream.

Apricots are cooked with lamb in the Middle East, where they are an everyday food staple.

ABOUT MINT

Spearmint and peppermint are the two most common and useful culinary mints; there is very little difference in their flavors. Both are native to Europe but they are fully naturalized in America. Gracious homes of the Old South always had a mint bed for adding to Bourbon whiskey.

Mint is a most cooling and refreshing herb. It is common in Arab countries to see people walking home from the market with large bunches of fresh mint stalks in their hands. It is made into mint tea, very strong and heavily sweetened. Roast lamb with mint jelly is a traditional English and American favorite.

ABOUT HONEY

Honey is the nectar of flowers collected and processed by bees. We get the sticky fluid by spinning the combs of the hives and extracting the honey.

Honey gets different flavors from the types of flowers from which the bees get their nectar. Clover is by far the most common, but there is also dark rich buckwheat honey, fragrant lavender honey, tupelo honey, and orange-blossom honey.

From a sugar-calorie standpoint, there is no difference between table sugar and honey. Honey just has a different taste. When using honey in cooking, a straight cup-for-cup substitution is acceptable, but honey will change the flavor, color, and liquidity of the dish.

It is best to store honey in a closed container at room temperature. If it crystallizes and hardens, place it in warm water until it liquefies.

Grilled Baby Lamb

Sauce:
¼ **cup minced mixed fresh herbs
(such as parsley, mint, chervil,
or tarragon)**
¼ **cup peanut oil**
¼ **cup rice wine vinegar**
1 **egg yolk**

Lamb:
1 **6-rib rack of lamb**
3 **tablespoons minced mixed
fresh herbs (such as parsley,
rosemary, mint, or chervil)
Freshly ground black pepper**
2 **tablespoons olive oil**

1 Mix the sauce ingredients in a blender. Set
aside.
2 Preheat the broiler. Season the rack of lamb
with the herbs and pepper and brush with
olive oil.
3 Grill the lamb for 5 to 7 minutes on each side.
4 Pour the sauce over the cooked lamb and
serve.

MAKES 3 SERVINGS

*Lamb is the symbol of Christ
and the traditional meat of
Easter. Muslims roast a whole
lamb to celebrate a new year
and the birth of children. Jews
eat lamb with unleavened bread
and bitter herbs at Passover.*

LAMB TRADITIONS

Lamb is young sheep. When lamb gets older it becomes the tougher and stronger-flavored mutton. The English like to eat mutton, but most of the rest of the world prefers lamb.

Our domesticated lamb is descended from the curly-haired wild mountain sheep. These animals were first domesticated tens of thousands of years ago in Kurdistan, a hilly region that stretches across Iraq, Iran, and Turkey. Lamb was the principal source of meat for the ancient developing civilizations in the Mediterranean, India, and Asia. Sheep could live almost anywhere, were very hearty, and provided wool to make clothes.

American lamb comes from an English breed of sheep. Most of it is raised by Spanish Basque herders in Texas, California, and Wyoming. The most delicate lamb on the market is the 6- to 10-week-old milk-fed baby lamb. The majority of lamb comes from animals that are 6 months to 1 year old.

Lamb is a good source of protein and B vitamins.

Continued . . .

WHAT'S COOKING TIPS: BUYING AND COOKING LAMB

1. Fresh young lamb should have firm flesh and white fat. The fat should be carefully trimmed away on all cuts. Lamb is covered with a thin membrane called the fell. The fell should be left on whole cuts like roasts or legs, but removed from chops.

2. Lamb is a tender meat and it can be cooked by the dry-heat method but can also be stewed with wine and vegetables. Lamb chops can be quickly broiled, grilled, or pan-fried. Leg of lamb can be roasted in the oven or on a spit barbecue.

3. A rack of lamb is the rib section of the lamb, which is between the loin and the shoulder. The rack makes a good roast for two to three people. Ask your butcher to crack the chine that connects the ribs so that you can carve the roast after you cook it.

4. A butterflied leg of lamb is one that has the bone taken out of it. The meat is then splayed open flat and trimmed so that it resembles a butterfly opening its wings. A butterflied leg of lamb is one of the most tender and flavorful cuts of meat. It tastes best roasted over coals in a barbecue.

5. Lamb shoulder is a firm and flavorful meat that needs long, slow cooking in liquid to tenderize it. Butchers say that an easy way to tell if a cut of meat is going to need moist cooking is to find out where it came from on the animal. If it comes from a part of the animal that moves—shoulder, hind leg, or shank—it will have muscle and will need slow cooking. If it comes from the back or rib section, which does not move, it will be tender and can be cooked by broiling, roasting, or baking with no liquid added.

Lamb and Cabbage Stew

1 Preheat the oven to 400° F.

2 Cut the lamb into slices.

3 Butter a heatproof casserole. Place a layer of the sliced cabbage on the bottom of the dish. Cover with a layer of the sliced lamb. Sprinkle with salt and pepper to taste. Repeat layering the cabbage and lamb until all is used. Place the bay leaves on the top of the casserole and add enough chicken stock to half-fill the casserole.

4 Cover and bake for about 1½ hours, or until the lamb is tender.

5 Remove the bay leaves and serve.

MAKES 8 SERVINGS

2 pounds lamb shoulder or leg, all fat removed
2 pounds green cabbage, sliced
Salt and freshly ground black pepper
2 bay leaves
Chicken stock

ABOUT CABBAGE

Cabbage is indigenous to western Asia and Europe. It is one of the oldest cultivated vegetables. The cabbage family, *Brassica,* also includes broccoli, Brussels sprouts, cauliflower, and kale. Settlers brought cabbage to America, where it was grown and eaten mostly by German and Dutch settlers in New York, Pennsylvania, Wisconsin, and Michigan.

The most common type of cabbage that is good for cooking is Dutch or white cabbage, which also has a special place in coleslaw.

Savoy cabbage, which has dark green crinkled leaves, is not quite as sweet as white cabbage, but is highly prized by French cooks. Chinese cabbage, or choy, has an elongated head and is much milder tasting than either white or savoy cabbage.

Red cabbage is similar to white cabbage, but contains a red pigment that gives it a different color and flavor.

Raw cabbage is very high in vitamin C and beta carotene, a building block for vitamin A which is now believed to inhibit the growth of cancer. Cabbage also has significant amounts of calcium, phosphorus, and potassium. A cup of finely shredded cabbage contains only 24 calories.

Stuffed Pork Tenderloin

1 2-pound pork tenderloin,
  trimmed of all fat
½ pound ground sausage
  Salt and freshly ground black
  pepper
2 tablespoons unsalted butter

Sauce:
  2 tablespoons vegetable oil
  1 cup sliced mushrooms
  ½ cup minced scallions
  2 tablespoons all-purpose
    flour
1½ cups warm milk
  2 tablespoons coarse-grain
    mustard

1 Preheat the oven to 350° F.

2 Cut a hole in the center of the pork and, using the long handle of a wooden spoon, continue the hole down the length of the central core of the tenderloin. Stuff with the sausage meat, using the spoon handle to push the sausage inside. Sprinkle with salt and pepper to taste.

3 In a sauté pan melt the butter over moderate heat. Add the pork tenderloin and brown well on all sides.

4 Place the meat in a roasting pan and roast until the tenderloin reaches an internal temperature of 170° F, about 35 minutes.

5 Meanwhile, in a sauté pan heat the oil and sauté the mushrooms and scallions for 5 minutes. Stir in the flour and blend well. Pour in the warm milk and whisk into a thick sauce. Blend in the mustard.

6 Remove the meat from the oven and carve on the diagonal into ½-inch slices. Spoon the sauce onto a serving plate and place the meat slices on top.

MAKES 8 SERVINGS

SAUSAGE

Sausage dates back to at least 850 B.C. on the Greek island of Salamis, from where we get our word salami. *The word* sausage *comes from the Latin word* salsus, *which means "salted meat."*

Dublin Coddle

This traditional Irish bacon and sausage–based stew has been popular as a Saturday night main dish since the 1700s. The word coddle *means to cook at a very low and gentle simmer.*

1 Layer the bottom of a 4-quart sauté pan with the potatoes. Continue layering with the carrots, leeks, onion, bacon, and sausages. Place the bay leaf on top. Season with salt and pepper to taste.

2 Add the stock, cover, and cook over moderate heat until the stock comes to a boil, about 10 minutes. Reduce the heat and simmer for 20 to 40 minutes, or until the sausages are cooked through.

3 Remove the bay leaf and serve.

MAKES 4 SERVINGS

4 medium all-purpose potatoes, peeled and sliced
3 medium carrots, peeled and sliced
2 leeks, trimmed, washed and sliced
1 medium onion, sliced
½ pound sliced bacon, cut into 1-inch pieces
8 pork sausages (about ½ pound)
1 bay leaf
Salt and freshly ground black pepper
2½ cups chicken stock

Stuffed Pork Chops

6 rib or loin pork chops, 1 to 1½ inches thick, trimmed of all fat (ask your butcher to cut a pocket in each, or do it yourself, following the directions below)

Stuffing:

¼ cup unsalted butter
1 medium onion, finely chopped
1 celery rib, finely chopped
.1 clove garlic, finely minced
3 large fresh mushrooms, finely chopped
1 teaspoon dried thyme or rosemary
1 cup dry bread crumbs
½ cup chopped fresh parsley
½ teaspoon salt
½ teaspoon freshly ground pepper
¼ cup vegetable oil
1 cup brown sauce or gravy, or 3 tablespoons all-purpose flour and.1 cup beef broth or bouillon

1 With a sharp knife cut a 2½-inch pocket in the fat-edged side of each pork chop that reaches deep into the meat, until the tip of the knife touches the bone. Set aside.

2 To prepare the stuffing, in a medium skillet melt the butter over moderate heat. Add the onion, celery, garlic, mushrooms, and thyme or rosemary. Cook, stirring, until the vegetables are softened, about 5 minutes. Stir in the bread crumbs, parsley, salt, and pepper. Blend thoroughly; the mixture should be fairly dry.

3 Using a teaspoon, fill the pocket in each chop with the prepared stuffing, dividing the mixture evenly. As each chop is stuffed, press the cut edges together to enclose the stuffing and secure the pocket with small skewers or wooden toothpicks.

4 Choose a skillet with a tight-fitting lid that is large enough to hold all the chops in a single layer. Warm the oil over moderately high heat. Add the stuffed chops and brown well on one side.

5 Carefully turn the chops, taking care not to disturb the stuffing, and brown the second side. Meanwhile, boil enough water to cover the bottom of the skillet.

6 Add the boiling water to the skillet, cover tightly, reduce the heat to low, and simmer for 25 minutes, adding additional water if necessary.

7 Carefully turn the chops, replace the lid, and simmer for 10 to 20 minutes longer, depending on the thickness of the chops. Chops should be tender but not dry. When cooked, transfer to a hot platter and keep warm.

8 With a large spoon, skim off any fat from the pan juices. Add the brown sauce or gravy to the pan and heat, stirring occasionally, just to a boil. Or, stir the flour into the pan juices, blend well, and cook for several minutes. Add broth or bouillon and stir over moderately high heat until the mixture thickens.

9 Taste and correct the seasonings; spoon the sauce over the chops. Remove the skewers or toothpicks and serve.

MAKES 6 SERVINGS

ABOUT PARSLEY

Fresh parsley is the most available, useful, and nutritious of all the herbs. Parsley can be kept in an airtight container for a week in the refrigerator. It is very high in vitamin C.

There are two main types of parsley. Curly leaf, the most common, has tight, compact curled leaves that should be separated from the stems, which are often bitter. Italian or flat leaf parsley is more pungent than regular parsley.

Chinese parsley is not parsley at all. It is the immature greens of the coriander spice plant. It resembles parsley but has quite a different and distinctive flavor (see page 19).

Butterflied Leg of Lamb

1 leg of lamb, boned and
  butterflied (ask your butcher
  to do this)
2 garlic cloves, minced
1 tablespoon crushed dried
  thyme
1 tablespoon crushed dried
  rosemary
2 tablespoons coarse-grain
  mustard
¼ cup vegetable oil
  Salt and freshly ground black
  pepper

1 Burn the coals in an outdoor grill or preheat
  the broiler.
2 Spread out the lamb on a board and rub it
  well with the garlic, thyme, and rosemary.
3 In a small bowl combine the mustard, oil, and
  salt and pepper to taste.
4 Place the lamb on the grill or on a rack in a
  broiling pan and grill or broil 4 to 5 inches
  from the heat, basting occasionally with the
  mustard sauce and turning once or twice, for
  40 to 50 minutes, depending on the desired
  degree of doneness. Internal temperatures for
  lamb can be checked with an instant-reading
  meat thermometer: rare at 140° F, medium at
  150° F, well at 160° F.
5 Remove the lamb to a cutting board and cut
  on the diagonal into ¼-inch slices.

MAKES 10 TO 12 SERVINGS

*Legend has it that the Virgin
Mary turned the color of
rosemary blossoms when she
spread her blue cloak over the
white-flowered bush and turned
the blooms to the color blue.*

ABOUT ROSEMARY OIL

The herb rosemary is the leaves of a fragrant perennial plant that grows in great bushes in Europe, especially the south of France and Spain. The herb has a sweet and bitter pungency which enhances the flavor of roast lamb and poultry. It is a powerful herb and should be used carefully.

Rosemary is a very oily plant and has long been prized as a hair conditioner. Rosemary oil is available in pharmacies and cosmetics stores. A drop or two on your brush is reputed to keep your hair fragrant and in good health.

Pork Chops in Country-Style Mustard Sauce

4 tablespoons unsalted butter
6 loin pork chops, cut 1¼ inches thick
Salt and freshly ground black pepper
3 tablespoons minced shallots or scallions
½ cup dry white wine
2 cups heavy cream
½ cup coarse-grain mustard

1 In a heavy skillet large enough to hold the pork chops in one layer, melt 2 tablespoons butter over moderately high heat until foamy. Add the pork chops and brown well on both sides. (If you do not have a pan large enough to prepare all the chops at one time, they can be prepared in smaller batches.)

2 Season with salt and pepper to taste. Reduce the heat to low, cover, and cook for 15 minutes. Transfer the chops to a platter; set aside and keep warm.

3 Pour off the fat from the skillet. Increase the heat to moderate, add the remaining 2 tablespoons butter and the shallots or scallions, and sauté for 30 seconds. Increase the heat to high, stir in the wine, and cook, scraping up the brown bits that cling to the bottom of the pan, until the liquid is syrupy and reduced by half, about 2 minutes. Blend in the cream and the mustard and cook, stirring, for 2 minutes more. Do not allow the sauce to boil.

4 Pour the sauce over the pork chops and serve.

MAKES 6 SERVINGS

ABOUT PORK

Pork is the meat of the pig, one of our oldest sources of meat. The wild boar is the pig's first ancestor, and some of the prehistoric cave paintings depict the wild boar hunt.

The first pork recipes stem from China, are dated about 500 B.C., and call for a suckling pig roasted in a pit. The Chinese and the Romans were adept at smoking and curing pork for use in the winter months. The tradition of slaughtering hogs for meat, sausages, ham, and lard continues to this day. Among the Cajuns of southwest Louisiana it is a community event called *la boucherie*. The Spanish conquistador Hernando de Soto brought the first pigs to Florida in 1525. The majority of pigs in the United States are raised in Iowa, Illinois, and Missouri.

The best cuts of pork for roasts are the hind legs, known as fresh hams, and the loin sections. Pork chops also come from the loin section. Bacon comes from the pork belly. Pork chops are cut from the center loin and the sirloin portion of the pig. Butterfly chops are boneless pieces cut from the top loin roast. Iowa chops are rib chops or loin chops that are cut at least 1½ inches thick.

Pork has become less fatty in recent years. A 3-ounce portion contains 200 calories, and 80 milligrams of cholesterol. Pork is also a good source of B vitamins and minerals.

People no longer need to fear trichinosis, a parasitical disease that used to be common in pork products. Modern breeding, production practices, and packing-house hygiene have virtually eliminated trichinosis. Furthermore, cooking pork to an internal temperature of 140° F kills the parasite and makes pork safe to eat. In terms of taste and tenderness, pork is best when cooked to 155° F.

The tenderloin is the most delicate and expensive cut of pork. Tenderloin tips run from the base of the ribs to the hip bone.

Pasta and Rice

Spaghetti Carbonara

Spaghetti carbonara is a popular Roman dish that mixes cooked bacon and eggs, cream, cheese, and pasta. The Italian word carbone *means "coal" and it is thought that dishes described as "carbonara" were particularly enjoyed by the men who delivered coal.*

Classic spaghetti carbonara is usually made with pancetta, the unsmoked Italian version of bacon. If you can't get pancetta, try using thinly sliced prosciutto ham, but even American bacon will still give you a delicious dish.

½ **pound spaghetti**
¼ **cup unsalted butter**
½ **cup chopped cooked bacon**
½ **cup thinly sliced, chopped pancetta or prosciutto**
2 **egg yolks**
½ **cup heavy cream**
   Freshly ground black pepper
¼ **cup freshly grated Parmesan cheese, plus extra as garnish**

1 In a large pot of boiling salted water cook the spaghetti until it's tender but still firm to the bite.

2 Meanwhile, in a large sauté pan or skillet melt the butter over moderate heat. Add the bacon and prosciutto and sauté for 2 minutes.

3 In a mixing bowl stir together the egg yolks, heavy cream, black pepper to taste, and the Parmesan cheese.

4 Drain the spaghetti and add to the bacon and prosciutto. Mix well and pour in the cream mixture. Cook, tossing, for 1 minute, until the pasta is well coated with the sauce. Season to taste with black pepper.

5 Serve hot, with Parmesan cheese on top.

MAKES 2 SERVINGS

WHAT'S COOKING TIPS: PASTA

1. Use a large pot, and at least 4 quarts water per pound of pasta.
2. Pasta should be cooked quickly, and the more hot water there is, the sooner it will come back to a boil after the pasta is added. Pasta should be added to the water all at once, and pushed under the water with a wooden spoon.
3. Fresh pasta can be ready in just a few seconds. Dried pasta usually takes from 6 to 8 minutes to cook, depending on the shape. The only way to know when it's done is to pull out a piece and taste it. It should be firm to the bite, not soft and mushy.
4. As soon as pasta is cooked, drain it in a colander, shake out the water, and put it back into the pot or serving dish with the sauce.

ABOUT "SPAGHETTI"

Pasta is an ancient dish that probably got its start in China. But it was the Italians, from Naples, who became big fans of spaghetti, and who brought pasta to America.

Until recently, spaghetti was a generic term used to describe a dish composed of boiled stringy noodles and a zesty tomato sauce. The name spaghetti comes from the Italian word *spago,* which means "string." Today, spaghetti is just one of dozens of popular pasta shapes.

Flat pasta shapes like ravioli and fettuccine are commonly made from freshly rolled dough. Spaghetti and other round shapes are extruded through special dies and dried for an extended period. Recent fashion has led some to believe that fresh pasta is superior to dried, when in fact, the appropriate type is usually determined by the particular dish or sauce.

Pasta with Tomato and Cream Sauce

½ cup unsalted butter
¼ cup finely chopped onion
¼ cup finely chopped carrot
¼ cup finely chopped celery
2½ cups canned Italian plum
   tomatoes, with their juice
¼ teaspoon sugar
   Salt
1 pound pasta
½ cup heavy cream

1 In a large saucepan melt the butter over moderate heat. Add the onion, carrot, and celery and sauté for 3 minutes. Stir in the tomatoes, sugar, and salt to taste. Reduce the heat to low and simmer, stirring from time to time, for 1 hour.

2 In a large pot of salted boiling water, cook the pasta until tender but still firm to the bite.

3 Meanwhile, puree the tomato sauce in a food mill, food processor, or blender. Return the sauce to the saucepan and bring to a simmer. Add the heavy cream and cook, stirring, for 1 minute more.

4 Drain the pasta and turn it into the sauce. Toss well and continue to heat for a minute. Serve immediately.

MAKES 4 SERVINGS

ABOUT PASTA AND HEALTH

The richest pasta has only about 210 calories a cup. Pasta is a high-complex-carbohydrate food that is filled with nutrients, including many of the B vitamins. Because pasta slowly releases sugar into your blood over several hours, your energy level is maintained, and your hunger is diminished. This is why pasta is among the foods recommended for those who participate in sports that require endurance, like marathon running.

When you eat high-complex-carbohydrate foods like pasta, your brain releases a chemical called serotonin that makes you feel safe and happy.

Low-Calorie Vegetable Pasta

1 In a pot of boiling salted water cook the pasta.

2 Meanwhile, in a large casserole or saucepan heat the vegetable oil. Add the onion and sauté for 2 minutes.

3 Add all of the remaining ingredients except the pasta and bring to a boil. Reduce the heat and simmer for 25 minutes, or until the carrots are tender.

4 Transfer the sauce to a blender or food processor. Cover and puree until smooth. Return to the saucepan.

5 Drain the pasta. Pour the pasta into the sauce and reheat for a few minutes. Serve at once.

MAKES 4 SERVINGS

1 pound pasta
2 tablespoons vegetable oil
3 cups thinly sliced onion
2 cups coarsely chopped celery
2 cups coarsely chopped carrots
1 green bell pepper, seeded and diced
1 red bell pepper, seeded and diced
1 35-ounce can peeled Italian plum tomatoes, chopped, with their juices
2 tablespoons tomato paste
½ tablespoon dried basil
½ teaspoon freshly ground black pepper
2 teaspoons sesame seeds
1 tablespoon sugar
Pinch of salt

ABOUT ZUCCHINI

Zucchini is a summer squash. Like all squashes, it originated in South and Central America and was introduced to Europe during the years of colonization in the sixteenth and seventeenth centuries. Zucchini was brought back to America in 1921 by Italian immigrants, who had a special fondness for the soft tender vegetable.

When buying zucchini, look for slender ones that are 3 to 6 inches long. At this size the seeds are edible and the flesh is sweet. The skin should be smooth and unblemished and either dark green or light green with dark green strips. Zucchini will last in the vegetable bin of the refrigerator for 2 to 3 days.

Roman Street Pasta

5 tablespoons olive oil
2 garlic cloves, minced
2–3 slices Italian bread, cut into ¼-inch cubes (about 1 cup)
8 anchovy fillets, finely chopped
4½ cups Italian plum tomatoes, drained, pureed in a food mill or processor
8 pitted black olives, sliced
1 teaspoon capers
1 tablespoon chopped fresh basil, or 1 teaspoon dried sweet basil
¼ teaspoon hot red pepper flakes
1 pound linguine or spaghettini

1 In a large saucepan heat 2 tablespoons oil over moderate heat and sauté the garlic and the bread cubes until the bread is crisp. Remove the croutons from the pan and set aside.

2 Add the remaining 3 tablespoons oil to the saucepan and stir in the anchovies. Add the tomato puree and simmer for 10 minutes.

3 Stir in the olives, capers, basil, and red pepper flakes. Simmer, uncovered, over low heat for 20 minutes, or until thickened.

4 Meanwhile, in a large pot of boiling water, cook the linguine until tender but still firm to the bite. Drain well.

5 Turn the pasta into the sauce. Blend well and heat for a few moments.

6 Top with the croutons.

MAKES 4 SERVING

OLIVE LORE

The olive tree is native to the borders of the Mediterranean Sea. It is probably the most significant nutritional and symbolic plant that grows there. The biblical Canaanites used olives for food, lamp fuel, medicine, and anointments. Jerusalem was founded at the foot of the Mount of Olives. The ancient Greeks gave their heroes olive wreaths. Cypriots worshiped olive trees in their temples. The Romans converted Spanish agriculture to huge olive oil plantations and fought naval battles to protect their control over the olive oil trade.

ABOUT OLIVES

Spain is the world's largest producer of olives and Seville is the olive capital of Spain. Endless olive plantations planted by the Moors surround Seville. There, in November, all olives are picked green and cured in caustic soda. Processing plants churn out "Spanish olives" complete with their pimiento center.

In general, green olives are immature and the black, purple, and dark red olives are ripe. All are cured either in salt water or oil or dried by the sun.

Olives are fairly low in nutritional value and calories and quite high in sodium because of the curing process.

ABOUT ANCHOVY

The salty brown strips of fish you find in tiny tins of anchovy were once 3- to 6-inch-long silvery fish swimming in the Mediterranean Sea. In Spain, fresh anchovies, called *boquerónes,* which means "big mouthed," are served whole or filleted as appetizers. The Spanish, Italians, and Portuguese are the main producers and consumers of anchovies.

The salting of anchovies goes back thousands of years. The Romans loved *garum,* a salty fish sauce made of anchovies; Worcestershire sauce is the modern version.

Try to buy the best whole fillets of anchovies rather than those that are chopped or mashed. If you love anchovies but you are on a sodium-restricted diet, rinse the anchovies in water to remove some of the salt, or buy the kind packed in oil.

Spring Pasta

1 pound spaghetti
3 tablespoons olive oil
1 cup cooked ham, cut into thin
   slivers about 2 inches long
1 cup zucchini, cut into thin
   slivers about 2 inches long
1 cup crushed canned Italian
   plum tomatoes
1 tablespoon chopped fresh
   basil, or 1 teaspoon dried
   sweet basil
   Salt and freshly ground black
   pepper
   Freshly grated Parmesan
   cheese

1 In a large pot of boiling water cook the spaghetti until tender but still firm to the bite.

2 Meanwhile, in a saucepan, combine the olive oil, ham, zucchini, tomatoes, and basil over moderate heat. Season with salt and pepper to taste and cook, stirring from time to time, for 7 minutes.

3 Drain the spaghetti and turn it into the sauce. Heat for a minute and toss to combine.

4 Serve with Parmesan cheese.

MAKES 4 SERVINGS

ABOUT PARMESAN CHEESE

Parmesan is a hard grating cheese that is made in and around the Italian city of Parma. True Parmesan cheese is labeled by Italian law as Parmigiano-Reggiano (and comes from the Emilia-Romagna region). Parmesan cheese is made from cows' milk and is aged 2 to 3 years. It is made in huge wheels that can weigh as much as 88 pounds.

Parmesan is a sharp, salty, tangy cheese, and when young is delicious as a table cheese. It is best to buy whole chunks of Parmesan and grate it yourself as you need it. You don't know how old pregrated Parmesan is, and it will continue to lose flavor rapidly. Grate it as you need it. Grated Parmesan should be kept in the refrigerator and then warmed to room temperature for serving.

Keeping a whole chunk of Parmesan fresh is easy. Wrap the cheese in a lightly damp cheesecloth or other thin muslinlike cloth. Wrap that in aluminum foil and keep it in the refrigerator.

ABOUT BASIL

Basil is a deep green plant with 2-inch-long glossy leaves. Thinly chopped fresh basil leaves strewn over fresh tomatoes and drizzled with olive oil makes a delicious summer dish, popular in the south of France and in Italy. Basil leaves are the main ingredient in the Genovese specialty, pesto sauce.

Basil originated in ancient India, where it was said to be sacred to the gods Vishnu and Shiva. The ancient Greeks, Romans, and Hebrews believed that basil had the power to give great strength.

Tortellini Salad

Tortellini can be served swimming in a rich chicken stock spiked with grated cheese and parsley, or topped with a sauce of tomatoes, meat, or cream. Modern cooks have been steaming or boiling tortellini until tender, cooling them, and mixing them with vegetables and a tangy salad dressing to make a variation on pasta salad. Here is one such preparation.

Vinaigrette Dressing:
- 2 tablespoons Dijon-style mustard
- ⅓ cup red wine vinegar
- ¾ cup olive oil
- 2 garlic cloves, finely minced
  Salt and freshly ground black pepper to taste

Salad:
- 1 pound meat- or cheese-filled tortellini, cooked and cooled
- 1 cup blanched broccoli flowerets
- ⅓ cup finely chopped red onion
- 1 red bell pepper, finely chopped
- ½ cup finely chopped fresh parsley
- 1 cup pitted black olives (optional)
  Freshly grated Parmesan cheese (optional)

1 To make the vinaigrette, in a mixing bowl whisk together all the ingredients.

2 Place the cooked tortellini in a serving bowl and toss with the vinaigrette dressing. Add the broccoli, onion, red pepper, parsley, and olives and toss again.

3 Cover and refrigerate for 30 minutes to allow the flavors to blend together.

4 Remove from the refrigerator and allow to come to room temperature. Serve with grated Parmesan cheese.

MAKES 4 SERVINGS

ABOUT TORTELLINI

Tortellini are little pasta packages filled with meat, cheese, herbs, vegetables, or seafood that originated in either Bologna or Modena, in Italy. The difference between tortellini and ravioli is that tortellini is made from a round circle of pasta which is filled and then twisted to look more like a little nugget, while ravioli is plain and flat, round or square in shape.

ABOUT VINAIGRETTE

Vinaigrette is the primary salad dressing of France. Classic vinaigrette is made of three to four parts vegetable oil whisked together with one part red wine vinegar, plus herbs and spices. Many people add dry or prepared mustard, lemon juice, and even blue cheese to a vinaigrette to enhance the flavor.

The classic way to make and serve green salad in France is to make the vinaigrette first in the bottom of a large salad bowl. Cross the salad forks over the vinaigrette to create a barrier and lay the lettuce leaves on top. When guests are assembled at the table, toss the lettuce with the vinaigrette for the freshest flavor. You do not want the vinegar to be in contact with the lettuce before you serve it because the acid breaks down the crisp consistency of the lettuce.

ABOUT BROCCOLI

Broccoli is an intensely green sprouting member of the cabbage family. We eat the flowering head of the plant before it flowers and turns yellow. Any yellow flowerets or open buds on your broccoli means that the plant is too mature and may be bitter and tough.

Broccoli is one of the most nutritious vegetables, a good source of vitamins A and B, calcium, iron, and potassium and more vitamin C than an equal amount of orange. Broccoli is best and most nutritious when it it still bright green and crunchy. Overcooking makes it soggy and destroys the vitamins. Steam broccoli or boil it briefly, then plunge it into a pan of cold water to stop the cooking process. A full cup of broccoli is high in fiber and has only 40 calories.

Broccoli was first made popular by the Italians around Naples. It was brought to England and the colonies in the eighteenth century. The wave of Italian immigration to the United States in the 1920s gave broccoli a big popularity push. Most of the broccoli we eat now is grown in California.

Cold Shells with Tuna

1 pound macaroni shells,
  cooked until just tender
1 6½-ounce can solid white
  oil-packed tuna, undrained,
  broken into chunks
1 medium tomato, peeled,
  seeded, and chopped
1 medium cucumber, peeled,
  seeded, and chopped
1 small zucchini, finely chopped
¼ cup capers, drained
  (optional)
2 tablespoons fresh lemon juice
1 cup mayonnaise
  Salt and freshly ground black
  pepper
2 tablespoons minced fresh
  parsley as garnish

1 In a mixing bowl combine the shells with the
tuna, its oil, the tomato, cucumber, zucchini,
and capers, if used. Add the lemon juice.
2 Stir the mayonnaise into the mixture. Season
with salt and pepper to taste. Chill for 1 hour.
3 Garnish with the parsley and serve.

MAKES 4 SERVINGS

ABOUT CAPERS

Capers are the pickled flower buds of the shrubby caper plant, which
grows wild in the countries that border the Mediterranean Sea. The best
capers are the tiny nonpareils. The larger capers are very tasty but are
stronger in flavor than the nonpareils and they need to be chopped for
most recipes. Capers are also available salted and dried.

ABOUT TOMATO

Tomatoes have not always been one of the world's most popular foods. They are native to the Andes mountains of South America and they were very popular in Mexico, where they got the name *tomatl*. When the Spanish conquistadors brought the tomato back to Europe in the sixteenth century, many people thought this new food was poisonous.

The Italians were the first Europeans to use tomatoes, which they called *pomoi d'oro,* or "golden apples," because tomatoes at that time were often yellow. The French called them *pommes d'amour,* or "love apples," because they were thought to be aphrodisiacs.

Thomas Jefferson popularized tomatoes in America when he grew them in his garden at Monticello. Tomato sauces and dishes became popular in America with the arrival of the Italian immigrants in the early years of the twentieth century.

Fresh tomatoes are high in vitamin C and fiber. They are a good source of vitamin A and potassium and contain iron, the B vitamins, phosphorus, and calcium. A medium-size tomato has about 27 calories.

Macaroni with Ham and Cheese

Dry bread crumbs
3 tablespoons unsalted butter, plus extra for topping
2 shallots, finely minced
3 tablespoons all-purpose flour
2 cups milk
Salt and freshly ground black pepper
2 cups cooked ham, cut into ¼-inch cubes
1 cup shredded Jarlsberg cheese
Dash of Tabasco sauce (optional)
½ pound elbow macaroni

1 Preheat the oven to 375° F. Butter a 6- to 8-cup baking pan, sprinkle with bread crumbs, and set aside.

2 In a saucepan melt the butter; add the shallots and cook for a few minutes to soften. Add the flour, stir, and cook for 2 minutes. Add the milk, stirring with a whisk, and cook until thickened.

3 Add the salt and pepper to taste, and stir. Fold in the ham and cheese, add Tabasco to taste, and set aside.

4 In a large pot of boiling water cook the macaroni until tender but still firm to the bite. Drain well and return to the empty pot.

5 Add the sauce and mix well. Turn the mixture into the prepared pan, sprinkle with the bread crumbs, and dot lightly with butter.

6 Cover with foil and bake for 30 minutes. Uncover, raise the heat to 425°, and bake for about 10 minutes longer, or until golden and bubbling.

MAKES 2 SERVINGS

STUCK A FEATHER IN HIS CAP AND CALLED IT MACARONI

During the 1700s, young Englishmen from upper-class families were sent to other parts of Europe to "polish off" their education. While in Italy, they were exposed to pasta cooking for the first time. They loved these "macaroni" dishes and tried to reproduce them upon their return to England. They came home not only with a passion for pasta but with many other ideas that appeared strange and foreign to their fellow countrymen. These graduates of the European Grand Tour seemed affected to the average Englishman and were often referred to with the derogatory term "macaroni," which was used both as a noun and as an adjective for a style of dress. When Yankee Doodle stuck a feather in his cap and called it macaroni, he was referring to this slang term of the era for a dandy.

ABOUT JARLSBERG CHEESE

Jarlsberg cheese is made in Norway and is very similar in taste and texture to Swiss cheese. It is a cow's milk cheese that originated in Oslo in 1959. Jarlsberg has a buttery and slightly nutty flavor accompanied by the familiar holes or eyes of Swiss cheese. Jarlsberg is a little less expensive than genuine Swiss cheese and is becoming quite popular in the United States.

ABOUT MACARONI

Most Americans know macaroni as the small elbow noodles that are boiled and mixed with cheese to make macaroni and cheese. The combination has been an American tradition since the English settlers first brought it to the colonies. A similar dish was popular in the north of Italy and that is probably where the English got the idea. Thomas Jefferson imported both macaroni and a macaroni-making machine from Italy and the first macaroni factory in America was opened—by a Frenchman—in Philadelphia in 1798. By the time of the Civil War, macaroni was popular as far west as Kansas.

In Italy, macaroni (*maccheroni*) has come to be a generic term for all types of dried unfilled pasta, including spaghetti, rigatoni, ziti, and linguine. Diners in working-class restaurants in some parts of Italy are bound to be asked if they want *zuppa* (soup) or macaroni as their first course. Macaroni is whatever pasta dish the cook has dreamed up that day. Old-fashioned grocery stores that make dried pasta in Brooklyn, New York, Philadelphia, and Boston, cities with large Italian populations, are called macaroni stores.

Ricotta, Spinach, and Noodle Pudding

6 ounces medium-size egg
   noodles (about 3 cups)
4 tablespoons unsalted butter
¾ cup finely chopped onion
½ teaspoon finely minced garlic
1 10-ounce package frozen
   chopped spinach, partially
   thawed
1 15-ounce container
   whole-milk ricotta cheese
1 teaspoon salt
¼ teaspoon freshly ground
   black pepper
¼ cup fine dry bread crumbs

1 Preheat the oven to 375° F. Butter a 1½-quart deep baking dish or soufflé dish.

2 In a pot of boiling water cook the noodles until not quite tender.

3 Meanwhile, in a large skillet melt 1 tablespoon butter over moderate heat. Add the onion and garlic and cook until softened, 3 to 5 minutes.

4 Drain the noodles. Turn into a large saucepan and toss with 2 tablespoons butter. Set aside.

5 Add the spinach to the onion and garlic and cook, covered, over moderate heat for 5 minutes. Uncover and cook briefly to evaporate most of the liquid.

6 Add the onion-spinach mixture to the noodles. Stir in the ricotta, salt, and pepper and mix well. Scoop the mixture into the prepared baking dish.

7 In a small skillet melt the remaining 1 tablespoon butter and stir in the bread crumbs. Sprinkle the crumbs evenly over the noodle mixture. Bake for 35 to 40 minutes, until the cheese is melted and the crumbs are lightly browned. Serve hot.

MAKES 3 TO 4 MAIN-COURSE SERVINGS OR 6 TO 8 SIDE DISHES

ABOUT RICOTTA CHEESE

Ricotta cheese is a fresh cheese similar to cottage cheese. It has a very mild flavor and delicate consistency, and heats well in dishes like lasagna. It is made from whey or buttermilk, and comes in regular and part-skim varieties. At 4 and 2 percent fat, they are both extremely low-fat cheeses, and are recommended in low-fat diets.

Ricotta is a healthy substitute for sour cream in some recipes.

Risotto

Risotto is a special Italian rice dish made with Arborio rice, which is grown in the Po River valley of northern Italy. Arborio is a wide-grained rice, almost round, that has a pearly white spot on it. The wonderful thing about Arborio is that it can absorb a large amount of liquid and still hold a firm texture. In making risotto, the rice is constantly stirred. The result is a creamy smooth dish with little nuggets of tender rice. Almost any meat, fish, shellfish, herb, vegetable, or spice can be added, and grated Parmesan cheese is often the final ingredient.

1 In a large saucepan heat the olive oil over moderate heat. Add the onions and sauté for 2 minutes.

2 Add the rice and stir until completely coated with the olive oil.

3 Stir in the vegetables and combine thoroughly with the rice.

4 Stir in 1 cup chicken broth and stir continuously over low heat until the broth is absorbed by the rice. Continue adding the broth, 1 cup at a time, and stirring until absorbed before adding more.

5 When the rice is tender, mix in the grated Parmesan cheese and the butter. Serve at once.

MAKES 4 SERVINGS

3 tablespoons olive oil
½ cup chopped onions
2 cups Italian Arborio rice
2 cups mixed fresh vegetables, chopped into small pieces and half cooked
5 cups chicken broth, boiling
½ cup grated Parmesan cheese
¼ cup unsalted butter, softened

RISOTTO: THE RICE OF ITALY

Risotto is mainly a dish served in the northern Italian cities. Because it is similar to Middle Eastern pilaf, some historians think rice was introduced to Italy by the Moors or by traders in Venice.

Spanish Rice

3 tablespoons unsalted butter
¼ cup finely chopped onion
1 garlic clove, finely chopped
2 cups long-grain rice
4 cups chicken stock
½ cup minced pimiento
½ cup cooked green peas

1 In a heavy saucepan melt the butter over moderate heat. Add the onion and garlic and sauté for 1 minute, without browning.
2 Add the rice, stir, and cook for 1 minute.
3 Add the chicken stock and cook, covered, over low heat, until all the stock is absorbed by the rice, about 20 minutes.
4 Stir in the pimiento and peas just before serving.

MAKES 6 SERVINGS

RICE HISTORY

Throughout Asia, rice has been a symbol of wealth and the sacred force that sustains life. In ancient Japan, rice was so highly prized that samurai warriors were paid in rice. Peasants in China before Mao had to mill their rice and give the polished kernel to the landlords; they were forced to eat only the hulls. When Mao took power, he gave whole rice back to the peasants. During the Cultural Revolution, bureaucrats were forced to eat rice hulls in the countryside at re-education camps.

ABOUT GREEN PEAS

Green peas originated in northern India. The best are considered to be the petits pois from France, which are small and sweet.

Split pea is a synonym for dried pea, because peas naturally split when they are dried.

ABOUT RICE

Rice, along with wheat and corn, is one of the world's three great grains. Mainly, Europeans eat wheat, North and South American Indians eat corn, and Asians eat rice.

Historians believe that rice was first cultivated in Neolithic China or Thailand over 5,000 years ago. The first documents relating to rice date back to 2800 B.C. in China. White rice as we know it today is rice that has had the hulls and outer shell polished off. In addition to food, rice is used to make alcohol, spirits, wine, and beer.

Turmeric Rice

Turmeric is a spice in the ginger family which is used in making curry powder and mustard. In this dish, it imparts a warm, yellow color and mild Oriental flavor to the rice.

This dish can also be prepared with polished or white rice, though you will be losing the superior nutritive value of the whole grain. Adjust the recipe in step 3, using the amount of liquid and cooking time recommended on the white rice package.

2 tablespoons vegetable oil
1 medium onion, minced
1 cup whole-grain (brown) rice
1 tablespoon turmeric
2 cups chicken stock or broth

1 In a saucepan combine the oil and onion and cook over moderate heat until the onion is translucent and milky in color, about 5 minutes.

2 Add the rice and turmeric and mix together.

3 Add the stock or broth. Bring to a boil over high heat, reduce the heat to low, and stir with a fork. Cover and cook for 45 minutes, without removing the cover during the cooking time. Fluff the rice with a fork.

MAKES 4 SERVINGS

ABOUT TURMERIC

Turmeric is a bright yellowish-orange member of the ginger family. What we use as a spice is the dried and ground roots of the turmeric plant. It is native to China and Indonesia, but it is grown widely in India, Haiti, and Jamaica.

Turmeric has a light fragrant taste but it is used more for its yellow coloring properties than its flavor and is one of the primary spices in blended curry powder. Turmeric is sometimes used as a substitute for the much more expensive saffron, imparting the color, if not the flavor. People in India and China also utilize turmeric as a dye for the brilliant yellow in many of their so-called saffron religious robes.

Rice and Nut Loaf

1 Preheat the oven to 350° F. Lightly grease a 9- × 5-inch loaf pan.

2 In a large mixing bowl combine all of the ingredients.

3 Spoon the mixture into the pan. Bake for 1 hour. Allow to sit for 10 minutes, slice, and serve.

MAKES 6 SERVINGS

2 cups cooked rice
1 cup chopped walnuts
1 cup tomato puree or sauce
2 medium onions, finely chopped
1 cup cracker crumbs or crushed saltines
2 tablespoons vegetable oil
½ teaspoon crushed dried sage
2 tablespoons chopped celery
1 tablespoon chopped fresh parsley
Freshly ground black pepper
Tabasco sauce to taste

ABOUT BOILING

Many recipes call for adding a pinch of salt to water that will be used to boil food. This raises the temperature of the water, so that the food cooks faster. Sugar will do the same thing—in fact any solid that you dissolve in the water will have this effect.

When you add alcohol to a dish, you lower the temperature at which it will boil, and you may have to add 10 percent more cooking time than you would need for the same dish without the alcohol.

Bacon Fried Rice

½ pound bacon, cut into
  ½-inch pieces
3 tablespoons vegetable oil
2 eggs, beaten
3 cups cold cooked rice (see
  Note)
1½ tablespoons soy sauce
½ cup scallions, green part
  only, coarsely chopped

1 In a skillet fry the bacon until crisp and drain on paper towels.

2 In a wok or large skillet heat 1 tablespoon oil. Add the eggs and cook, stirring, just until firm. Remove from the pan and reserve.

3 Heat the remaining 2 tablespoons oil in the pan and add the rice. Mix well. Add the soy sauce and mix well. Mix the eggs into the rice, breaking them into smaller pieces as you stir. Add the scallions and bacon. Mix again to combine and serve.

MAKES 4 SERVINGS

NOTE: The rice should be cooked at least several hours ahead, or the day before, and refrigerated. It should be completely cold to be used for fried rice.

This dish can be kept in a casserole in the oven at 140° F for about 40 minutes without drying out. It makes a good dish to serve with a main course that needs last-minute preparation.

WHITE RICE

1 cup long-grain white rice
1¾ cups water

1 Pour the rice into a 2-quart saucepan. The pan must have a heavy bottom and a tight-fitting lid.

2 Cover the rice with 1¾ cups water and set the saucepan over a high heat, uncovered, until the water comes to a boil.

3 Cover the pot, lower the heat to very low, and simmer the rice for 15 minutes.

4 Turn off the heat and let the rice rest for 10 minutes. Don't stir the rice until you are ready to serve it. Stir the rice with a fork, as spoons tend to make it stick together.

FRIED RICE

Fried rice is thought to have originated in the Yangchow province of China, and combines rice, onions, soy sauce, and just about anything else, fresh or leftover. If one major ingredient is used, the dish is given that name, as in Chicken Fried Rice. If many major ingredients are used, it is called subgum—or many varieties— fried rice. In China it was at one time considered rude to serve fried rice to your guests because it is almost always made from leftovers.

Wild Rice Griddle Cakes

½ cup yellow cornmeal
½ cup all-purpose flour
1 tablespoon baking powder
1½ teaspoons brown sugar
1 egg, lightly beaten
½ cup milk
3 tablespoons unsalted butter
½ cup wild rice, cooked just until tender and drained well
2 tablespoons chopped pecans
2 medium baking apples, peeled, cored, and finely diced
2 tablespoons minced scallions
Salt (optional)
Applesauce, warmed

1 In a mixing bowl combine the dry ingredients.

2 Blend in the egg and milk and set the batter aside for 2 minutes.

3 On a griddle or in a fry pan melt the butter over moderately high heat until it foams and turns a light nutty brown.

4 Lightly chop the wild rice. Add the wild rice, pecans, apples, and scallions and sauté for 1 minute. Season with salt, if desired, and stir the rice mixture into the batter.

5 Spoon 2 heaping tablespoons of the batter onto the buttered griddle and cook until the edges are firm. Turn and cook the other side for 1 minute more.

6 Serve with warm applesauce.

MAKES 6 CAKES

WHAT'S COOKING TIPS: GRIDDLE, JOHNNY/HOE CAKES

Griddle cakes are pancakes that are cooked on a flat, sideless skillet called a griddle. Johnnycakes or hoecakes were early frontier griddle cakes that were often cooked on a garden hoe over an open fire.

1. When making the batter for griddle cakes, don't overbeat. Whip the ingredients together quickly. Ignore the lumps. They will disappear. Flours differ and so will the consistency of your batter. If it is too thin, add more flour. If too thick, add more liquid.
2. Make sure the griddle is made of heavy metal and is well seasoned and thoroughly heated before you start cooking.
3. Drop the batter from a spoon 1 or 2 inches above the griddle surface. Cook for 2 to 3 minutes or until little bubbles appear. Flip and brown the other side.

ABOUT WILD RICE

Wild rice is not a rice at all. Also known as Indian rice and Canadian rice, it is actually a tall grass that grows in lakes, rivers, and streams in the northern United States, especially Minnesota. Traditionally, wild rice was harvested by Indians who paddled their canoes into a wild rice paddy and shook the kernels off the plants and into their boats.

True wild rice is quite expensive, so it is sometimes mixed with long-grain rice to make it go farther. Wild rice has a deep brown color and a light nutty flavor. It tastes especially good in combination with maple syrup, mushrooms, game meats, nuts, and duck.

Vegetables

Green Beans Provençale

The French term à la Provençale *usually refers to dishes prepared with garlic and tomatoes.*

1½ pounds fresh green beans, trimmed
2 garlic cloves
  Salt
1 tablespoon olive oil
4 ripe tomatoes, quartered and coarsely chopped
3 tablespoons tomato paste
¼ teaspoon dried oregano (optional)
½ cup chopped fresh parsley

1 In a pot or steamer steam the beans for 6 minutes. Refresh the beans under cold running water.

2 Chop and crush the garlic with a little salt to make a paste.

3 In a large skillet or saucepan warm the olive oil over moderately high heat. Add the garlic paste, tomatoes, tomato paste, and oregano, if used. Cook, stirring, for 3 to 4 minutes. Reduce the heat to moderately low and stir in the beans. Cook, tossing, until heated through.

4 Stir in the chopped parsley and serve hot.

MAKES 8 SERVINGS

ABOUT OREGANO

Oregano is a more highly flavored variety of marjoram; both are members of the mint family. Oregano grows as a compact bushy plant with tiny dark green leaves and lovely purple and white blossoms. The greater part of the crop is harvested and marketed dried, but fresh oregano is beginning to be available as well. Greek oregano is thought to be the most flavorful, and it can sometimes be purchased with the leaves still on, and the stems tied together in a bouquet.

Oregano is a well-known herb in Italian and Greek kitchens, and is also an ingredient in prepared chili powder.

ABOUT FRUIT VERSUS VEGETABLE

Strictly speaking, a fruit contains the seeds of a plant. By this botanical definition, green beans, eggplants, peppers, and other seed-containing edibles are fruits, but they are commonly called vegetables. Common usage tends to classify fruits and vegetables by the way they are used and by their relative sweetness, rather than by botanical guidelines. But botanists do sometimes refer to "vegetable-fruits," acknowledging their typical use.

Braised Red Cabbage

3 tablespoons vegetable oil
2 cups sliced onions
2 heads red cabbage (about 4
   pounds), cored, and cut into
   bite-size pieces
½ cup red wine vinegar
¾ cup water
½ tablespoon caraway seeds
¼ cup brown sugar

1 In a large saucepan heat the vegetable oil over moderate heat and cook the onions for 2 minutes.
2 Add the cabbage, cover, and cook for 5 minutes.
3 Add the vinegar, water, caraway seeds, and brown sugar and braise the cabbage, covered, for 45 minutes, or until tender.

MAKES 8 SERVINGS

ABOUT CABBAGE AND CRUCIFEROUS VEGETABLES

We've known for a long time that cabbage is a good source of dietary fiber and vitamin C. Now we are learning that cabbage is also high in beta-carotene, a building block for vitamin A. Scientists believe that eating cabbage may help prevent cancer. In fact, all the vegetables in the cabbage clan—broccoli, Brussels sprouts, and cauliflower—have been found to help the body's defense system. These vegetables are called cruciferous vegetables because they have a crosslike structure at their base or stem.

Broccoli Puree

This side dish is wonderful with roasted or grilled meats.

1 Using a vegetable peeler peel away the tough skin from the broccoli stems. Cut off the flowerets. Cut the stems crosswise into ½-inch rounds.

2 In a pot or steamer steam the stems and flowerets for 5 minutes, or until tender.

3 Place the broccoli in a food mill or food processor. Add the heavy cream, butter, nutmeg, and lemon juice and blend until smooth.

MAKES 4 SERVINGS

2 bunches broccoli
¼ cup heavy cream
2 tablespoons unsalted butter
¼ teaspoon grated nutmeg
1 teaspoon fresh lemon juice

Amish Carrots

The largest Amish communities are in Pennsylvania and Ohio. Though the Amish of Pennsylvania are often described as Pennsylvania Dutch, they are not from Holland, but from Germany, or "Deutsch"land. The Amish life-style is marked by separation from modern technology and the outside world.

6 carrots, scrubbed or peeled
½ cup mayonnaise
2 tablespoons prepared white
   horseradish
¼ cup water
   Freshly ground black pepper
¼ cup sliced almonds

1 Preheat the oven to 350° F.
2 Cut the carrots into strips. In a pot or steamer steam for 8 minutes.
3 While the carrots are steaming, mix together the mayonnaise, horseradish, and water.
4 Turn the carrots into a baking dish, pour in the mayonnaise mixture, and mix to coat evenly. Season lightly with pepper and sprinkle the sliced almonds over the top.
5 Bake for 10 minutes, and serve immediately.

MAKES 4 SERVINGS

ABOUT CARROTS AND NUTRITION

Carrots contain carotene, which is changed by our liver into vitamin A. Vitamin A is necessary for healthy skin and mucous membranes, and promotes the proper functioning of our immune system. It also may be helpful in preventing certain types of cancer, such as lung and bladder cancer.

ABOUT HORSERADISH

Horseradish is the pungent root of a member of the cabbage family. It's called horseradish because it looks like a giant beige-colored radish. Native to southeastern Europe and western Asia, most of the horseradish grown in the United States comes from Illinois farm country, just across the Mississippi River from St. Louis.
   Freshly ground horseradish has a much brighter and more pungent flavor than horseradish that has been preserved in vinegar.

Monterey Jack Corn Fritters

For fritters the batter should be slightly thicker than pancake batter. Fritter batters hold better to foods that have been patted dry, and are close to room temperature, rather than cold.

1 In a mixing bowl blend together all the ingredients except the butter.

2 Place a griddle over moderately high heat until hot. Lightly butter it and, using about ¼ cup of the batter at a time, pour circles of batter onto the griddle. Cook until bubbles come to the surface. Flip the fritters and cook for a few minutes more.

MAKES ABOUT 14 CAKES

1 cup yellow cornmeal
1 cup creamed corn
½ cup buttermilk
½ cup vegetable oil
1 cup shredded Monterey Jack cheese
¾ teaspoon baking soda
Salt, to taste
2 teaspoons finely chopped jalapeño pepper
1 egg
3 scallions, green part only, finely chopped
Unsalted butter

BUTTERMILK IS BETTER MILK

Buttermilk should really be called better milk. Contrary to what the name implies, it is actually lower in fat and calories than whole milk. Buttermilk is made with skim or low-fat milk and has less than 1 percent milk fat and only 90 to 100 calories per cup.

Originally, buttermilk was the whey left over from making butter. Before refrigeration, the buttermilk was left to clabber or thicken naturally. The modern technique blends skim milk with a buttermilk culture that causes the milk to thicken. Buttermilk is often made with salt added. If you are on a salt-restricted diet, look for buttermilk that is labeled NO SALT ADDED. In some soup recipes buttermilk is an ideal low-calorie substitute for cream.

Eggplant Mozzarella

Vegetable oil
1 cup all-purpose flour
1 medium eggplant (about 1½ pounds), trimmed, peeled, and cut into ¼-inch-thick slices
1 cup tomato sauce
2 tablespoons chopped fresh basil, or 1 teaspoon dried basil
Salt and freshly ground black pepper
12 ounces mozzarella cheese, sliced ¼-inch thick
¼ cup freshly grated Pecorino cheese
1 tablespoon olive oil

1 Preheat the oven to 375° F.

2 In a large skillet heat ¼ inch of vegetable oil over medium flame.

3 Lightly flour the eggplant slices on both sides. Fry the eggplant on both sides until golden brown, about 2 minutes. Drain on paper towels.

4 Coat the bottom of a 1½-quart heatproof dish with some of the tomato sauce. Sprinkle in one-third of the basil. Layer with half of the eggplant slices. Sprinkle lightly with salt and pepper.

5 Cover the eggplant with a layer of tomato sauce. Sprinkle with half of the remaining basil. Layer with half of the mozzarella cheese; sprinkle on 2 tablespoons Pecorino cheese. Layer on the remaining eggplant and season lightly with salt and pepper. Cover with the remaining tomato sauce and sprinkle with the remaining basil. Put the remaining mozzarella cheese on top, and sprinkle with the remaining 2 tablespoons Pecorino cheese. Sprinkle the olive oil over all.

6 Bake for 15 minutes. Then place the dish under the broiler for 1 to 2 minutes, until the top is golden brown. Serve at once.

MAKES 4 SERVINGS

ABOUT EGGPLANT

Eggplants originated in China and India, where they have been grown for thousands of years. They are called eggplants because the early varieties were small and egg-shape. They are available year-round, and can be baked, broiled, sautéed, stuffed, or fried. A small eggplant can be cooked whole, and often has better flavor than the large ones.

ABOUT PECORINO CHEESE

In Italy, pecorino cheese is made from sheep's milk—the Italian word for sheep is *pecora*. About 15 percent of the cheese made in Italy is Pecorino.

Fresh Pecorino Romano is a pungent table cheese. When it is aged and hard, it is the favored grating cheese of southern Italians. The hard grating Pecorino cheese of Sardinia is called Sardo. Fresh Pecorinos are made all over Italy but they are highly perishable and rarely exported.

ABOUT MOZZARELLA CHEESE

Mozzarella is a soft fresh cheese usually used to top pizza. Most mozzarella is made from cow's milk, but the most authentic is made in Italy from the milk of water buffaloes. Buffalo mozzarella has a tangier taste than mozzarella made from cow's milk.

The cheese is usually shaped like a baseball, but when very fresh, it may be too soft to hold a shape. It is sweet, slightly tangy, and creamy tasting, with a springy, pillow-like texture. Fresh mozzarella and packaged mozzarella are two very different products. Both have the essence of fresh whole milk in their flavor, but fresh mozzarella, available at Italian groceries as well as other "gourmet" food and cheese shops, is preferable.

Bermuda Onions Braised with Madeira

2 tablespoons olive oil
2 tablespoons unsalted butter
4 large Bermuda onions, sliced
  1 inch thick
  Salt and freshly ground black
  pepper
¼ cup beef stock or broth
¼ cup Madeira wine

1 In a heavy sauté pan melt the oil and butter over high heat. Add the onions and sear on one side for 2 minutes.

2 Turn the onions and season with salt and pepper to taste. Add the stock or broth, cover, and reduce the heat to low. Simmer for 10 minutes, or just until tender.

3 Add the Madeira and cook until the sauce is reduced, slightly caramelized and sweet.

MAKES 4 SERVINGS

ABOUT WHITE ONIONS

Most medium and large white onions are called Bermuda onions or Spanish onions. The onions are quite sweet and can be eaten raw, or used to make onion rings. Look for firm unbruised onions.

Ratatouille

1 Heat the olive oil in a 4-quart saucepan over medium heat. Add the onion, garlic, and oregano and cook until the onion is tender, stirring often. Stir in the eggplant, bell pepper, and zucchini. Cook for 10 minutes or until eggplant is tender.

2 Stir in the V-8 juice and cook for 3 minutes. Add salt and pepper to taste. Serve warm or chilled, with toasted French bread or pita bread wedges.

MAKES 3½ CUPS OR 4 TO 6 SERVINGS

¼ cup olive oil
1 large onion, chopped
2 medium garlic cloves, minced
1 teaspoon oregano
1 small eggplant, cut into ¼-inch cubes (about ¾ pound)
1 large red bell pepper, cut into ¼-inch pieces
1 small zucchini, cut into ¼-inch cubes
¾ cup V-8 vegetable juice
Salt and freshly ground black pepper
Toasted French bread or pita bread wedges for serving

Potatoes Gratin

The word gratin *refers to the thin crust that is formed over a sauced dish when it is browned in the oven or broiler. The term* au gratin *first appeared in eighteenth-century French cookbooks, where it applied to foods that were sauced and cooked in the same dish until the sauce "caught" at the bottom and sides of the dish. Today we use "gratin" and "au gratin" to refer to a shallow, crumb-topped preparation of food, usually in a sauce, and also to the dish or pan containing the food. The gratin dish does not have to be heavy-duty like a saucepan, but it should be attractive enough to go directly to the table from the oven. Potatoes gratin is one of the great rustic French side dishes.*

1½ cups milk
1½ cups heavy cream
 1 teaspoon salt
½ teaspoon freshly ground
   black pepper
 2 garlic cloves, finely minced
 1 tablespoon whole-grain
   mustard
 2 pounds baking potatoes,
   peeled, thinly sliced
¼ cup freshly grated Parmesan
   cheese

1 Preheat the oven to 400° F. Lightly butter an 8-inch round heatproof baking dish or pan.

2 In a large saucepan combine the milk, cream, salt, pepper, garlic, and mustard.

3 Put the potato slices directly into the milk-cream mixture to prevent them from turning brown.

4 Set the saucepan over moderate heat and stir until the liquid comes just to the boiling point. Watch carefully and stir to prevent scorching.

5 Pour the mixture into the prepared pan and sprinkle with the Parmesan cheese. Bake for 1 hour, or until a knife easily pierces the potatoes. Remove to a rack to rest for about 15 minutes before serving.

MAKES 4 TO 6 SERVINGS

Baked Sliced Potatoes with Cheese and Mustard

1 Preheat the oven to 425° F. Butter a heat-proof dish or pan that can be used as a serving dish.

2 In a small bowl blend the butter, mustard, salt, and pepper together to form a smooth paste.

3 Arrange one-third of the potatoes in the dish. Dot the potatoes with one-third of the mustard mixture and one-third of the cheese.

4 Repeat this layering process twice again, until all of the potatoes and mustard mixture are used, ending with a layer of the remaining cheese.

5 Pour the chicken stock over the potatoes and place the baking dish on a baking sheet. Bake for 1¼ hours, until bubbling and lightly browned. The baking sheet will catch any spillover from the baking dish.

MAKES 6 SERVINGS

¼ cup unsalted butter, at room temperature
½ cup prepared mustard
    Salt and freshly ground white pepper to taste
2 pounds baking potatoes, peeled and thinly sliced
4 cups shredded Swiss cheese
1¼ cups chicken stock

Shrimp-Stuffed Potatoes

4 baking potatoes, washed and
  patted dry
2 egg yolks
¼ cup milk
¼ cup heavy cream
1 tablespoon crushed dried
  chives
1 cup coarsely chopped cooked
  shrimp (see Note)
¼ cup minced fresh parsley
¼ cup grated Cheddar cheese

1 Preheat the oven to 375° F.

2 Bake the potatoes for 45 minutes, or until a thermometer inserted into the center of a potato reaches 210° F.

3 Slice off one end of each potato. The cut should be about 1 inch in from the potato's tip. Scoop the center of the pulp out of the potatoes and place it in a mixing bowl. Leave enough pulp against the inside of the skin so that the side walls remain firm; about ¼ inch should be sufficient.

4 Beat the egg yolks, milk, and cream into the potato pulp and continue beating until the mixture is smooth. An electric mixer is the best tool for the job, but it can be done with a fork. Blend in the chives, shrimp, and 2 tablespoons parsley.

5 Spoon the mixture into the hollow potato shells. Sprinkle 1 tablespoon cheese on each potato. Press the bottom end of each potato against your work surface to flatten the base so the potato will stand up. Arrange the potatoes in a heatproof dish, open ends up.

6 Bake for 20 minutes until the cheese has melted and turned a golden brown and the stuffing is heated. Sprinkle with ½ tablespoon remaining parsley on each potato and serve immediately.

MAKES 4 SERVINGS

NOTE: The shrimp can be cooked by boiling them in water for 3 minutes.

WHAT'S COOKING TIP: MAKING THE PERFECT BAKED POTATO

1. A potato for baking should be oblong and uniform in shape so that it cooks evenly. The Idaho Russet Burbank, Eastern Maine, and Long Island potatoes are good bakers, but don't bake red potatoes. They have a waxy flesh that is better for boiling.
2. Never bake potatoes wrapped in aluminum foil. This traps the potato's moisture and causes it to steam rather than bake. A baked potato should be free to bake in dry heat. Baking a potato at 400° F for an hour will yield a crisp skin and fluffy inside.

Tomato-Stuffed Potatoes

4 baking potatoes, washed and
  patted dry
2 tablespoons unsalted butter
½ cup tomato puree
½ cup sour cream
  Salt and freshly ground black
  pepper
1 cup grated sharp Cheddar
  cheese

1 Preheat the oven to 400° F.
2 Bake the potatoes for 45 minutes, or until a
   thermometer, inserted into the center of a
   potato reaches 210° F.
3 Split the potatoes lengthwise and scoop out
   the pulp into a mixing bowl. Leave enough
   pulp against the inside of the skin so that the
   side walls remain firm; about ¼ inch should
   be sufficient.
4 Add the butter, tomato puree, and sour cream
   to the potato pulp and mix until smooth. Add
   salt and pepper to taste, and blend in the
   cheese. Mound the mixture into the potato
   shells.
5 Put the filled shells on a baking sheet about
   8 inches under the broiler and cook for about
   5 minutes, or until the mixture is heated.

MAKES 4 SERVINGS

ABOUT POTATOES

The potato is probably the most widely used vegetable in the world. Potatoes are native to the mountains of northern South America, where Indians domesticated wild potatoes and used them in all of their cooking. Spanish conquistadors brought potatoes back to Europe and they became particularly popular as a crop for European peasants because they grew underground, well hidden from invading troops who regularly pillaged farms for food. Ireland was the first European country to cultivate potatoes; in time the Irish diet became so dependent on potatoes that when the potato famine hit in 1845, thousands of people died and thousands more sailed to America to escape.

There are over fifteen varieties of potatoes grown in the United States but they can be separated into four major groups. The round white, also known as the Cobbler, Kennebec, and Katahdin, are good for boiling, frying, and baking. The round red or waxy red is very good for boiling. The long white potato is grown mainly in the western states and is good for boiling, frying, and baking. The long Russet or Burbank potato is considered by many as the best baking potato available.

The volcanic soil and climatic conditions make potatoes grown in Idaho among the best in the world. Nutritionally, potatoes are a very good source of dietary fiber. They are low in calories if you don't put butter and sour cream on them (a single Russet averages 100 calories), and they are a good source of vitamin C.

Danish Sugar-Browned Potatoes

1 pound small new potatoes,
   scrubbed clean
6 tablespoons unsalted butter
2 tablespoons vegetable oil
3 tablespoons sugar

1 In a pot of lightly salted boiling water boil the potatoes for 12 to 15 minutes, or until they are tender but not too soft.

2 Rinse the potatoes under cold water to stop the cooking. When the potatoes have cooled, peel them.

3 Melt the butter in a large frying pan and add the vegetable oil. Stir in the sugar and cook until the sugar is light brown, about 3 minutes. Add the potatoes and cook until they have an even coating of the sugar mixture. Do not let the sugar scorch. Stir the potatoes in the pan until they have a light brown color. Serve immediately.

MAKES 4 SERVINGS

ABOUT NEW POTATOES

New potatoes are the tiny first potatoes that the potato plants produce, usually in the spring. They can be either red or white. They are succulent, tender, and sweet. Before the long-term storage techniques we have today, people kept potatoes in the cellar. As spring approached, they got pretty tired of eating last year's shriveled old potatoes, so when the ground warmed and the new crop of potatoes began to swell underground, they could not wait for the potatoes to reach maturity and enjoyed the tender new crop. For some, new potatoes are no less a sign of spring than asparagus. New potatoes are excellent for egg salad.

Rosti Potatoes

Rosti or roesti are Swiss fried potatoes and their full name in Swiss German is kartoffelrosti. *True rosti comes as a flat pancake that is browned on both sides. Before Switzerland became the wealthy industrial country it is today, there were hard times in the valleys, and people counted on a plate of rosti, often times topped with melted cheese, to make a meal. Today, the Swiss-born chef of the Four Seasons restaurant in New York has elevated roesti to the heights of luxury by topping it with crème fraîche and caviar.*

Rosti is a simple dish, but needs to be made carefully. It can be fried in lard, bacon, butter, or oil. Rosti with breaded veal cutlets is a typical everyday dish in German-speaking Switzerland.

1 In a pot of water boil the potatoes until just tender when pierced with the tip of a sharp knife, about 20 minutes.

2 Drain the potatoes, peel, and chill for at least 2 hours.

3 Coarsely grate the cooled potatoes.

4 In a large nonstick frying pan heat the oil over a moderate flame. Add the bacon and cook for 1 to 2 minutes. Add the onion and cook until the bacon is crisp and the onion softened, about 2 minutes. Add the potatoes and mix the ingredients together. Pat the ingredients into a disk.

5 Cook for about 4 minutes, or until the underside is light brown. Hold a plate on top of the pan and invert the plate and the pan together. Then slide the potato cake (cooked side up) off the plate and back into the pan. Place the pan on the heat again and cook for 3 minutes, until the surface is lightly browned.

6 Season with salt and pepper to taste. Slide the rosti out of the pan, onto a plate. Serve immediately.

MAKES 4 SERVINGS

1 pound baking potatoes
2 tablespoons vegetable oil
2 strips bacon, chopped
2 tablespoons chopped onion
Salt and freshly ground black pepper

Irish Colcannon

Colcannon is an Irish dish traditionally made with equal amounts of cooked chopped kale and cooked mashed potatoes. Cabbage is often substituted for kale; here we extend the variations on the theme to include broccoli. The mixture is blended with hot milk or cream and chopped leeks or green onion tops. Some make patties of the mixture and fry them in bacon fat until crisp on both sides.

Colcannon is a traditional dish on Halloween, when a ring is often stuck in the mixture. Whoever gets the ring will supposedly be married within a year.

¼ cup unsalted butter
4 medium potatoes, peeled, cooked, and mashed
2 cups chopped, steamed broccoli (see Note) or cooked cabbage
¼ cup heavy cream
1 cup thinly sliced onion
3 tablespoons chopped fresh parsley
Salt and freshly ground black pepper

1 Preheat the oven to 325° F.
2 In a medium sauté pan melt the butter. Add the mashed potatoes and broccoli or cabbage. Blend in 2 tablespoons heavy cream. Add ¾ cup sliced onion and 2 tablespoons parsley. Season with salt and pepper to taste. Cook over a moderate heat for 10 minutes, stirring often.
3 Spoon the vegetable mixture into a 2½-cup heatproof baking dish and smooth the surface. Top with the remaining 2 tablespoons heavy cream, ¼ cup onion, and 1 tablespoon parsley.
4 Bake for 20 minutes, or until lightly crusted.

MAKES 4 SERVINGS

NOTE: Broccoli should be steamed only for 3 minutes.

Turmeric Potatoes with Green Peppers

1 In a pot of water boil the potatoes in their jackets until cooked but still firm. Plunge them into cold water for a minute and peel. (The peeling is optional.) Cut into 1-inch cubes.

2 Quarter the peppers; remove the stems and seeds. Cut into 1-inch pieces.

3 In a large frying pan heat the oil over a moderately high flame. When the oil is very hot, add the turmeric, and immediately add the potatoes and peppers. Sprinkle with salt, if used, and sauté, turning and tossing for 3 to 4 minutes. Sprinkle 2 to 3 tablespoons of water over the vegetables, reduce the heat, and cook, covered, until the peppers are cooked but still very crisp, 5 to 10 minutes.

4 Uncover, and raise the heat to evaporate any excess moisture remaining in the pan and to brown the vegetables. Cook and stir for about 5 minutes.

MAKES 6 SERVINGS

8 medium boiling potatoes (about 2 pounds)
4 medium bell peppers (red, green, and/or yellow; about 1 pound, the more colors the better)
3–4 tablespoons vegetable oil
1½ teaspoons ground turmeric
1½ teaspoons kosher salt (optional)
2–3 tablespoons water

Creole Vegetable Sauté

2 tablespoons olive oil
1 large onion, minced
2 tablespoons chopped garlic
2 cups okra, sliced ½ inch thick
2 large tomatoes, peeled, seeded, and chopped
½ cup chopped celery
½ cup thinly sliced carrots
1 tablespoon tomato paste
1 tablespoon crushed dried basil
2 tablespoons red wine vinegar
1 teaspoon sugar
Salt and freshly ground black pepper

1 In a saucepan or sauté pan heat the oil over a medium flame. Add the onion and garlic and sauté for 3 minutes. Add the okra and cook for 2 minutes. Add the tomatoes, celery, carrots, tomato paste, and basil and cook until the okra and carrots are just tender, 15 to 20 minutes.

2 Remove from the heat and stir in the vinegar, sugar, and salt and pepper to taste. Serve hot or cold.

MAKES ABOUT 3 CUPS

ABOUT OKRA

Okra is a member of the Hibiscus family. The finger-shape pods grow on 3- to 4-foot-tall plants. Okra is very popular throughout the American South, where it was introduced by black African slaves who brought the seeds from West Africa. Today okra is grown and eaten wherever black Africans were carried as slaves. It is sometimes called gumbo in the United States from the African *ochinggômbo,* and it has given its name to the spicy stew popular in Louisiana in which it is a frequent ingredient; when stewed, okra has a gelatinous texture, and acts as a thickener for gumbo, which is a characteristic almost as important as the flavor imparted.

When buying okra, look for 3-inch-long green pods that are clean and firm. Okra is sometimes, but rarely, red. It is a source of calcium, as well as phosphorus, potassium, iron, and vitamins A and C. Okra contains only 140 calories per pound.

ABOUT TOMATO PASTE

Tomato paste is the thickest and most concentrated tomato product. Paste is produced by cooking whole tomatoes for several hours, pureeing them, and cooking them until they reach the characteristic thick pasty consistency. You can make tomato paste out of any tomato but the best paste comes from tomatoes that are thick walled, meaty, and not very juicy, such as Italian plum tomatoes.

Tomato paste is commonly used to thicken tomato-based pasta sauces, but a tablespoon added to brown gravy or a thickened cream sauce is a wonderful flavoring and coloring agent.

If you don't use the whole can of tomato paste in a single recipe, you can save the leftover part by placing individual tablespoonfuls wrapped in plastic wrap in the freezer. Tubed tomato paste is the most convenient form, and usually better quality.

ABOUT CAJUN AND CREOLE CUISINE

Paul Prudhomme, the portly potentate of Louisiana cooking, says that the difference between Cajun and Creole food is that Cajun is country food and Creole is city food. Specifically, Creole food is the cooking of New Orleans and Cajun is the cooking of the people who live in the French parishes on the bayous west of New Orleans.

Creole is the oldest style of cooking in New Orleans. The word *Creole* comes from the Spanish word *criollo,* which means "native to this place." The first Creole colonists in New Orleans did not have the ingredients they were accustomed to in Europe, so local Indian and black African slave foods and techniques were combined with French and Spanish cooking methods.

Cajuns are the descendants of French Canadian Acadians who were forced out of Canada in the 1750s and finally settled on the prairies and swamps of southwest Louisiana. Longfellow's poem "Evangeline" is the story of the Acadian diaspora. The name Acadian was eventually contracted to Cajun. Cajun food has a strong, down-home country flavor; it is the cooking of rural people. It is often hot, peppery, pungent, and spicy all at once. Cajun food is based on one-pot meals that often start with roux, a flour and oil gravy. Rice, smoked meat, and seafood are important to Cajun cooking.

Creole cooking, which is also a French derivative, is more formal and often based on cream sauces.

Some of the most well-known Cajun dishes are jambalaya, crawfish pie, étouffée, filé gumbo, and seafood boiled in hot pepper mash. Creole dishes are trout Amandine, oysters Bienville, shrimp Creole, and pecan pralines.

Salads

Sunset Salad with Lorenzo Dressing

Sunset salad with Lorenzo dressing was for many years a house staple at the "21," a restaurant that has been very much a club for New York's rich and powerful. Lorenzo dressing is named after one of the "21's" longtime maitre d's, who helped develop the sauce. "21," at 21 West 54th Street in midtown Manhattan, was opened during prohibition, a speakeasy run by Jack Kreindler and Charlie Berns who unabashedly served booze. "21," often referred to as "Jack and Charlie's" by its regulars, was a sort of private hangout for the likes of John Steinbeck, Ernest Hemingway, Frank Sinatra, Richard Nixon, and Cary Grant.

The restaurant is famous for the depth and quality of its wine cellar and for the Sunset salad with Lorenzo dressing, chicken hash and chicken potpie, prime beef, and its "21" hamburger which, by the way, now costs more than $21.

Salad:
½ head green cabbage
½ head iceberg lettuce
5 thin slices cooked beef tongue or ham
2 chicken breasts, poached, skin and bone removed, or 1 pound skinless cooked turkey

Lorenzo Dressing:
1 cup chili sauce
½ cup finely chopped watercress
½ cup French dressing

1 Cut all of the salad ingredients into thin match-size strips. Combine them in a large bowl. Just before serving, toss the salad with the Lorenzo dressing.
2 To make the dressing, combine the chili sauce and the watercress. Add the French dressing and blend thoroughly.

MAKES 4 SERVINGS

ABOUT WATERCRESS

Watercress is a peppery-tasting green leafy plant that grows along streams and creeks. It is a member of the nasturtium family, whose edible leaves and petals offer a similar peppery flavor.

Watercress has been used as a food for over 3,000 years, since the ancient Greeks ate it. It is a good source of vitamins C and A.

Watercress is very perishable. Look for bright green bunches where the leaves and stems are as undamaged as possible. Wash them and store in a plastic bag in the refrigerator for only 1 or 2 days.

Watercress makes an excellent addition to a salad. It is mixed with cream cheese and spread on thinly sliced white bread for tea sandwiches in England. Watercress loses its color and texture quickly when cooked, so add it at the very last minute in Chinese stir-fried dishes and soups.

Tomato, Onion, and Green Bean Salad

2 pounds trimmed fresh green beans
3 large ripe tomatoes
2 tablespoons vegetable or olive oil
1 tablespoon red wine vinegar
1 small red onion, sliced

1 In a pot or steamer steam the green beans for 7 minutes.

2 Slice the tomatoes and arrange them in an attractive pattern along the outside rim of a plate or platter.

3 Refresh the green beans under cold water. Pat dry and place them in the center of the tomatoes.

4 Pour the oil over the beans and tomatoes and sprinkle with vinegar.

5 Garnish with a few slices of red onion.

MAKES 8 SERVINGS

WHAT'S COOKING TIP: STORING TOMATOES

Never store tomatoes in the refrigerator. Temperatures below 50° F interfere with ripening. A refrigerated tomato will turn red but it will not become sweet and juicy. Store fresh tomatoes at room temperature, stem end up, or the bumpy shoulders of the stem end, which are the most tender part, will bruise from the weight of the fruit.

ABOUT HARICOTS VERTS

Haricots verts are French green beans. They are the most tender and succulent green beans you can buy, because they are very thin, and only 3 to 4 inches long. Fresh-picked haricots verts can be eaten raw. Avoid overcooking them—they take only a fraction of the cooking time of larger green beans.

Because of their rarity in the United States, they are expensive. But they are as easy to grow as regular green beans and available in many seed catalogs.

Siena Summer Salad

3 cups stale Italian bread, broken into 1-inch cubes
1 cup water
1 cup chopped lettuce
1 tomato, cut into ½-inch cubes
¼ cup minced fresh basil, or 1 teaspoon dried basil
¼ cup finely chopped scallions (optional)
¼ cup finely chopped gherkin pickles or cornichons
1 tablespoon chopped anchovy fillets or anchovy paste
1 tablespoon capers
¼ cup olive oil
2 tablespoons red wine vinegar

1 In a bowl soak the stale bread pieces in the water. Let the bread soak thoroughly for a moment, then drain and squeeze the bread until it is as dry as possible. Place the bread into a mixing bowl.

2 Add the lettuce, tomato, basil, scallions, gherkins, anchovies, and capers and mix together. Add the olive oil and vinegar and mix again.

MAKES 4 SERVINGS

ABOUT ANCHOVY PASTE

Anchovy paste is a savory condiment that is made from mashed anchovy fillets. Europeans commonly stuff anchovy paste into tubes that look like toothpaste tubes. These tubes are convenient, and increasingly available in the United States.

Waldorf Salad

Waldorf salad is a mixture of apples, celery, and nuts blended with mayonnaise. It was developed by chef Oscar Tschirky at the Waldorf Astoria Hotel in 1893, on the occasion of the very first Waldorf banquet given in the United States. The affair was a charity fundraiser organized by Mrs. William Vanderbilt.

1 In a bowl sprinkle the apple with lemon juice to prevent it from turning brown.

2 Add the celery and mayonnaise and mix well.

3 Arrange lettuce leaves on 2 serving plates. Spoon the apple and celery mixture onto the lettuce leaves and garnish with walnuts.

4 Serve with jelly sandwiches.

MAKES 2 SERVINGS

1½ cups red apple, cored, seeded, and diced
1 tablespoon fresh lemon juice
1 cup diced celery
½ cup mayonnaise
Lettuce leaves
Shelled walnuts
Jelly sandwiches

Wilted Spinach Salad

Salad:
- 1 10-ounce bunch of fresh spinach, washed thoroughly, and trimmed of stems
- 1 red onion, thinly sliced
- 1 cup thinly sliced fresh mushrooms

Dressing:
- 1 tablespoon unsalted butter
- 2 tablespoons Dijon-style mustard
- 4 strips bacon, cooked and crumbled
- 6 tablespoons brandy
- 3 tablespoons Cointreau
  Juice of ½ lemon
- ⅓ cup vegetable oil
- 3 tablespoons red wine vinegar
  Freshly ground black pepper
- ½ cup grated Parmesan cheese

1 In a serving bowl toss together the spinach, onion, and mushrooms.

2 In a sauté pan melt the butter. Mix in the mustard, cooked bacon, brandy, and Cointreau. Heat this mixture for a minute, then carefully ignite with a long match. Cook, shaking the pan, until the flame subsides.

3 Stir in the lemon juice, oil, and vinegar. Add fresh pepper to taste and the Parmesan cheese.

4 Pour the hot dressing over the salad. Hold the sauté pan over the salad bowl as a lid for 1 minute. This will help wilt the spinach and warm the cheese.

5 Toss the salad and serve immediately.

MAKES 4 TO 6 SERVINGS

ABOUT COINTREAU

Cointreau is the brand name of a distilled orange-flavored liqueur from France. It is made from the peels of the Curaçao orange, a very flavorful orange grown on the island of Curaçao in the Dutch West Indies. Cointreau is an elegant version of white Triple Sec, which is the clear version of Curaçao.

Cointreau can often be enjoyed as an after-dinner drink with coffee or used in the making of crepes suzette.

ABOUT OILS

All cooking oils are a combination of saturated fats and unsaturated fats. Highly saturated fats are thought to be a major cause of heart disease. When buying oils, it is healthiest to choose those with a high proportion of unsaturated fat.

The following is a list of oils, each ranked by its proportion of unsaturated fat to total fat.

1. Canola oil   .93
2. Safflower oil   .86
3. Sunflower oil   .85
4. Corn oil   .83
5. Sesame oil   .82
6. Olive oil   .81
7. Soybean oil   .81
8. Peanut oil   .78
9. Coconut oil   .07

Caesar Salad

Caesar salad was invented in 1920 in Tijuana, Mexico, by a restaurateur named Caesar Cardini. Cardini was an Italian immigrant, so the salad is Italian, not Mexican, in nature. It is traditionally made with romaine lettuce, olive oil, lemon juice, Parmesan cheese, fresh garlic, anchovy, and a whole egg, coddled. It is usually topped with homemade croutons.

2 egg yolks
2 anchovy fillets, chopped
2 tablespoons prepared mustard
2 garlic cloves, chopped
Juice of ½ lemon
1 tablespoon red wine vinegar
¼ cup vegetable oil
1 large head of leaf lettuce, washed, dried, and chopped into bite-size pieces
1 cup Garlic Croutons (see below)
3 tablespoons grated Parmesan cheese
3 drops of Tabasco sauce
5 drops of Worcestershire sauce

1 In a mixing bowl blend together the egg yolks, anchovies, mustard, garlic, and lemon juice to make a paste.

2 Add the vinegar and slowly blend in the vegetable oil.

3 Add the remaining ingredients and toss to coat thoroughly.

MAKES 4 SERVINGS

GARLIC CROUTONS

3 garlic cloves, finely minced
⅓ cup olive oil
6 slices bread, crusts removed, cut into ½-inch cubes

1 In a small container, combine the garlic and oil together. Cover and let marinate for 3 hours or longer.

2 Preheat the oven to 400° F.

3 Place the bread cubes in a single layer in a sauté pan or baking pan. Pour the garlic and oil mixture over the bread and stir to coat.

4 Bake for 10 minutes, or until golden brown.

MAKES 2 CUPS

NOTE: The croutons can be stored in a covered container in the refrigerator for 2 weeks.

New Potato Salad

1 In a large saucepan combine the potatoes, salt, caraway seeds, and garlic. Add water to cover and cook over moderately high heat for 20 minutes, or until the potatoes are tender. Drain and cool.

2 Quarter the potatoes and place in a mixing bowl. Add salt and pepper to taste and stir in the sour cream or yogurt and dill.

3 Line a serving bowl with lettuce leaves, add the potato salad, and garnish with tomato wedges and a sprig of dill.

MAKES 6 SERVINGS

3 pounds new potatoes, scrubbed
2 tablespoons salt
1 tablespoon caraway seeds
1 garlic clove
Salt and freshly ground black pepper
1 cup sour cream or plain yogurt or a combination of the two
¼ cup minced fresh dill
Lettuce leaves
Tomato wedges, and a sprig of dill as garnish

Low-Calorie Sour Cream Substitute

Combine the ingredients in a blender for 5 seconds. Use the same amount as you would of sour cream.

MAKES 1¼ CUPS

1 tablespoon fresh lemon juice
⅓ cup buttermilk (made with skim or low-fat milk)
1 cup low-fat cottage cheese

Classic American Coleslaw

The word coleslaw comes from the Dutch koolsla, kool *meaning "cabbage," and* sla *meaning "salad." Coleslaw was known in the United States as early as 1792.*

Dressing:
- 1½ **cups mayonnaise**
- ¼ **cup prepared mustard**
- 3 **tablespoons white wine vinegar**
- 1½ **teaspoons dried tarragon**
- ¼ **teaspoon celery seed**
  Freshly ground black pepper to taste

- 10 **cups shredded green cabbage, about 2 large heads**

1 In a large bowl combine the dressing ingredients.
2 Add the cabbage to the dressing and mix until all the cabbage is evenly coated.
3 Cover and refrigerate briefly before serving.

MAKES 10 SERVINGS

WHAT'S COOKING TIPS: CHOOSING AND STORING CABBAGE

1. Cabbage heads should feel solid, and be heavy in relation to their size. They should be closely trimmed, with stems cut close to the head and only three or four outer or wrapper leaves. The cabbage should show no discolored veins and the outer leaves should have a fresh appearance, with no sign of puffiness or wormholes, and bright color.
2. Undamaged, unwashed heads can be stored in a plastic bag in the refrigerator for a week to 10 days.

FOR LEAFY FOODS, COLOR CAN BE A NUTRITIONAL GUIDE

Leafy green vegetables are turning out to be one of the healthiest food groups. Lettuce, chicory, spinach, watercress, kale, turnip, and collard greens are low in calories, sodium, and fat, and high in vitamin C and carotene, a building block for vitamin A. They are good sources of fiber, calcium, and iron.

In general, the darker the green of the leaf, the greater the nutritional value of the vegetable. Iceberg is one of the most popular lettuce varieties in America, but it is one of the poorest nutritionally. Loose-leaf lettuce has up to six times as much vitamin C and eight times as much vitamin A as iceberg. Try using romaine, endive, arugula, or escarole lettuce in salads.

In cooking greens, it's important to remember that the less you do, the more nutrients remain in the food. Vitamin C is water soluble and heat sensitive, so it will leach out of vegetables that are overcooked or are soaked in lots of water.

White Bean Salad

1½ cups (about 10 ounces)
   dried cannellini beans
¼ cup olive oil
2 tablespoons white wine
   vinegar
2 tablespoons chopped onion
   (see Note)
2 tablespoons chopped fresh
   parsley
   Salt and freshly ground
   black pepper

1 Cover the beans with cold water 2 inches above the level of the beans and soak them for 8 hours or overnight.

2 Drain the beans. Place them in a saucepan and add cold water to cover by at least 2 inches. Bring to a boil. Reduce the heat to low and simmer for 1 hour, or until tender. Drain well.

3 In a large bowl whisk together the olive oil and vinegar. Add the beans and toss gently.

4 Add the onion and parsley to the beans and mix thoroughly. Season with salt and pepper to taste.

MAKES 4 TO 6 SERVINGS

NOTE: The onions can be cooked in a little oil to reduce the strength of their flavor. Some cooks add 2 crushed garlic cloves to the onions and/or 2 tablespoons tomato paste when sautéing them.

WHAT'S COOKING TIP: PRE-PARING DRIED BEANS

Cooking dried beans is a two-step process. They must be soaked to rehydrate them, and then they must be cooked.

1. Sort the beans to remove any pebbles or other foreign matter. Place the beans in a large pot and add enough cold water to cover the beans by at least 2 inches (extra water won't hurt). Set aside at room temperature to soak for 6 to 10 hours.

2. An alternative to long soaking is to bring the beans and water to a boil in a large pot. Cover and boil for 2 minutes. Uncover and let soak for at least 1 hour. This method is preferred because fewer nutrients are lost.

3. To cook the beans, drain off all of the soaking water. Add fresh water to cover by 2 inches, and set over high heat. Bring the water to a boil. Reduce the heat to low and simmer until the beans are tender but firm, 35 minutes to 2 hours, depending on the bean. Chick-peas generally require 1 to 1½ hours of cooking. Soybeans take even longer.

Cucumber Salad

3 cucumbers, scrubbed, thinly
  sliced
1 cup white vinegar
¼ cup sugar
½ tablespoon freshly ground
  white pepper
2 tablespoons chopped fresh
  dill

1 Place the cucumbers in a bowl and weigh down with a plate. Let stand at room temperature for 2 hours. Drain the cucumbers.

2 In a mixing bowl combine the vinegar, sugar, white pepper, and dill.

3 Pour the mixture over the cucumber slices, cover, and chill for 4 hours.

MAKES 4 SERVINGS

People have been making vinegar for more than 10,000 years. It's talked about in the Bible.

Roman legions used vinegar to purify their drinking water.

In 40 B.C. the Egyptian queen Cleopatra made a bet with Mark Antony that she could eat and drink the equivalent value of a million dollars at one meal. She knew that vinegar was a great solvent, so she dropped a few priceless pearls into a glass of vinegar. When they dissolved she drank the mixture.

WHAT'S COOKING TIPS: CUCUMBERS

1. Cucumbers are 96 percent water, which makes them an ideal food for dieters. Some cookbooks suggest cut cucumbers be mixed with salt in order to draw out their water content. That may have been necessary at one time, but today's varieties have a much different texture, and generally do not need salting.
2. Cucumbers are best stored unwashed, in a plastic bag in the refrigerator. Put a few holes in the bag to allow some air circulation. They hold well for about 5 days.

10,000 YEARS OF VINEGAR

Vinegar is a 4 to 6 percent solution of acetic acid, produced from the action of bacteria on alcohol. The name comes from *vin aigre,* French for "sour wine."

Vinegar is often made from the distilled juice of fruits or rice. Their various flavors give different vinegars distinct characteristics.

Vinegar holds better if shielded from air, light, and cold. Vinegars are made from most wines, and in hundreds of flavorings. It is easy to make your own flavored vinegars by adding herbs to the bottles.

Cauliflower Salad

1 head of cauliflower, cut into flowerets

Dressing:
2 teaspoons peanut oil
2 teaspoons olive oil
1 tablespoon white wine vinegar
Juice of ½ lemon
Freshly ground black pepper
Pinch of chopped garlic
¼ cup plain yogurt
¼ cup mayonnaise
1 tablespoon chopped fresh mint (optional)

Lettuce leaves
Fresh chives, chopped, as garnish

1 In a pot blanch the cauliflower in boiling water for 3 minutes. Drain and set aside.
2 Make the dressing by combining the peanut oil, olive oil, vinegar, lemon juice, pepper to taste, and garlic. Pour over the cauliflower and set aside to marinate for 30 minutes.
3 Stir in the yogurt, mayonnaise, and mint.
4 Serve the cauliflower salad on a bed of lettuce leaves and sprinkle with chives.

MAKES 4 SERVINGS

ABOUT CAULIFLOWER

Cauliflower is a blooming cabbage. Most cabbages put their energy into growing leaves, but cauliflower is devoted to its blossom. It has been grown since at least 600 B.C. in Asia Minor. Mark Twain called cauliflower a "cabbage with a college education." It grows best in cool growing seasons, as a late fall crop in the United States and a winter crop in the Mediterranean.

The type of cauliflower we eat today was first introduced into Europe by the Arabs in the twelfth century. Cauliflower is still a very popular vegetable in Spanish cooking, especially on the island of Mallorca (Majorca) where the national dish, sopa Mallorquina, is a stew of cauliflower and bread.

Nutritionally, 1 cup of cauliflower has as much vitamin C as one whole orange, and only 30 calories. It is a good source of dietary fiber. A cruciferous vegetable (a vegetable with a crosslike mark at its base), cauliflower, like others in this category, is believed to help fight cancer.

When shopping for cauliflower, look for heads that are dense and compact with clear white flowerets. Avoid discoloration. The leaves at the base should be green and fresh.

Mandarin Chicken Salad

Mandarin cooking is the cuisine developed by chefs in Peking, China's Imperial City. The word comes from the Chinese word mandar, *which means to govern, and was often used to describe people in positions of power. Peking is a port city located on the northeast coast of China. As the seat of government and the center of culture in China, many of the best cooks migrated there. Peking became the culinary capital of China and Mandarin cooking became the most influential style in the country.*

This is a perfect warm-weather picnic dish. There is no mayonnaise to worry about and the longer the salad marinates in its sauce, the better it tastes.

3 chicken breasts, poached,
  bones and skin removed
2 cups fresh bean sprouts

Dressing:
2 tablespoons soy sauce
1 tablespoon white wine
  vinegar
1 tablespoon sesame oil
½ teaspoon chili oil
½ teaspoon sugar

1 Coarsely shred the cooked chicken breasts.
2 In a medium saucepan boil the bean sprouts for 2 minutes. Drain and refresh under cold water.
3 In a mixing bowl combine the dressing ingredients.
4 Place the shredded chicken in a serving bowl, and add the bean sprouts and the dressing. Stir together and serve.

MAKES 4 TO 6 SERVINGS

ABOUT MANDARIN COOKING

Mandarin cooking is very inventive. It is known for steamed dumplings, wheat noodles, sweet bean sauce, and duck. Mandarin cooking is very stylish and complicated, but it is not highly spiced or hot like Szechuan or Hunan. Peking duck and mu shu pork are two famous Mandarin dishes. As Peking is located in the north of China where the winters are cold, Mandarin cooking tends to be hearty and characteristically there is a greater use of wheat than rice.

Curried Chicken Salad

1 In a large bowl blend together the yogurt and mayonnaise. Stir in the curry powder.

2 Add the chicken to the dressing and combine thoroughly. Stir in the apple, walnuts, and raisins.

3 Cover the bowl and refrigerate for 1 hour.

MAKES 6 SERVINGS

½ cup plain yogurt
½ cup mayonnaise
2 teaspoons curry powder
4 cups diced skinless, boneless cooked chicken breast
1 cup chopped apple
1 cup coarsely chopped walnuts
½ cup raisins

ABOUT RAISINS

In 1873, a California grape grower had his entire crop scorched by very hot sun. Instead of throwing out the dehydrated grapes, he brought them to a local grocer and convinced him that he was selling raisinated grapes, a rare Persian delicacy. That was our first California raisin crop.

Raisins are grapes that have been dried to a point that prevents the development of enzymes that cause spoilage, which means they keep for a long time. To store raisins properly, remove them from the carton they come in, and place them in an airtight container in the refrigerator. To plump out raisins that have become too dry, soak them in water or fruit juice.

Chicken, Potato, and Tomato Salad with Basil Mayonnaise

2 pounds boneless, skinless chicken breasts, cooked and completely cooled
3–4 cups freshly cooked new potatoes, cooled
¼ cup tightly packed fresh basil leaves
1 tablespoon olive oil
⅔ cup chilled mayonnaise
Salt and freshly ground black pepper
Fresh lemon juice
4 large ripe tomatoes

1 Cut the chicken into 1-inch pieces. Cut the potatoes into 1-inch cubes and place both the chicken and potatoes in a large bowl.

2 In a blender or food processor puree the basil with the olive oil; there will be about 2 tablespoons of the puree. Mix the puree into the mayonnaise.

3 Add the mayonnaise mixture to the chicken and potatoes and toss lightly; season with salt, pepper, and lemon juice to taste.

4 Slice the tomatoes and arrange them on the outside rim of a serving dish.

5 Spoon the salad into the center of the dish and serve.

MAKES 6 SERVINGS

Blender Mayonnaise

2 egg yolks
½ teaspoon dry mustard
½ teaspoon salt
2 tablespoons vinegar (any flavor desired) or fresh lemon juice
1 cup vegetable oil

1 Place the egg yolks, mustard, salt, vinegar or lemon juice, and ¼ cup of the oil in the container of an electric blender.

2 Cover and turn on the motor for 10 seconds. Remove the cover and add the remaining oil in a slow steady stream.

3 The mayonnaise will become thick and creamy. Remove from the blender and store in a clean glass jar in the refrigerator. It will keep up to 1 week.

MAKES 1½ CUPS

WHAT'S COOKING TIP: STORING LEMONS

1. Place lemons in a plastic bag and keep the bag in the refrigerator. That should keep them moist for about 2 weeks.
2. A sliced lemon can hold for about 10 days if the exposed side is covered with plastic wrap and kept in a small tightly closed container.

Turkey and Apple Salad

2 cups diced cooked turkey (or chicken)
2 cups apples, peeled, cored, and coarsely diced, tossed with 2 tablespoons fresh lemon juice
½ cup chopped scallions
½ cup chopped celery
¼ cup vegetable oil
¼ cup plain yogurt
½ cup mayonnaise
¼ teaspoon chili powder
2 teaspoons minced fresh dill
2 tablespoons chopped fresh parsley
Salt and freshly ground black pepper
4 slices bacon, cooked crisp and crumbled

1 In a bowl combine the turkey, apples, scallions, and celery.
2 In another bowl blend together the oil, yogurt, mayonnaise, and chili powder until smooth, and fold into the turkey mixture.
3 Add the dill, parsley, and salt and pepper to taste.
4 Transfer to a serving bowl or dish, sprinkle with the bacon, and serve.

MAKES 4 TO 6 SERVINGS

TALKING TURKEY

The turkey is an excellent source of food but it has a bad image problem. Not a single sports team in the free world is named after the turkey. You've got cardinals, beavers, bears, colts, dolphins, and rams. Even razorback hogs. But no turkeys take the field, at least no turkeys who put that name on their jacket. There are movies that are turkeys, books that are turkeys, and people who are turkeys.

The turkey's bad image goes back to certain American Indian tribes who thought the turkey was dumb and cowardly. They refused to eat turkey meat because they thought they would become as dumb as turkeys. Turkeys are one of the few animals that will drown themselves by opening their beaks and tilting their heads back during rainstorms. During the 1930s Americans began to use the word to describe a person who could be easily tricked.

Benjamin Franklin wrote a letter to his daughter in which he said, ". . . I wish that the bald eagle had not been chosen as the symbol of our country; he is a bird of bad moral character. The turkey is a much more respectable bird and a true native of America." The native American wild turkey is a forefather of the much changed bird we eat today. The wild turkey is much scrawnier, with almost all dark meat. Some American Indians insist that it was venison, not turkey, that their ancestors brought to the first Thanksgiving.

Steak Salad

Dressing:
4 red bell peppers, roasted, peeled, and cut into small strips
6 anchovy fillets, minced
¾ teaspoon crushed red pepper flakes
Salt and freshly ground black pepper to taste
½ teaspoon minced garlic
½ cup olive oil
½ cup red wine vinegar

Salad:
1 red onion, sliced
4 tomatoes, cut into wedges
1 cup sautéed mushrooms
3 scallions, trimmed and sliced
2 tablespoons grated Parmesan cheese
1 head lettuce, cleaned, separated, and dried
½ cup blanched string beans

2 pounds steak, cooked, trimmed of all fat, and cut into thin bite-size slices

1 In a bowl combine all of the ingredients to make the dressing. Mix well. Set aside.
2 In a second bowl mix together the onion, tomatoes, mushrooms, and scallions. Stir in the Parmesan cheese, lettuce, beans, and the steak.
3 Add some of the dressing and toss to coat well. Serve the remaining dressing on the side.

MAKES 4 TO 6 SERVINGS

ABOUT LETTUCE

Lettuce is the most popular salad green in America. The most familiar form of lettuce is iceberg, a crisp head lettuce that is crunchy and juicy, but lacking in distinctive flavor. It chops well for use in tacos and pita sandwiches.

The second most popular lettuce is romaine, an ancient flavorful type that was grown and eaten by the Greeks and Romans. Romaine has long crunchy leaves.

The Boston or Bibb and other leaf lettuces have long been a staple of home gardens and French restaurants. The tender buttery leaves are now becoming popular in supermarkets as well.

California is the nation's largest producer of lettuce. Some growers are starting to produce lettuce in soil-free hydroponic systems. The advantage of hydroponic lettuce is that it is dirt and grit-free and is not sprayed with herbicides or pesticides. Lettuce is low in calories and is a good source of fiber.

Dressings, Sauces, and a Relish

Russian Dressing

1 cup mayonnaise
½ cup ketchup
½ cup chili sauce
2 tablespoons finely chopped
  scallions
2 tablespoons fresh lemon juice
3 tablespoons pickle relish
2 teaspoons Worcestershire
  sauce

Mix all ingredients together thoroughly and chill.

MAKES 2 CUPS

Walnut Dressing

1 In a bowl mix together the lemon and orange juices, mustard, and garlic.

2 Slowly whisk in the vegetable oil and continue whisking until well mixed.

3 Stir in the salt and walnuts.

MAKES 1 CUP

2 tablespoons fresh lemon juice
⅓ cup fresh orange juice
2 teaspoons prepared mustard
1 garlic clove, finely chopped
⅓ cup vegetable oil
Pinch of salt
⅓ cup chopped walnuts

Thousand Island Dressing

For many years Thousand Island has been the most popular salad dressing in the United States, valuable information when you're making a salad dressing for new guests.

1 cup mayonnaise
½ cup chili sauce
1 egg, hard-cooked, finely chopped
1 tablespoon chopped dill pickle
1 teaspoon minced fresh parsley
1 teaspoon Worcestershire sauce

In a mixing bowl combine the mayonnaise and chili sauce. Stir in the remaining ingredients.

MAKES ABOUT 1½ CUPS

ABOUT PICKLES

Pickles in America most often refer to the sweet or sour cucumbers that are pickled and packed in jars. Pickling is a process of preserving food in a salt-and-vinegar brine. Corned beef actually means pickled beef. Hard-cooked eggs are pickled and served at English bars. Pickled pigs' feet are popular bar snacks in the Midwest. Onions, cauliflower, olives, and green walnuts are popular pickling foods in other countries.

Henry J. Heinz began pickling his 57 varieties of cucumber pickles near Sharpsburg, Pennsylvania, in 1869. The main varieties of pickles in the United States are dills, sweet pickles, New York deli half-sours, gherkins, sweet and sour, and Polish dills. Generally, sweet pickles and dills are most popular. All American pickles are cured in a vinegar or salt brine. Sugar is added to make sweet pickles and gherkins. The French make tiny cornichons with white wine vinegar and tarragon.

The New York deli pickle is a sour pickle that is made by mixing kirby cucumbers with fresh garlic, water, vinegar, and salt. Add dill to make dill pickles. The bright green half-sours have only been cured for a few days, the full sours for a few weeks. True Polish pickles are the same as New York deli pickles.

Blue Cheese Dressing

1 In a bowl mix together the blue cheese, mustard, vinegar, and pepper until completely blended.

2 Add the mayonnaise or yogurt and mix well. Cover and refrigerate for up to 10 days.

MAKES 2 CUPS

½ cup crumbled blue cheese
1 teaspoon dry mustard
¼ cup red wine vinegar
Freshly ground black pepper, to taste
2 cups mayonnaise or plain yogurt, or 1 cup of each

WHAT'S COOKING TIP: STORING BLUE CHEESE

1. A small 4-ounce piece of blue cheese will hold properly in the refrigerator for about 1 month. The larger the block of blue cheese the better it stores.
2. Wrap the cheese in a piece of moist cheesecloth. Wrap the cheesecloth with plastic wrap and place it into a tightly closed container. Each week, open the container, moisten the cheesecloth, rewrap, and refrigerate the container. The cheese will keep for 2 months or longer.
3. Cut off only what you are going to use and keep the cheese under almost constant refrigeration.

Creamy Tarragon Dressing

1 egg
1 tablespoon Dijon-style
   mustard
2 cups vegetable oil
¼ cup red wine vinegar
1 tablespoon dried tarragon
   Salt and freshly ground black
   pepper, to taste

1 In a food processor or blender or in a bowl with a whisk, beat together the egg and mustard until foamy. Very slowly add the oil until thickened. Add the vinegar and beat until thoroughly combined.

2 Stir in the tarragon and salt and pepper.

MAKES 2 CUPS

WHAT'S COOKING TIPS: USING HERBS

1. Fresh herbs can stick together and hold fast to the side of the knife. After you wash them you should dry them with a piece of absorbent paper toweling or a cloth towel.

2. Use a very sharp knife, with a blade long enough to span the bunch of herbs, and cut down on them like a guillotine. Steady the bunch of herbs with one hand, fingers tucked under, and chop them with the knife held in the other hand. Use a rocking motion.

3. When you are substituting a fresh herb for a dry one, you need twice as much of the fresh herb as you do of the dry. The reason is that dried herbs have less moisture than fresh herbs and are more concentrated in volume and flavor.

4. Dried herbs are better cooked in heavy sauces; fresh herbs are preferred in salads and fish dishes.

Roquefort Cream Dressing

1 In a bowl combine the cheese, mustard, vinegar, and pepper. Mix until well blended.

2 Fold in the mayonnaise and yogurt. The dressing will keep, refrigerated, for up to 10 days.

MAKES ABOUT 2½ CUPS

¼ cup packed crumbled Roquefort cheese (about 2 ounces)

1 teaspoon dry mustard

⅓ cup red wine vinegar

Freshly ground black pepper, to taste

1 cup mayonnaise

1 cup plain yogurt

Creole Mayonnaise

This Creole mayonnaise is ideal as a dip for fresh vegetables. Mixed with shredded cabbage it makes a very tasty coleslaw. Put a light coating over fish or poultry before broiling. Use it as a dipping sauce for seafood, poultry, or vegetables.

The Creole mustard listed here is a spicy mustard originally produced by the Creole inhabitants of southern Louisiana, but any other hot mustard will suffice.

¼ cup chopped celery
2 tablespoons chopped fresh parsley
2 tablespoons chopped onion
1 teaspoon Worcestershire sauce
2 tablespoons red wine vinegar
¼ cup Creole mustard or other hot and spicy mustard
2 tablespoons prepared white horseradish
2 tablespoons paprika
1 teaspoon salt
½ teaspoon freshly ground black pepper
2 cups mayonnaise

In a large bowl combine all of the ingredients and mix thoroughly. Cover and refrigerate.

MAKES 3 CUPS

Garlic Mayonnaise

This sauce can be made in a blender or food processor, if you desire. Serve with broiled fish and meat, potatoes, hard-cooked eggs, and vegetables.

In a mixing bowl whisk together the egg yolks, lemon juice, salt, and garlic. Slowly whisk in the olive oil until the mayonnaise thickens and is very smooth.

MAKES ABOUT 1½ CUPS

3 egg yolks
1 tablespoon fresh lemon juice
½ teaspoon salt (optional)
8 garlic cloves, minced
½ cup olive oil

Creamy Raspberry Dressing

1 egg
2 cups vegetable oil
½ cup red wine vinegar
1 10-ounce package frozen
  raspberries, thawed

1 Whip the egg until it starts to foam. Begin adding the oil very slowly. When it starts to thicken, add the vinegar until thoroughly combined.
2 In a food processor puree the raspberries.
3 Add the oil mixture and process until combined.

MAKES 1 QUART

NOTE: If the raspberries are tart, a little sugar may be added.

WHAT'S COOKING TIP: FROZEN FRUITS

Frozen fruits have a tendency to thaw very rapidly. It is a good idea to buy all frozen foods at the end of your shopping. Keep them on top of your groceries and get them into your freezer as quickly as possible. In a freezer that is kept at 0° F or below, frozen fruit will keep for 9 months to a year.

Low-Cal Yogurt Curry Dressing

Serve as a dressing for salads or as a dip for raw vegetables.

In a bowl whisk together all of the ingredients.

MAKES ABOUT 1 CUP

1 cup plain low-fat yogurt
2 tablespoons low-fat mayonnaise
1 tablespoon curry powder (see Note)
½ teaspoon dry mustard

NOTE: Try toasting the curry powder in a dry skillet over low to moderate heat just until fragrant, 1 to 2 minutes. The flavor will be different but quite delicious.

Yogurt, Honey, and Cream Cheese Dressing

Serve with fresh fruit.

3 tablespoons honey
Juice of ½ lemon
2 tablespoons cream cheese, at room temperature
1 cup plain yogurt
3 tablespoons toasted sesame seeds (see sidebar)

WHAT'S COOKING TIP: TOASTING SESAME SEEDS

Sesame seeds can be toasted by placing them on a baking sheet in a 350° F oven for 10 minutes or in a small skillet on the stovetop. Stir or shake once and remove from heat when golden brown.

1 In a mixing bowl blend together the honey and lemon juice. Add the cream cheese and yogurt and whisk until smooth. Stir in the sesame seeds.

2 Refrigerate for 30 minutes before serving.

MAKES 1 CUP

Low-Cal Fresh Strawberry Dressing

Serve with fresh fruit.

In a blender combine the strawberries and fructose.

MAKES 1 CUP

NOTE: Fructose can be purchased in most pharmacies.

1¼ cups sliced fresh strawberries
2 tablespoons fructose (see Note)

Creole Sauce

Serve with any poultry or seafood, or over rice.

2 tablespoons vegetable oil
1 cup minced onion
1 cup minced green bell pepper
3 cups chopped tomatoes
½ teaspoon dried thyme
2 bay leaves
2 tablespoons chopped fresh
   parsley
1 tablespoon paprika
1 teaspoon Tabasco sauce

1 In a skillet combine the oil, onion, and bell pepper. Sauté over low heat for 15 minutes.

2 Add the remaining ingredients and simmer for 30 minutes.

3 Scrape the sauce into a jar or bowl and cover. Refrigerate overnight to allow the flavors to develop.

MAKES ABOUT 2½ CUPS

ABOUT SAUCE

No cuisine in the world has as many sauces as French. The French cooks have created hundreds of sauces and written volumes of books about them. The Gauls made a primitive form of sauce for their meats. Medieval Frenchmen made sauces thickened with bread and seasoned with spices from the Orient. Modern French sauces began when Catherine de Medici brought her Italian cooks to France when she became the wife of the French King Henry II in the sixteenth century. But it was not until the early years of the eighteenth century that modern French sauces, some thickened with a flour-based roux, began to be formulated.

Escoffier's *Guide Culinaire* in 1921 defined and categorized the French sauces that we know today. The sauce maker, or *saucier,* is second only to the head chef in status and prestige in French restaurants.

French sauces are divided up into families:

béchamel—made with roux and milk
velouté—made with roux and fish or poultry stock
brown sauce—made with roux and beef or veal stock
hollandaise—made with egg yolks and melted butter
tomato sauce—made with chopped vegetables and tomatoes
mayonnaise—made with egg yolk and vegetable oil

Adding different seasonings to these bases creates hundreds of French sauces.

Mustard Coating for Roasted Meats and Poultry

1 In a blender combine all of the ingredients.
2 Brush the surface of meat or poultry with the coating about 10 minutes prior to roasting.

MAKES ABOUT ¾ CUP

2 garlic cloves, minced
½ teaspoon salt (optional)
6 tablespoons Dijon-style mustard
½ cup light olive oil or peanut oil

Salsa

Serve with meat, fish, or poultry.

2 cups tomatoes, peeled, seeded, and diced
1 red onion, minced
1 red bell pepper, seeded and minced
1 green bell pepper, seeded and minced
2 tablespoons fresh lime juice
¼ cup chopped fresh parsley
1 jalapeño pepper, roasted, peeled, and chopped
3 drops of Tabasco sauce
    Freshly ground black pepper, to taste

1 In a mixing bowl combine all of the ingredients and mix well.
2 Cover and refrigerate for 30 minutes.

MAKES ABOUT 3 CUPS

HOW THE LIMEYS GOT THEIR NAME

In the sixteenth, seventeenth, and eighteenth centuries, when the British navy ruled the waves, extended ocean voyages were typical. But the restricted diet of hardtack and salted meat left the sailors weak and sick from a disease called scurvy. British navy doctors started giving the men limes to eat and their illnesses disappeared, though it was not quite clear at the time why this was so. Modern science has revealed that it was the vitamin C in the limes that kept the men healthy. Sailors from other countries noticed this peculiar habit among their English counterparts and began calling the English sailors limeys.

Remoulade

Remoulade is a French creamy mayonnaise-based sauce that is served on cold cooked shellfish, meats, eggs, and vegetables. According to Larousse Gastronomique, a remoulade sauce is made with a mustard-spiked mayonnaise to which is added tiny chopped cornichon pickles, capers, parsley, chervil, scallions, and fresh tarragon. Sometimes a dash of anchovy is added to give bite to the sauce.

In New Orleans, shrimp remoulade is one of the most popular first courses. It is made with local spicy Creole mustard.

This sauce also makes an excellent dip for raw vegetables or a dressing for salads.

6 tablespoons prepared Creole mustard or other hot and spicy mustard
1 teaspoon prepared white horseradish
3 tablespoons chopped garlic
⅓ cup chopped celery
⅓ cup chopped dill pickles
3 tablespoons chopped fresh parsley
⅓ cup chopped scallions
⅔ cup vegetable oil
⅓ cup white wine vinegar
Dash of Worcestershire sauce
5 drops of Tabasco sauce

In a mixing bowl combine the mustard, horseradish, garlic, celery, pickles, parsley, and scallions. Blend together. Whisk in the remaining ingredients.

MAKES 1½ CUPS

Low-Cal Orange-Yogurt Dressing

Delicious with fresh fruit salad.

In a bowl whisk together all of the ingredients.

MAKES 1¼ CUPS

1 cup plain low-fat yogurt
¼ cup fresh orange juice
¼ teaspoon vanilla extract

Cocktail Sauce

¾ cup chili sauce or ketchup
1 tablespoon prepared white
   horseradish
2 teaspoons Worcestershire
   sauce
   Juice of 1 lemon
   Dash of Tabasco sauce
   (optional)

Combine all ingredients and mix well.

MAKES ALMOST 1 CUP

Mexican Cocktail Sauce from Oaxaca

Combine all ingredients and mix well.

MAKES ALMOST 1 CUP

¾ cup chili sauce or ketchup
1 medium fresh jalapeño
   pepper, seeded and minced
2 tablespoons freshly minced
   parsley or cilantro
   Juice of 1 lime
1 tablespoon mescal or tequila
   (optional)

Ginger-Soy Dressing

¾ cup V-8 vegetable juice
⅓ cup vegetable oil
2 tablespoons soy sauce
2 tablespoons red wine vinegar
1 tablespoon sugar
1 tablespoon grated fresh
   ginger
1 tablespoon dry sherry

In a jar with a cover combine all ingredients. Shake until well blended. Cover and refrigerate for 2 hours. Shake again before using. Serve over salad greens or pasta salads.

MAKES 1½ CUPS

Oriental Magic Mustard Sauce

Serve with grilled meats or vegetables.

1 Mix the mustard into the hot water to make a paste.

2 In a blender combine the sesame seeds and the mustard paste. Add the soy sauce and garlic and blend at high speed until smooth.

3 Scrape into a bowl and stir in the whipped cream until completely blended.

MAKES 1¼ CUPS

3 tablespoons dry mustard
2 tablespoons hot water
1 tablespoon toasted sesame seeds (see sidebar, page 250)
¾ cup soy sauce
1 garlic clove, crushed
3 tablespoons whipped heavy cream

Tartar Sauce

⅔ cup white wine
⅔ cup tomato puree
1 teaspoon minced garlic
1¼ cups mayonnaise
2 hard-cooked eggs, chopped
1 tablespoon chopped onion
2 tablespoons sweet relish
1 teaspoon crushed dried
　　tarragon
　　Dash of Tabasco sauce
1 teaspoon minced fresh
　　parsley
　　Freshly ground black pepper
　　to taste

1 In a saucepan combine the wine, tomato puree, and garlic over moderate heat. Cook until very thick and reduced by half, about 10 minutes. Let cool to room temperature.

2 Blend in the remaining ingredients. Cover and chill before serving.

MAKES ABOUT 2 CUPS

NOTE: This sauce is best when made a day ahead of time and chilled.

Tuna Sauce

This sauce is traditionally served over cooked veal for the classic Italian dish vitello tonnato, but it is excellent over any cooked meat. It's also terrific over pasta or, serve at room temperature or chilled, as a dip for fresh vegetables.

Combine all of the ingredients in the container of a blender. Blend until smooth.

MAKES 2 CUPS

1½ cups regular or low-cal mayonnaise
1 6½-ounce can water-packed white tuna, drained
5 anchovy fillets
Juice of 1 lemon
2 tablespoons drained capers
1 tablespoon cold water

Pesto Sauce for Pasta

Pesto is a bright green uncooked pasta sauce native to Genoa, Italy. It is made with fresh, leafy basil that is blended with garlic, olive oil, and grated cheese. Pesto dates from the Renaissance when pignoli nuts, walnuts, or hazelnuts were often added to recipes. The term pesto *is the Italian word for* pounded; *the word is related to the pounding action of the pestle in the mortar when making the sauce.*

The type of cheese used in pesto is important. The Genovese use Sardinian sheep's milk cheese mixed with cow's milk Parmigiano. Pecorino Romano can be substituted for the sheep's milk cheese, but a good pesto is usually made from a blend of sharp and mellow grated cheese.

Pine nuts are the best nut to use in pesto. They have a mild, almost buttery flavor, and a mealy texture that helps thicken the sauce. The nuts are plucked from fresh unopened pine cones that grow on the pine trees of the Mediterranean. They are white, pea-sized, and oblong.

Today, pesto is easily made in blenders or food processors. To preserve pesto, leave the cheese out of the recipe. Then it can be frozen or placed in clean glass jars and covered with olive oil. Just add the cheese at the last minute, before serving on pasta, boiled potatoes, or in minestrone soup.

2 cups packed fresh basil
leaves
½ cup olive oil
2 tablespoons pine nuts
(pignoli)
2–4 tablespoons chopped garlic
1 teaspoon salt (optional)
½ cup grated Parmesan
cheese
3 tablespoons unsalted butter,
softened

1 In a food processor or blender combine the basil, olive oil, pine nuts, garlic, and salt. Blend for 15 seconds, until well pureed.
2 Stir in the cheese and butter. Scrape into a bowl and cover with plastic wrap.

MAKES ABOUT 1¼ CUPS

Barbecue Sauce

1 In a large sauté pan, heat the oil. Sauté the onions until soft and translucent, about 10 minutes. Stir in all of the remaining ingredients.

2 Bring the sauce to a boil. Reduce the heat and simmer for 20 to 30 minutes, until thickened slightly. Remove from the heat and let cool to room temperature. Cover and store in the refrigerator. It can keep for up to 1 month.

MAKES ABOUT 2 QUARTS

¼ cup olive oil
2 large onions, chopped, and pureed in a food processor
4 bay leaves
4 teaspoons cayenne pepper
½ cup Frank's Original "Durkee Redhot" Cayenne Pepper Sauce
1 teaspoon salt
2 teaspoons freshly ground black pepper
5 cups tomato puree
1 cup packed dark brown sugar
¼ cup fresh lemon juice
3 cups water

Curried Onion Relish

This relish can be served as a condiment with any meat, fish, or poultry. It is also excellent as a marinade for chicken or pork.

4 fresh jalapeño peppers, or 2 tablespoons chopped pickled jalapeño peppers
¼ cup olive oil
4 cups minced onions (about 2½ pounds)
2 tablespoons minced garlic
½ cup raisins
1 tablespoon curry powder
Juice of 1 lemon
Juice of 1 lime
1½ cups honey
1½ cups white wine vinegar
¼ cup chopped cilantro
Salt and freshly ground black pepper

1 If using fresh jalapeño peppers, slice the peppers in half. Remove the seeds and ribs. Mince.

2 In a large sauté pan heat the oil over medium heat. Add the onions, jalapeños, garlic, raisins, and curry powder. Sauté for 5 minutes. Scrape the mixture into a bowl.

3 Using the same sauté pan over high heat, cook together the lemon and lime juices, the honey, and vinegar. Bring to a boil. Reduce the heat to low and simmer for 5 minutes. Pour the liquid over the onions. Stir in the cilantro. Season with salt and pepper to taste. Blend well and set aside to cool and thicken. It can be stored in the refrigerator for at least 2 weeks.

MAKES 1½ QUARTS

ABOUT RELISHES AND CONDIMENTS

Relishes and condiments are savory sauces that bring color and texture to otherwise bland foods. There are long lists of differences between the two, but in general, relishes tend to be chunky and condiments tend to be fluid. Pickle relish is a classic relish and ketchup is a typical condiment.

Relishes are finely chopped fruits and/or vegetables that are flavored with vinegar. Some American favorites are chopped sweet pickle, watermelon pickle, thick homemade chili sauce, tart corn relish, chowchow, and picalili. Mexicans like red and green salsas and relishes. Dutch Americans in the Hudson Valley, central and upper Iowa, and southern Michigan lay out extended relish platters that are family-style displays of vinegared bean salads, pickled cucumbers and fresh vinegared cucumbers, pickled fish, sour-creamed vegetables, plus raw radishes and green onions.

Mango and other fruit chutneys are also relishes. Condiments, on the other hand, are usually cooked or fermented sauces that are added at the stove or at the table. Tomato ketchup, mustard, soy sauce, sesame oil and hot chili oil, Mexican green and red chili sauces, Brazilian piripiri, Argentine churrasco, English HP, and American A.1. sauce, Worcestershire, and Thai nam pla (fish sauce) are all condiments.

Desserts

Danish Snowball

1 pint cherry vanilla ice cream, softened

¼ cup finely grated dark sweet chocolate

2 cups pitted sweet dark cherries, drained

½ cup cherry liqueur or the heavy syrup from the cherries

1 In a bowl blend together the ice cream and the chocolate.

2 In another bowl combine the cherries and liqueur.

3 Scoop the ice cream and chocolate mixture into a glass or dish. Pour the cherry mixture on top and serve.

MAKES 2 SERVINGS

ABOUT CHERRIES

The cherry tree is a member of the rose family. It originated in Asia but became widely distributed throughout Europe and North America. The United States is the world's leading producer of cherries, with Michigan, California, and Oregon leading the way.

Cherries are either sweet or sour. Sour cherries can be eaten raw but they are better cooked with sugar and made into jams or pies. They are bright red. Sweet cherries tend to be larger and darker, sometimes even a mahogany red. They can be cooked but they are better raw. An excellent sweet cherry is the Bing cherry, named after Bing, the Chinese horticulturist who developed it in 1875.

When buying fresh cherries, always look for those that are firm, unblemished, and have a bright, clear color. Overripe cherries will deteriorate very quickly, which is fine if you are going to cook them right away. Slightly underripe cherries will ripen if kept at room temperature in a dark place.

Vanilla Ice Cream

1 In the container of a blender or food processor fitted with a steel blade combine the vanilla bean and sugar. Process until the vanilla bean is chopped into fine specks. Set aside.

2 Place the egg yolks in the top of a double boiler, not over heat, and beat with an electric hand mixer until foamy and light colored. Add the half and half and the vanilla-flavored sugar. Place over simmering water and beat with an electric hand mixer on medium-low speed until the mixture is approximately double its original volume, about 8 to 10 minutes.

3 Remove the top of the double boiler from the heat and place in a large bowl filled with iced water. Stir often until the mixture is cooled. Add the heavy cream and salt; stir to combine. Transfer the cream mixture to your ice cream machine and freeze according to the manufacturer's instructions.

MAKES 1½ QUARTS

1 vanilla bean, cut in ½-inch pieces
¾ cup sugar
5 large egg yolks
1 cup half and half
2 cups well-chilled heavy cream
Dash of salt

ICE CREAM HISTORY

When Marco Polo dined on frozen desserts in the mysterious East, ice cream was already several centuries old. Alexander the Great and the Roman emperor Nero froze their ice cream with snow brought to them by couriers from the nearby mountain peaks.

George Washington owned a "cream machine for making ice" and Thomas Jefferson's recipe for making ice cream is still used today.

In 1846, Nancy Johnson took a wooden bucket, filled it with ice and salt, and fitted within it a metal can equipped with beaters powered by a crank. Unfortunately for her, Nancy didn't patent her invention and imitators proliferated.

German immigrants spread their love of ice cream in the 1880s and 1890s when they began opening candy stores, soda fountains, and ice cream stores across the United States.

Praline Sauce for Ice Cream

Great over vanilla ice cream.

- ⅔ cup pecan halves
- ½ cup firmly packed light brown sugar
- ½ cup dark corn syrup
- 1 tablespoon unsalted butter

1 Into a pot with boiling water drop the pecans and boil for 5 minutes; drain and set aside.

2 Combine the sugar, corn syrup, and butter in the top of a double boiler. Place over boiling water. Heat and stir until the sugar has completely melted and the mixture is blended.

3 Stir in the pecans.

MAKES 4 TO 5 SERVINGS

WHAT'S COOKING TIP: STICKY MEASURING

When you have to measure honey, molasses, corn syrup, or other sticky liquids, coat the surface of the measuring tool with a little butter or corn oil. The liquid will all pour out easily, and you will have a more accurate measure.

Brennan's Bananas Foster

Bananas Foster is a flaming dessert sauce that is spooned over ice cream. It was developed at Brennan's restaurant in New Orleans in 1950. In the late 1940s, New Orleans was the nation's largest banana port. There were bananas all over the French Quarter. Owen E. Brennan, Sr. commissioned his chef Paul Blange to create a dish using bananas. The dish Blange developed is named after Richard Foster, a New Orleans businessman who was a regular customer and friend at Brennan's.

1 In a sauté pan combine the butter, sugar, and cinnamon over moderate heat. Stir and cook for about 3 minutes, until the sugar dissolves.

2 Add the bananas to the mixture and cook for 30 seconds. Stir in the rum. Cook for 1 minute. Very carefully, use a long match to ignite the sauce. Shake the pan until the flames subside.

3 Spoon the sauce over vanilla ice cream.

MAKES 4 SERVINGS

¼ cup unsalted butter
1 cup brown sugar
   Pinch of ground cinnamon
4 bananas, peeled and halved
   lengthwise
¼ cup rum (optional)
   Vanilla ice cream

Coffee-Dusted Ice Cream

2 scoops vanilla ice cream
1 heaping tablespoon finely
    ground dark roast or espresso
    (see Note)
1 tablespoon Scotch whiskey or
    fruit juice

1 Scoop the ice cream into a serving glass or bowl.
2 Sprinkle the ground coffee over the ice cream.
3 Pour the Scotch on top and serve.

MAKES 1 SERVING

NOTE: You can make powdered espresso by pulverizing coffee beans in a coffee mill or blender. Or you can use instant espresso coffee powder.

COFFEE FACTS AND FOLKLORE

The beverage we drink as coffee is the roasted, ground, and brewed nuts of the coffee tree. The first coffee beans came from Ethiopia, shipped from the port of Kaffa (Kefa). This port city or the Turkish word kavheh gave coffee its name. No one coffee bean has the ultimate combination of flavor and aroma that people like and so most coffees are blends of different beans.

The origins of drinking coffee are traced to an Arab goat herder who saw how active his goats were after eating coffee beans and coffee leaves. He used the beans to keep himself awake during his prayers. Arab nobility picked up the practice and soon became the first confirmed coffee drinkers. Coffee became popular in seventeenth-century Europe and was a fashionable drink at the court of Louis XIV. Coffeehouses sprang up in London and New York in the late 1600s.

After the Boston Tea Party, Americans began drinking coffee to protest the British and their tea. But coffee remained expensive until after the Civil War, when American businessmen began importing raw beans directly from Brazil.

Chase & Sanborn were the first men to put ground roasted coffee in a can.

Maxwell House coffee got its name from the Maxwell House hotel in Nashville, Tennessee. When President Theodore Roosevelt was breakfasting there one day, he commented that the coffee was "good to the last drop." His description became the company's slogan.

The decaffeinated coffee Sanka got its name from the French expression sans caféine, "without caffeine."

Brazil is the largest producer of coffee, followed by Colombia, Costa Rica, Cuba, India, and Java. Java is a slang term that was used by Americans as early as the mid-nineteenth century to describe all coffee. Mocha is a port city on the Arabian peninsula and the first city from which coffee was exported to Europe.

Continued . . .

Instant coffee was developed in 1906 by an Englishman living in Guatemala. Instant coffee is made by brewing the liquid and then removing the water by evaporation.

Decaffeinated coffee is made by steaming the unroasted beans and extracting the caffeine with a solvent. The Swiss water-processed decaffeinated coffee is made by steaming the beans and rubbing off the caffeine-laden outer layers of the coffee bean.

Different coffees achieve their flavor and aroma by blending different beans and roasting them to the desired darkness. American coffee is an aromatic brew that is not very dark or strong. French and Vienna roasts are much darker and made for a drip filter system. Espresso is made from very dark oily beans that are ground to a fine powder and brewed in a steam pressure machine that "expresses" the vapors through the coffee and into the cup. In New Orleans, coffee is brewed with ground roasted chicory roots.

The darkness of the coffee bean is a function of the roasting time—the longer the roasting, the darker the color.

WHAT'S COOKING TIPS: BROWN SUGAR SAVERS

1. The best way to store leftover brown sugar is in an airtight container. Add a slice of apple or a lettuce leaf to it before closing it up. The moisture in the apple or lettuce will help keep the moist texture that you find in fresh brown sugar.
2. You can also use this technique to soften brown sugar that has hardened. To soften hard sugar immediately, put it into a blender or food processor.

ABOUT BROWN SUGAR

Brown sugar, in most cases, is white refined sugar with molasses added to it. Light brown sugar has a little molasses, dark brown sugar has more. Pure white sugar is made by refining away the molasses from sugar cane—in brown sugar, it is returned.

In England it is common to find turbinado, West Indian, or Barbados sugar. They are rare in the United States, but can be found. These are all the same name for a coarse granulated brown sugar that is less refined than white sugar; in other words, some molasses is naturally still present.

Udder Delite Ice Cream Drinks

Each of the following drinks makes 1 serving.

RUM RUNNER

½ pint rum raisin ice cream
½ ounce crème de menthe

Blend the ingredients in the container of a blender until smooth. Serve immediately.

BERRY BERRY GOOD

½ pint strawberry ice cream
1 cup plain or vanilla yogurt
2 tablespoons amaretto

Blend the ingredients in the container of a blender until smooth. Serve immediately.

JACOCO

¼ pint coconut ice cream
¼ pint chocolate ice cream
2 tablespoons Kahlúa

Blend the ingredients in the container of a blender until smooth. Serve immediately.

CHOCOMINT

1 cup chocolate ice cream
½ cup chocolate milk
2 tablespoons crème de menthe

Blend the ingredients in the container of a blender until smooth. Serve immediately.

ESKIMO PIE

½ pint chocolate chip ice cream
½ cup chocolate milk
½ ounce crème de menthe

Blend the ingredients in the container of a blender until smooth. Serve immediately.

JAMOCHO

¼ pint chocolate ice cream
¼ pint coffee ice cream
2 tablespoons Kahlúa

Blend the ingredients in the container of a blender until smooth. Serve immediately.

Cool Mint

Blend the ingredients in the container of a blender until smooth. Serve immediately.

1 cup vanilla ice cream
2 tablespoons Kahlúa
1 tablespoon crème de menthe

Bananaquit

Blend the ingredients in the container of a blender until smooth. Serve immediately.

1 cup vanilla ice cream
1 ripe banana, peeled and sliced
2 tablespoons amaretto

WHAT'S COOKING TIPS: ICE CREAM

1. Freezing diminishes most flavors, so flavor more heavily than you would for hot dishes.
2. If you cooked ingredients together, let them cool to under room temperature before adding them to the ice cream maker. Extracts, fruits, and liqueurs lose some of their flavor when heated, and should only be added after the mix has cooled.
3. Ice cream loses its flavor and texture about a week after it is made, and should not be stored more than a month.
4. If your frozen dessert is not too firm, chill your serving dishes for 5 minutes in the freezer before using them.
5. A fork is the best tool for digging into ice cream that is too hard to scoop.

Carmello Dip

1 14-ounce can sweetened
condensed milk, *unopened*
Fresh fruit, sliced

1 In a saucepan of boiling water submerge the
unopened can of milk. Reduce the heat to low.
Simmer for *3½ hours*, adding more water to
the pot as needed to keep the can completely
covered with water.

2 Remove the can from the water and allow to
cool to room temperature. Chill the can in the
refrigerator or in a bowl of ice water.

3 Open the can. The sugar and the milk will
have caramelized and thickened to the consistency of a jam.

4 Spoon the carmello dip onto a serving plate
and surround with sliced fresh fruit for dipping.

MAKES ABOUT 1½ CUPS

Pecan Maple Crunch Topping

Serve the crunch over ice cream, fruit salad, or as a topping on cheesecake.

1 Preheat the oven to 375° F.

2 Place the pecans in a baking pan. Sprinkle the nuts with the maple sugar or brown sugar, then pour on the maple syrup. Bake for 10 minutes.

3 Pour the liquid crunch onto a marble slab or baking sheet, spreading it out with a spatula. Let cool and break into small pieces.

MAKES 1 CUP

1½ cups coarsely chopped pecans
¼ cup maple sugar or brown sugar
¼ cup maple syrup

Crème Caramel

Crème caramel is a rich custard pudding that is baked with a caramelized sugar syrup. In Spain, a similar dessert is called flan, and is made and served in individual cups. It is the national dessert of the country.

1½ cups sugar
¼ teaspoon fresh lemon juice
4 cups milk
1 vanilla bean, split
4 whole eggs, at room temperature
8 egg yolks, at room temperature

1 Preheat the oven to 350° F.

2 In a saucepan over very low heat combine ¾ cup sugar and the lemon juice. Cook, stirring constantly, for about 10 minutes, or until the sugar becomes a light, golden caramel color.

3 Working very quickly, because the sugar will harden almost immediately, pour the caramel into a shallow 1½-quart mold. Tilt and swirl the caramel to be sure it covers the bottom of the mold.

4 In another saucepan combine the milk and the vanilla bean. Heat to just before the boiling point. Remove from the heat.

5 Meanwhile, in a mixing bowl combine the whole eggs, egg yolks, and the remaining ¾ cup sugar. Remove the vanilla bean from the milk and gradually stir the hot milk into the egg mixture. Strain this "custard" mixture into the caramel-coated mold.

6 Set the filled mold into a deep pan. Fill the outside pan with hot water to reach three-quarters of the way up the side of the mold.

7 Set the baking pan with the custard-filled mold in the oven. Bake for 40 minutes. Let the custard cool to room temperature.

8 When the custard has come to room temperature, dip the mold into hot water for 2 minutes. Invert the mold onto a plate and serve.

MAKES 4 SERVINGS

WHAT'S COOKING TIP: WHIPPING EGGS

Eggs that are allowed to come to room temperature before they are beaten will have greater volume.

ABOUT VANILLA AND VANILLA EXTRACT

Vanilla is the pod of a climbing vine and a member of the orchid family. Vanilla extract is made from whole vanilla beans that have been soaked in alcohol. Vanillin is an artificial vanilla flavoring chemically made from wood waste. By United States law, pure vanilla extract must be made from vanilla. Imitations must be labeled. When using imitation instead of pure vanilla extract, double the amount called for in the recipe.

The very best vanilla flavor comes from steeping the vanilla bean in the liquid you are using for cooking. Place a whole vanilla bean in a jar of sugar and it will give the sugar the flavor of vanilla. Long, dark brown vanilla beans can be used a number of times. Just rinse them, dry them off, and keep them in an airtight container.

Veiled Country Lass

½ cup unsalted butter
3½ cups unseeded fresh rye or
   pumpernickel bread crumbs
3 tablespoons sugar
2 cups chunky applesauce
2 cups sweetened whipped
   heavy cream
   Sweet chocolate shavings

1 In a large skillet melt the butter over medium heat. Add the bread crumbs and sugar and stir with a wooden spoon. Reduce the heat to low and continue stirring until the bread crumbs are crispy. Remove from the heat and set aside.

2 Cover the bottom of a serving bowl with ½ inch of the bread crumbs. Add a layer of applesauce. Continue layering with another layer of bread crumbs and applesauce and more bread crumbs.

3 Top with sweetened whipped cream and chocolate shavings.

MAKES 4 SERVINGS

ABOUT SUGAR

There are dozens of types of sugar and sweeteners but the most common is white granulated sugar derived from sugarcane. Cane sugar products were used in Asia before they were brought to Europe by the Arabs and returning Crusaders. Columbus planted sugar cane in the New World. The resulting sugarcane industry became a source of bloody wars and the main reason for slavery in the West Indies. A flourishing trade developed sending sugar, molasses, and rum from the West Indies to New England, which sent other products to Europe. Many American slaves were previously from sugarcane plantations in the West Indies. Abolitionists discouraged eating cane sugar because of the cruelty to the slaves on the sugar plantations. Before cane sugar became popular in America with the lifting of tariffs in the 1880s, Americans used honey and sorghum molasses as sweeteners.

Powdered sugar is a finer grain of granulated sugar. Powdered or superfine sugar can be made by processing granulated sugar in a blender for 60 seconds. Confectioners' sugar is granulated sugar that has been highly refined and enriched with cornstarch. It is commonly used to make icings or frostings for cakes. Do not substitute confectioners' sugar for granulated in baking.

Raw sugar is a light brown sugar that is produced when molasses has been removed from white sugar but before it is refined into granulated white table sugar.

Besides making foods sweet, sugar gives dough a tenderness. When added to yeast for bread, it helps the action of the yeast. It also adds a golden-brown crust to baked goods.

Rice Pudding

6¾ cups milk
1 cup long-grain white rice, washed
⅓ cup sugar
1 cinnamon stick, broken in half
1 cup raisins
1 cup heavy cream
5 egg yolks

1 In a large saucepan bring the milk to a simmer. Add the rice, sugar, and cinnamon. Simmer, stirring, for 45 minutes.

2 Remove the pan from the heat. Discard the cinnamon stick. Stir in the raisins and ½ cup heavy cream.

3 In a small bowl beat the remaining ½ cup cream until peaks form. Whisk in the egg yolks.

4 Ladle the rice pudding into individual heat-proof baking dishes. Spread a small amount of the egg yolk and whipped cream mixture on top of each and place under the broiler until lightly browned.

MAKES 6 TO 8 SERVINGS

ABOUT CINNAMON

Cinnamon is the dried bark of a tree that is native to Ceylon and parts of southern India. The cinnamon tree is a deep green evergreen that has leaves and blossoms like the orange tree, and papery bark like a cork or birch tree. In biblical times, cinnamon was used as perfume.

Most people know cinnamon as a sweet spice that is used in cakes, cookies, and pies. But Greeks used cinnamon in meat sauce for moussaka. Mutton and lamb dishes and chicken pies in Middle Eastern and North African cooking are spiced with cinnamon.

ABOUT MILK

Animal milk has been consumed by humans since we first began to domesticate animals thousands of years ago. Milk is the liquid nourishment that lactating female mammals produce for their young. Cow's milk is by far the most popular, but goat's milk and even sheep's milk have their fans. Cheese and butter can be made from any mammal's milk.

Almost all the milk we get at the grocery store is cow's milk. Almost all of it has been pasteurized, a process that raises the temperature of the milk in order to kill all the enzymes and bacteria. The milk has also been homogenized, which means that the milk and the cream have been permanently combined. The milk in our stores comes in four basic types: whole milk, 2 percent, 1 percent, and skimmed milk. Whole milk has 3 to 4 percent of its volume as butterfat. It has the richest taste and the most calories—150 per cup. Two percent milk is 2 percent milk fat and 120 calories per cup. One percent has 1 percent butterfat and 100 calories per cup. Skimmed has only ½ percent butterfat and 90 calories. Doctors suggest that after the age of 2 years, we should all be drinking skim milk, but before that we need whole milk.

Evaporated milk is whole milk that has had half of its water content removed by evaporation. It should be kept in the refrigerator once the can or container is opened and should not be held in any case for more than 6 months.

Condensed milk is evaporated milk that has been sweetened with sugar or corn syrup. It is used primarily as a shortcut for making puddings and custards. It keeps well because it has a high sugar content.

Nondairy coffee creamer is a type of milk that is made with cornstarch and other chemicals to approximate milk's creamy whiteness. It is not as perishable as fresh milk and it is used as a convenience.

Bread Pudding with Whiskey Sauce

The pudding family has both a sweet and savory wing. Bread pudding is a sweet pudding that has many variations. Basically it is slices of bread spread with butter, then layered in a casserole. A custard mixture is poured over the bread and the pudding is baked until the custard is set. Raisins, sugar, and cinnamon may be added.

5 whole eggs
1 egg yolk
½ cup sugar
2 cups milk
1 cup heavy cream
4 tablespoons plus 1 teaspoon ground cinnamon
⅛ teaspoon freshly grated nutmeg
1 cup raisins
1 large loaf day-old French bread, cut into 4 slices, the remainder cut into bite-size pieces
Whiskey Sauce (see below—optional)

PUDDING

The word pudding *probably stems from the old French word* boudin *for "sausage." Blood sausages are still called puddings. The earliest puddings were meats and grains stuffed in an animal gut and boiled or baked. Eventually the gut was replaced by cheesecloth bags. Nowadays, puddings mostly refers to milky, creamy desserts.*

1 Preheat the oven to 300° F.

2 In a mixing bowl whisk together the eggs and egg yolk. Whisk in the sugar, milk, cream, 4 tablespoons cinnamon, and the nutmeg.

3 Sprinkle the remaining 1 teaspoon cinnamon on the bottom of an 8-inch-square heatproof baking pan. Sprinkle with ⅓ cup raisins.

4 Sprinkle a single layer of the bite-size bread on the bottom of the prepared pan. Spoon some of the egg mixture over the bread, pressing the liquid into the bread pieces with the back of a spoon. Continue the layering process with the raisins, pieces of bread, and egg mixture and ending with the remaining 4 slices of French bread on top.

5 Cover with aluminum foil. Bake for 45 minutes. Remove the foil and bake for another 5 minutes.

6 Serve the bread pudding with the whiskey sauce, if desired.

MAKES 6 TO 8 SERVINGS

WHISKEY SAUCE

In New Orleans bread pudding is typically topped with a silky smooth whiskey sauce. The food of New Orleans is based on French cooking and French bread pudding is often covered with a sweet sabayon sauce made of powdered sugar and egg yolks whipped into a froth. New Orleans whiskey sauce is made with whipped eggs, sugar, melted butter, and topped off with Bourbon.

1 In a heavy saucepan mix the cornstarch and sugar, gradually add the milk and whiskey. Heat, stirring constantly, until the mixture almost boils.

2 Reduce the heat and simmer, uncovered, for 3 minutes, stirring occasionally. Add the butter, vanilla, and nutmeg and stir until the butter melts and is well blended.

3 Serve hot over the bread pudding.

MAKES 2 CUPS

2 tablespoons cornstarch
½ cup sugar
1¾ cups milk
1¾ cups whiskey
¼ cup unsalted butter
½ teaspoon vanilla extract
Pinch of grated nutmeg

ABOUT SCOTCH WHISKEY

Scotch whiskey is made by distilling the liquid "spirit" of fermented grain. The Scots use barley that has been sprouted and roasted, a process called malting, to give that familiar smokey flavor of Scotch whiskey, which is why it is sometimes called malt whiskey.

When first distilled, Scotch is clear. It is put in oak barrels to age and develop color. All of the mainstream Scotches—Dewar's, Johnnie Walker, Ballantine's, et cetera, are blends of whiskeys, each with its own special flavor, but there are some single malt, or unblended Scotches on the market. Many Scotch whiskey authorities prefer the single malts, believing that they are of the quality of a fine brandy.

Zabaglione with Fresh Strawberries

Zabaglione (or zabaione) is a sweet Italian custardlike dessert. It is made with egg yolks and sugar and fortified with Marsala wine. In France it is called sabayon, and there are dozens of variations, including champagne in place of the Marsala. Zabaglione can be poured over bread pudding or fresh fruit, but in Italy it is usually served straight in a stemmed glass.

1 pint fresh strawberries, washed and stemmed (see Note)
8 egg yolks
½ cup sugar
½–⅔ cup Marsala or sweet sherry wine

1 Divide the strawberries among 6 stemmed glasses.

2 In the top of a large double boiler combine the egg yolks, sugar, and wine and place over simmering water. Cook, beating the mixture rapidly and constantly with a wire whisk until it becomes a thick creamy custard. Do not let the mixture come near the boil or it will curdle.

3 Immediately pour the custard over the strawberries and serve at once.

MAKES 6 SERVINGS

NOTE: If strawberries are not available, substitute sliced fresh, frozen, or canned peaches, pitted fresh or canned apricot halves, or sliced bananas. Be sure to fully drain frozen or canned fruit of their juices before serving.

ABOUT STRAWBERRIES

An Englishman once said of the strawberry, "Doubtless the Almighty could make a better berry—but he never did." Strawberries grow wild on many continents. They were so abundant in New England that an early colonist said that you couldn't put your foot down without stepping on one.

Strawberries were always the first fruit of spring in temperate zones. The strawberry season used to last from 1 to 3 months, but with new breeds and methods, it now runs from February through November in California. Production is greatest in May.

When buying strawberries, look for clean, bright berries with a uniform red color. Their green stem caps should be attached. Don't wash or remove the stems until right before you eat them. Strawberries should be used the day of purchase.

Strawberry Soufflé

Generally a soufflé is a combination of a custard base lightened by the addition of whipped egg whites. When the mixture is baked, it puffs up. When it cools it falls or contracts. Guests should be at the table waiting for the soufflé, not the other way around.

1½ cups chopped fresh or
    frozen strawberries
7 tablespoons sugar
1 tablespoon Grand Marnier
    or other orange-flavored
    liqueur
3 tablespoons unsalted butter
2 tablespoons all-purpose
    flour
½ cup milk
6 eggs, separated

1 In a bowl combine the strawberries, 2 table-spoons sugar, and the liqueur. Let stand for about 15 minutes.

2 Preheat the oven to 400° F. Lightly butter a 9-inch soufflé mold or deep baking dish. Sprinkle it with sugar, tilting the dish to coat thoroughly.

3 In a saucepan melt the butter over moderate heat and stir in the flour. Cook, stirring constantly for 2 to 3 minutes. Gradually add the milk and stir until the mixture is thickened and smooth.

4 Remove from the heat. One at a time, beat in the egg yolks and 3 tablespoons sugar. Stir in the strawberry mixture. Set aside.

5 About 30 minutes before serving, beat the egg whites until almost stiff. Add the remaining 2 tablespoons sugar and beat for 1 to 2 minutes, until combined. Gently fold the egg whites into the strawberry mixture.

6 Pour the mixture into the prepared mold and bake for 20 to 25 minutes without opening the oven during the baking time. Serve immediately.

MAKES 6 SERVINGS

WHAT'S COOKING TIPS: HOW TO MAKE A PERFECT SOUFFLÉ

1. The equipment used to beat the egg whites should be immaculately clean.
2. The egg whites should be at room temperature and have no egg yolk in them.
3. Beat the whites in a glass, stainless steel, or copper bowl. Aluminum may discolor the whites.
4. Have the base and all the ingredients ready before you beat the whites.
5. As soon as the whites are ready, add them to the custard with a folding motion. The base sauce should be lukewarm. Don't beat the whites into the base or you will press the air out of them.
6. Use the size soufflé dish that the recipe calls for. A soufflé dish too small will spill; too large and the soufflé won't puff up properly.
7. When a soufflé batter is heated, it starts to rise up along the walls of the soufflé mold. If the walls are smooth, the batter will slip back a little as it goes up. If you butter the inside of the mold and then give it a little coating of sugar or bread crumbs (depending upon the type of soufflé) and refrigerate the mold for 30 minutes, the texture of the inside surface will then be like sandpaper. The rough texture gives the batter a ladder to climb. The soufflé will stay up better.
8. Don't open the oven door during the baking of a soufflé. The change in temperature might cause the soufflé to fall.
9. Put a baking sheet under your soufflé. The sheet will conduct heat more evenly, and will catch any spills.

Hot Chocolate Soufflé

1½ tablespoons powdered instant espresso coffee, or 2 tablespoons instant coffee powder

1½ tablespoons boiling water

6 ounces unsweetened chocolate, grated or broken into small pieces

⅓ cup cornstarch

1½ cups milk

1½ cups plus 2 tablespoons sugar

7 eggs, separated
Pinch of salt

¼ teaspoon cream of tartar
Heavy cream, whipped and sweetened, or vanilla ice cream

1 Preheat the oven to 350° F.

2 Lightly butter and sugar an 8-inch soufflé mold, tapping on all sides to coat evenly with the sugar. Chill until needed.

3 In the top of a double boiler set over simmering water, dissolve the instant coffee in the boiling water. Add the chocolate and stir until just melted. Set aside to cool.

4 In a saucepan combine the cornstarch and ¼ cup milk. Whisk until smooth, then whisk in the remaining 1¼ cups milk and 1½ cups sugar. Set over moderate heat and bring to a boil, whisking constantly to prevent scorching. Boil for 30 seconds.

5 Transfer the mixture to a large bowl, and beat in the egg yolks, one at a time, incorporating thoroughly after each addition. Mix in the melted chocolate mixture.

6 In another bowl beat the egg whites with an electric mixer at high speed until they start to foam. Add the salt and cream of tartar. Continue beating at high speed until the whites are stiff but not dry. Add the remaining 2 tablespoons sugar and beat just to incorporate.

7 Fold the egg whites into the chocolate mixture with a rubber spatula. Pour the batter into the prepared soufflé mold and bake for 40 minutes, without opening the oven during the baking time.

8 Serve immediately with sweetened whipped cream or vanilla ice cream.

MAKES 6 SERVINGS

WHAT'S COOKING TIPS: WHIPPING CREAM

Whipping thick cream to firmness can be a delicate operation. Whip it too much and it turns to butter; too little, and it will be runny.

1. You should keep the cream, beaters, and bowl cold. Put them in the refrigerator 2 hours before you plan to whip. In the summer, place the bowl over a large bowl of ice cubes.
2. Never try to whip cream in a blender. Place the cream in a cold bowl. Turn the electric hand blender to high and whip the cream until it starts to thicken. Turn the switch to medium low, and watch the cream carefully. Don't overwhip. Cream can be whipped in a food processor.

ABOUT CREAM OF TARTAR

Cream of tartar is a purified form of argol, the crusty deposit that forms in wine casks. It is the acid potassium tartrate, and it is used as an ingredient in baking powder. Mixing cream of tartar with bicarbonate of soda in the presence of liquid forms carbon dioxide, which acts as a leavening agent in baking. Cream of tartar is an optional ingredient in meringue. Before the age of the electric hand mixer, cream of tartar was always added to meringue to help form the stiff peaks of the whipped egg whites.

White Chocolate Mousse

¼ pound white chocolate
2 eggs, separated
¼ cup milk
½ teaspoon vanilla extract
1 cup heavy cream
1 9–10-ounce package frozen
   raspberries
   Chocolate dessert cups
   (optional)
   Chocolate shavings as
   garnish

WHAT'S COOKING TIPS: BAKING PANS

1. When you are baking in oven-proof glass, such as Pyrex, reduce the temperature by 25 degrees. This is because clear glass transmits heat better than does metal.
2. If you're using black metal bakeware, decrease your cooking temperature by 10 degrees.

1 In the top of a double boiler melt the white chocolate over hot water. Remove from the heat and allow to cool down so you don't end up cooking the eggs that you add next.

2 Pour the melted chocolate into a mixing bowl. Add the egg yolks, milk, and vanilla; mix together.

3 Beat the egg whites until thick peaks form.

4 In another mixing bowl whip the heavy cream until stiff. Beat half of the white chocolate mixture into the whipped cream. Blend the remaining white chocolate mixture into the egg whites. Blend the two mixtures together.

5 Refrigerate for 1 hour, or until thickened.

6 In a food processor or blender puree the raspberries. Pour ¼ cup of the puree on a serving plate, place a chocolate cup on top of the raspberries, and fill the cup with the white chocolate mousse. Alternately, scoop out 2 small balls of mousse and place on the raspberry sauce.

7 Garnish with the chocolate shavings and serve.

MAKES 4 SERVINGS

Chocolate Chip Mousse

1 In the top of a double boiler or in a large metal bowl set over simmering water combine the egg whites and the sugar. Beat constantly until the sugar dissolves and the mixture is heated through, about 3 minutes. The mixture should be hot to the touch.

2 Remove from the heat and beat for 3 to 5 minutes, or until the mixture cools to 115° F or less.

3 Pour the melted cooled chocolate into the egg white mixture and stir together.

4 Whip the heavy cream until very thick and stiff.

5 Gently fold the whipped cream into the chocolate mixture with a spatula.

6 Fold in the chocolate bits.

7 Pour the mixture into a serving bowl or individual glasses and refrigerate for at least 1 hour. Just before serving, top with whipped cream.

MAKES 4 SERVINGS

4 egg whites
1 cup sugar
½ pound milk chocolate, melted and cooled
2 cups heavy cream
3 ounces semisweet chocolate, chopped into small bits
Heavy cream, whipped and sweetened

WHAT 'S COOKING TIP: FOLDING IN INGREDIENTS

Many recipes call for ingredients to be folded in, usually thicker, heavier ingredients with light and fluffy ones such as beaten egg whites. Try not to break up the lightness of your fluffy ingredients. Many cooks prefer using a long-handled rubber spatula for this, but the best tools are your hands.

Place the heavier ingredients in the bottom of a large round-sided mixing bowl. Add the fluffy ingredients on top. Now, flatten your hand like a spatula blade. Run your hand down the inside edge of the bowl to the heavy ingredients at the bottom. Twist your hand and bring some of the heavy ingredients to the top in a turning motion. Do this lightly but firmly. Continue until all the ingredients are folded in. The hand is best because it gives you a greater grasp of the ingredients and control over the mixture.

Chocolate Island with Vanilla Sauce

1⅛ pounds semisweet chocolate
½ pound plus 2 tablespoons
   unsalted butter
 2 tablespoons Grand Marnier
 2 tablespoons rum
 8 eggs, separated
½ cup sugar
   Vanilla sauce (see below)

1 In the top of a double boiler over barely simmering water melt the chocolate and ½ pound butter. Blend in the Grand Marnier and rum and stir until smooth. Set aside to cool slightly.

2 Choose a 9- ×5- ×3-inch rectangular mold or another straight-sided mold with a 6-cup capacity. Coat it generously with the remaining 2 tablespoons butter. Butter the wax paper and line the mold with it, buttered side down.

3 In an electric mixer beat the egg yolks with the sugar until the mixture is doubled in volume and light in color, about 2 minutes. Pour this mixture into the chocolate and fold in.

4 Whip the egg whites until they form soft peaks. Fold into the chocolate. Pour into the mold, cover with plastic wrap, and freeze for at least 6 hours.

5 To unmold, dip the outside of the mold in hot water for 5 seconds. Dry the outside of the mold. Invert the mold onto a plate, remove the wax paper, and slice the island with a knife that has been dipped in hot water.

6 To serve, ladle a pool of vanilla sauce onto each plate. Place a slice of the chocolate island on the sauce.

MAKES 8 TO 10 SERVINGS

NOTE: The chocolate island can be wrapped tightly and frozen for up to 1 month.

VANILLA SAUCE

This sauce can be served as is or flavored with 2 tablespoons liqueur, such as Grand Marnier, Kahlúa, or Cointreau. Coffee concentrate or grated orange zest is an excellent nonalcoholic flavoring agent.

1 In a heavy saucepan over low heat bring 2 cups half and half to just under the boiling point.

2 In a mixing bowl whisk together the egg yolks and the sugar until smooth and light, about 1 minute. Whisk in the cornstarch. Gradually whisk the heated half and half into the egg mixture. Rinse out the saucepan and return the mixture to it. Place the pan over low heat.

3 Cook the sauce, stirring constantly, over low heat, until the mixture is thick enough to coat the back of a wooden spoon lightly, about 5 minutes. Do not let the sauce rise above 165° F. Remove from the heat.

4 Strain the mixture through a sieve, into a bowl that is sitting in a bed of ice. Quickly whisk in the remaining ¼ cup half and half and the vanilla to help cool the sauce. Set the bowl in the refrigerator to continue cooling.

2¼ **cups half and half**
10 **egg yolks**
½ **cup sugar**
1 **teaspoon cornstarch**
1 **teaspoon vanilla extract**

MAKES 3 CUPS

ABOUT GRAND MARNIER

Grand Marnier is the brand name of a French liqueur that has the flavors of both brandy and orange. It is made by the Marnier-Lapostelle company, a Cognac producer in Bourg-Charente, France. The reason Grand Marnier is different from other orange-flavored liqueurs is that it is made by marinating bitter Haitian orange peels in a very high-quality young clear Cognac. This liquid is distilled and then blended with mature, aged Cognac and bottled. Grand Marnier is an afterdinner drink and a classic topping for sweet crepes.

Continued . . .

WHAT'S COOKING TIPS: MELTING CHOCOLATE

1. The best way to melt chocolate is in the top of a double boiler. Make sure that the water in the bottom of the double boiler is not boiling, because chocolate should be melted by the water's heat, not by steam, which can burn chocolate.

2. Water does not mix well with melting chocolate. Any pots and utensils used in working with chocolate should be completely dry. Even a small amount of water can cause melted chocolate to thicken and tighten. If by accident you end up with thickened chocolate, you can correct the problem by adding a small amount of vegetable shortening to the chocolate and whisking everything back to a smooth consistency.

3. If you are melting a very small amount of chocolate, put the chocolate into a piece of aluminum foil and pop it in the oven. The temperature of the oven should be under 110° F. The low heat will melt the chocolate without scorching it. Chocolate can be melted in a microwave oven, on a microwave-safe dish.

Coffee Mousse

1 With an electric mixer beat the cream, 2 tablespoons sugar, and the instant coffee until stiff peaks form and the cream is very thick. Stir in the chocolate.

2 In another bowl beat the egg white with the remaining 2 teaspoons sugar until stiff.

3 Gently fold the egg white mixture into the coffee mixture and combine. Spoon the mixture into a bowl or stemmed glasses. Chill for 2 hours.

MAKES 4 SERVINGS

1 cup heavy cream
2 tablespoons plus 2 teaspoons sugar
1½ teaspoons powdered instant coffee
2 ounces semisweet chocolate, melted
1 egg white

ABOUT CHOCOLATE AND HEALTH

Chocolate is perfectly acceptable as part of a balanced diet. A 1-ounce milk chocolate bar contains 147 calories. Furthermore, studies have shown that bacteria in the skin, not chocolate, is the cause of acne in teen-agers. Eating chocolate does not increase your chances of getting cavities any more than any other food.

A 1.5-ounce milk chocolate bar contains 9 milligrams of caffeine. That is only one-tenth of the amount in a cup of coffee. Researchers have also disproven the idea that chocolate inhibits the body's ability to use calcium and that chocolate causes hyperactivity in children.

Chocolate Loaf

3 cups heavy cream
1¼ pounds semisweet
  chocolate, grated
4 egg yolks
½ cup unsalted butter, at room
  temperature
½ cup blanched and slivered
  almonds
  Strawberries or raspberries
  Heavy cream, whipped and
  sweetened

1 Lightly butter a 9- ×5- ×3-inch loaf pan. Line the inside with wax paper, cut to fit.

2 In a small saucepan scald the cream until hot but not boiling. Remove from the heat. Add the chocolate and whisk until smooth and melted. One at a time, add the egg yolks, whisking after each addition. Cover and refrigerate to cool completely.

3 When cooled, whisk in the butter. Add the almonds and pour the mixture into the prepared loaf pan. Refrigerate overnight.

4 To serve, dip the sides of the loaf pan into warm water for 30 seconds, to loosen the loaf from the pan. Remove the pan from the water, dry the outside of the pan, and invert it onto a serving plate to free the loaf. Remove the wax paper.

5 Serve plain or slice and decorate with strawberries or raspberries and sweetened whipped cream.

MAKES 8 SERVINGS

ABOUT RASPBERRIES

Raspberries are sweet little fruits that grow on thorny raspberry bushes. They grow better in countries in northern latitudes. Most raspberries are red, but they can also be black, yellow, golden, or white. Raspberries are a good source of vitamin C. They have naturally high amounts of pectin, which makes them perfect for jams and jellies.

Apple and Raisin Crunch

1 Preheat the oven to 400 ° F. Lightly butter a 10-inch pie pan and a sheet of aluminum foil.

2 In a small bowl cover the raisins with boiling water. Set aside to soften.

3 As you slice the apples, toss with lemon juice in a bowl, to prevent browning. Add the lemon zest, sugar, cinnamon, and nutmeg and mix well. Set aside.

4 In another bowl combine the bread crumbs and butter. Mix thoroughly.

5 Drain the raisins.

6 Spread about one-third of the bread crumbs in the bottom of the prepared pan. Top with half of the apple slices, and half of the raisins. Repeat the process, ending with bread crumbs. Cover with the sheet of buttered aluminum foil.

7 Bake for 25 minutes. Remove the foil and bake for about 10 minutes or until golden.

8 Serve warm, as is, or with ice cream.

MAKES 6 SERVINGS

½ cup raisins

½ cup boiling water

6 tart apples (such as Granny Smiths), cored, peeled, and sliced

Grated zest and juice of 1 lemon

¼–½ cup sugar, depending on the sweetness of the apples

1 teaspoon ground cinnamon

½ teaspoon grated nutmeg

4 cups packed fresh, unflavored white bread crumbs (about ¾ loaf with crusts removed and run through a food processor or blender)

½ cup unsalted butter, melted

Ice cream (optional)

ABOUT ZEST

Zest is the grated outer peeling of lemons, oranges, limes, and grapefruits. The best way to add zest to your cooking is to rub the whole fruit against the tiny holes on a small hand grater or a zester.

The zest is more flavorful than the juice of the fruit because it has a very high oil content. Be sure to use only the colorful outer rind because the white connective tissue right underneath is very bitter.

Blueberry Buckle

Topping:
1¼ cups sugar
2 teaspoons ground cinnamon
1 cup plus 3 tablespoons all-purpose flour
¾ cup cold unsalted butter, cut into bits

Batter:
1¾ cups all-purpose flour
1 tablespoon baking powder
¾ cup sugar
½ cup unsalted butter
¾ teaspoon salt
¾ cup buttermilk
1 teaspoon vanilla extract
4 egg yolks

  Sweet pastry dough for 4 individual 10-ounce custard cups
3 cups fresh blueberries or frozen blueberries, thawed and drained well, or canned blueberries, drained well
  Heavy cream (optional)

1 Preheat the oven to 400° F. Butter four 10-ounce custard cups.

2 To prepare the topping, in a bowl combine the sugar, cinnamon, and flour. Add the butter and mix at medium speed until the dough begins to clump slightly. Cover and refrigerate until ready to use.

3 To prepare the batter, in a mixing bowl sift together the dry ingredients. Add the butter and salt and cut together with an electric mixer until the mixture resembles fine meal. In another bowl whisk together the buttermilk, vanilla, and eggs yolks. Pour into the flour mixture and blend together.

4 Roll out the pastry dough and cut the dough to fit the custard cups. Line the cups with the dough.

5 Divide half of the blueberries among the pastry-lined cups. Top with the batter, using all of it. Add another layer, using the remaining blueberries. Sprinkle evenly with the topping.

6 Bake for 30 minutes. Reduce the oven temperature to 350° F and bake for 20 minutes more, or until the topping is golden brown and crisp. Serve with cream, if desired.

MAKES 4 SERVINGS

ABOUT BLUEBERRIES

There are two types of blueberries in America. There are high bush blueberries that grow to 10 feet tall and produce large round berries that are sweet enough to eat just as they are or with cream. Michigan and New Jersey produce the bulk of this type of blueberry. These are the blueberries you find in pint containers in supermarkets. Then there are the Maine blueberries, tiny little vine bushes that grow in bogs in Maine. The Maine blueberries are essentially wild and have been harvested in much the same way since the Indians controlled the eastern seaboard. In August, when they are ripe, people walk through the fields with special harvesting rakes and scoop the berries off the vines. Maine blueberries are tiny and tart. They make the best pies, cobblers, and pancakes. The blueberry harvest in summer is festival time in "downeast" Maine, where churches have blueberry-pie sales and young women vie for the title of Blueberry Queen.

Banana Betty

1¼ cups finely ground
    gingersnaps
3½ tablespoons sugar
 ¼ cup melted unsalted butter
 2 cups heavy cream
 4 egg yolks
 1 tablespoon dark rum
    (optional)
½ teaspoon vanilla extract
 2 large ripe bananas, peeled,
    halved crosswise and
    lengthwise

GINGERSNAP

"Snap" probably referred to the ease with which these cookies of ginger and molasses can be made. The name gingersnap first appeared in print in 1805, in The Buckeye Cookbook, *which warns that "Snaps will not be crisp if made on a rainy day."*

1 Preheat the oven to 350° F.

2 In a mixing bowl combine the ground gingersnaps, 2 tablespoons sugar, and the melted butter. Mix until the mixture holds together. Set aside.

3 In a saucepan bring the heavy cream to the boiling point and remove from the heat.

4 In another mixing bowl whisk together the egg yolks and the remaining 1½ tablespoons sugar. Stir ¼ cup of the hot cream into the egg yolks to warm them. Gradually blend in the remaining hot cream. Add the rum and vanilla.

5 Place the saucepan with the cream and egg yolk mixture over low heat and cook, stirring, for 2 minutes, just until it thickens enough to coat the back of a spoon.

6 Sprinkle the bottom of four 10-ounce custard cups with some of the gingersnap mixture. Place 2 banana halves over the crumbs and pour in the custard sauce. Top with the remaining gingersnap crumbs.

7 Place the custard cups in a deep roasting pan and pour enough hot water into the pan to reach halfway up the outside of the custard cups. Bake for 30 minutes. Serve warm or at room temperature.

MAKES 4 SERVINGS

ABOUT RUM

Rum is a distilled alcoholic beverage made from fermented sugarcane and molasses. The rum business got started in the Americas when Christopher Columbus first planted sugarcane in the West Indies. The Spanish brought their distillation process over and began making rum. African slaves were brought in to grow the sugarcane and produce the molasses. The molasses was shipped to New England, where the rum was made. Rum was the staple drink of the American colonies until the British enacted the Molasses Act and the Sugar Act, unpopular taxes that led to the American Revolution.

There are two types of rum, light and dark. Light rums are preferred by Americans for mixed drinks. Most light rum is produced in Puerto Rico and the Virgin Islands, and is made with a continuous still that produces a whiter product with less impurities. Dark rum is produced in a pot still and preferred in Jamaica, Barbados, and Martinique. Dark rum is better in cooking because of its richer flavor.

Apple Pandowdy

12 slices firm white bread
  Softened butter and
  granulated sugar for the
  bread
5 large baking apples, cored,
  peeled, and cut into ¼-inch
  slices
3 tablespoons molasses
½ cup light brown sugar
½ teaspoon ground cinnamon
¼ teaspoon freshly grated
  nutmeg
2 tablespoons plus 2 teaspoons
  dark rum (optional)
2 tablespoons fresh lemon juice
1 tablespoon vanilla extract
5 tablespoons unsalted butter,
  cut into small pieces
  Heavy cream and sweetened
  whipped cream, or ice cream
  (optional)

1 Preheat the oven to 375° F.
2 Butter six 10-ounce custard cups.
3 Cut the bread into rounds to fit the bottoms of the custard cups. Butter both sides of the bread and sprinkle one side of the bread with sugar. Place a bread round, sugared side down, in each custard cup.
4 Toss the apple slices with the molasses, brown sugar, cinnamon, nutmeg, rum, lemon juice, vanilla, and butter.
5 Divide the apples among the custard cups. Pour any remaining liquid over the slices. Top each custard cup with a second bread round, sugared side up.
6 Place the custard cups in a roasting pan. Place the pan on the center rack of the oven and pour 1 inch of hot water around the custard cups. Bake for 25 minutes, or until the bread is golden brown.
7 Serve with whipped cream or ice cream, if desired.

MAKES 6 SERVINGS

PANDOWDY

A pandowdy is made by layering fresh or dried apples in a baking dish and covering them with a dumpling, biscuit, or flaky rolled crust. The pandowdy is similar to cobblers, slumps, grunts, buckles, brown bettys, and other dishes that have the fruit on the bottom and the crust on the top and are made in a baking dish. All of these terms date back to colonial New England, but some form of this dessert is served in every state.

ABOUT MOLASSES

Molasses is the thick black syrupy residue left from the process of refining white sugar. It was a profitable export from the West Indies to colonial New England, and an important sweetener in those days when white sugar was very heavy and expensive to transport. Famous early American dishes like Boston baked beans and Indian pudding are made with molasses.

In the Middle West and South molasses was made from the tall canes of the sorghum plant and called sorghum molasses. This thick brown syrup is not as bitter as sugarcane molasses, and can be used as a good substitute. Sorghum molasses is made with a horse-drawn grinder that squeezes the juice out of the sorghum canes. The syrup is then boiled like maple syrup for kitchen use. Self-sufficient farmers, such as the Amish, still make sorghum molasses the old-fashioned way.

There are three grades of molasses. First boil, the finest, is used as a table molasses. Second boil is darker and less sweet. Blackstrap molasses is very black, and a tablespoon of it contains one-third of the adult minimum daily requirement for iron.

In baking, molasses is usually used with baking soda. It adds sweetness to ginger bread and molasses cookies. It also acts as a natural preservative and keeps cakes moist for long periods of time.

Baked Apples

¾ cup packed light brown sugar
1 teaspoon ground cinnamon
¼ teaspoon grated nutmeg
⅓ cup raisins
⅓ cup cinnamon red hot candies
6 baking apples, cored but not peeled
½ cup maple syrup

1 Preheat the oven to 350° F. Lightly butter a loaf pan or square baking pan large enough to hold all the apples.

2 In a bowl mix together the sugar, cinnamon, nutmeg, raisins, and red hot candies. Spoon this mixture into the cores of the apples.

3 Place the apples in the prepared pan. Pour the maple syrup over the apples. Bake for 30 to 40 minutes, or until tender.

MAKES 6 SERVINGS

NOTE: Baking time can vary slightly with the variety and size of the apples.

ABOUT MAPLE SYRUP

Maple syrup is the sweet amber-colored nectar that is created when the sap from a maple tree is boiled down. True maple syrup is very expensive—as much as $10 a pint. Many of the so-called maple syrups that we pour over our pancakes are really corn syrups with a limited amount of maple syrup or maple flavoring added. Pure maple is thin, not thick.

The American Indians in New England taught the colonists how to make maple syrup. The colonists upgraded the process by boiling the sap in kettles. In March, when the days are warm and the nights still freeze, the sap begins to run in the maple forest or sugar bush. The trees are tapped with a spike and the sap is collected and boiled in a shallow metal pan over a fire fueled with wood or oil. The old way of hand gathering with buckets has been replaced with a network of plastic tubing that transports the sap from the trees to a sugarhouse.

Maple syrup is graded as light amber, medium amber, and dark amber, with medium being the most popular. The last dregs of making maple syrup are unpalatable and are often sold to tobacco companies for flavoring cigarettes. It takes 30 to 40 gallons of sap to produce 1 gallon of syrup. Maple sugar is syrup that has been crystallized. It was used by colonists to replace expensive West Indian sugar.

Poached Pineapple in Maple Syrup

1 Slice the pineapple crosswise into ½-inch slices.

2 In a heavy saucepan bring the maple syrup to a boil. Add the sliced pineapple and remove the pan from the heat. Allow the pineapple and maple syrup to sit in the saucepan until the syrup is cool, about 20 minutes.

3 Serve the pineapple at room temperature, with a few tablespoons of maple syrup on top (see Note). Serve the yogurt on the side as a topping.

MAKES 6 SERVINGS

NOTE: You may reuse the remaining maple syrup but be sure to keep it under refrigeration until you do so.

1 large pineapple, peeled and cored
2 cups maple syrup
2 cups plain yogurt

WHAT'S COOKING TIPS: STORING PINEAPPLES

1. The best way to store a whole ripe pineapple is in a closed plastic bag in the refrigerator. The pineapple will keep for about 4 days.

2. If you need to hold the pineapple for a longer period of time, cut off the fruit's outer skin, remove the core, and cut the meat into 1-inch chunks. Store the pineapple pieces and their juices in a tightly closed container in the refrigerator. The chunks will hold for about 1 week.

Cakes, Pies, Tarts, Cookies, and Candies

Harry's New York Cheesecake

The three main types of cheesecakes in America are the cottage cheese with graham cracker crust cake popular in the Midwest, the cream cheese cake, also known as New York cheesecake, and Italian cheesecake made with ricotta cheese. Midwest cheesecakes are often topped with sweet cherries in syrup or chocolate. New York and Italian cheesecakes are usually flavored with the zests of oranges and lemons, but Harry's is made with juice.

6 8-ounce packages cream cheese (3 pounds), at room temperature
2¼ cups sugar
6 eggs
3 tablespoons cornstarch
1½ cups heavy cream
¼ cup unsalted butter
1 tablespoon vanilla extract
Juice of 1 lemon

1 Preheat the oven to 350° F. Butter a 12- × 18-inch oblong baking pan or two 10-inch springform pans.

2 In the bowl of an electric mixer combine all of the ingredients. Beat until fluffy and well mixed.

3 Pour the mixture into the prepared pan and set the pan into a larger pan. Add enough water to the outside pan to reach halfway up the outside of the cheesecake pan. Bake for 1 hour. To prevent cracking, do not open the oven during baking.

4 Remove the cheesecake pan to a rack and allow the cake to cool completely before serving.

MAKES ABOUT 20 SERVINGS

ABOUT CREAM CHEESE

Cream cheese is a soft, fresh, cow's milk cheese with a smooth, creamy texture made by mixing cow's milk of a very high cream content with rennet until it coagulates. (Rennet is a digestive enzyme taken from the stomachs of cows or sheep. It causes milk to coagulate and form curds.) The mixture is then drained and pressed into blocks or placed in containers. The method of making cream cheese has changed little in hundreds of years. Modern techniques simply speed up the process and add ingredients to make it firmer and prolong shelf life.

Commercial cream cheese in the familiar 8-ounce blocks was first made by the Lawrence dairy in upstate New York at the turn of the century. The name Philadelphia cream cheese came from another upstate New York dairyman who made such good cream cheese that he named it after the gracious city of Philadelphia. It should be noted that at that time Philadelphia was famous for the high quality of its dairy products. When the New York farmer called his cheese Philadelphia it was a clear case of false advertising.

Hazelnut Cheesecake

3 8-ounce packages cream
   cheese (1½ pounds), at room
   temperature
1 cup sugar
3 eggs
1 cup finely chopped hazelnuts
1 teaspoon vanilla extract
1 cup heavy cream
2 tablespoons rum
   Plain bread crumbs

1 Preheat the oven to 375° F.

2 In the bowl of an electric mixer beat the cream cheese until fluffy. Add the sugar, eggs, hazelnuts, vanilla, heavy cream, and rum; beat until well combined.

3 Butter a 10-inch springform pan and coat the sides and bottom with bread crumbs.

4 Pour the batter into the prepared pan. Set the springform pan in a larger pan and add hot water to the outer pan to reach halfway up the side of the springform. Bake for 1 hour. Turn the oven off and leave the cheesecake inside for 1 hour, without opening the oven door. The cool air may cause the cheesecake to crack.

5 Remove the cake from the oven and allow it to cool completely.

MAKES 10 TO 12 SERVINGS

New York Chocolate Cheesecake

1 Preheat the oven to 350° F. Lightly butter a 9-inch springform pan. Line the bottom with a circle of wax paper and butter the paper.

2 Melt the chocolate in the top of a double boiler set over hot water. Set aside.

3 In a large bowl beat the cream cheese with an electric mixer at high speed until fluffy. Gradually add the sugar, and beat until the mixture is smooth and the sugar is dissolved. Add the eggs, one at a time, mixing well after each addition, and scrape the batter down the sides of the bowl with a rubber spatula. Stir in the vanilla.

4 In a bowl combine one-quarter of the cream cheese mixture with the melted chocolate.

5 Pour the remaining cream cheese mixture into the prepared mold.

6 Pour the chocolate–cream cheese mixture into the center of the mold. With a knife, draw lines through the batter to mix in the chocolate and give the cake a marbleized look.

7 Set the pan into a larger pan. Add enough water to the outer pan to reach halfway up the sides of the springform pan. Bake for 1¼ to 1½ hours, until a wooden toothpick inserted in the center comes out clean. Allow to cool on a rack.

8 When the cake is completely cool, invert it onto a dish, then invert again onto a serving plate. Cover with plastic wrap to prevent the cake from absorbing odors. Set it to chill in the refrigerator for at least 2 hours.

MAKES 8 SERVINGS

6 ounces bittersweet chocolate, grated or broken into pieces

4 8-ounce packages cream cheese (2 pounds), at room temperature

1¾ cups sugar

4 eggs

1 teaspoon vanilla extract

Chocolate Cheesecake

Crust:
1 **cup crushed graham crackers**
¼ **cup unsalted butter, melted**
2 **tablespoons sugar**

Filling:
2 **8-ounce packages cream cheese (1 pound), at room temperature**
¾ **cup sugar**
3 **eggs**
2 **tablespoons milk**
2 **tablespoons heavy cream**
½ **cup sour cream**
2 **teaspoons vanilla extract**
5 **ounces bittersweet chocolate, melted**

Decorations:
1 **cup chocolate sprinkles**
Heavy cream, sweetened and whipped
Chocolate shavings

1 Preheat the oven to 350° F. Butter a 9-inch round cake pan.

2 To make the crust, in a bowl blend together the ingredients and press the mixture into the bottom of the cake pan. Refrigerate for 1 hour.

3 To make the filling, in a bowl cream together the cream cheese and sugar. Add the eggs, one at a time, blending well after each addition. Blend in the milk, heavy cream, and sour cream. Fold in the vanilla and melted chocolate.

4 Pour the filling into the prepared pan and bake for 45 minutes. Turn off the heat and let the cheesecake sit in the oven for 1 hour. Do not open the oven door. The cool air may cause the cheesecake to crack.

5 Let the cake cool completely. Invert the cake to unmold it. Press the chocolate sprinkles into the sides and decorate the top with swirls of whipped cream and chocolate shavings.

MAKES 10 SERVINGS

ABOUT GRAHAM CRACKERS

Graham crackers are sweet whole-wheat crackers made from graham flour. Graham flour is whole-grain wheat flour with the husk or bran and center or germ left in. The Reverend Sylvester Graham (1794–1851) gave his name to the flour because of his rigid views on temperance and the virtue of eating whole grain and unadulterated foods. The Reverend Graham believed that a healthy diet would produce better citizens of superior moral fiber.

ABOUT CHOCOLATE HISTORY

Chocolate has its historical roots in South America, where the Aztecs used the bean to make a drink. Columbus noted the drink on his fourth voyage, but it was not brought back to Europe until Cortez took some home to Spain with him in 1526. The Spanish kept chocolate a secret to such a degree that when Dutch and English pirates saw chocolate on board Spanish ships, they dumped it overboard, thinking that the beans were sheep droppings. The secret was out by 1657, when the first chocolate house opened in London, but the heavy import taxes on cocoa kept it a luxury until the 1830s.

WHAT'S COOKING TIPS: SHAVINGS AND GRATINGS

1. To make chocolate shavings or curls, take a vegetable peeler, warm the blade for a moment over a burner, and draw it over the smooth surface of a bar of chocolate.

2. Make a fabulous Italian dessert called tartufo by rolling chocolate ice cream in chocolate shavings and top with whipped cream. Cover with grated chocolate.

3. Make grated chocolate by chilling a bar of chocolate in a plastic bag in the refrigerator for 30 minutes. Put the chocolate into a hand grater and grate it just like you would a piece of cheese.

Fudge Cake with Vanilla Buttercream Icing

Fudge Cake:
- 1 cup all-purpose flour
- 1 cup unsweetened cocoa powder
- 1 tablespoon plus 1 teaspoon baking powder
- ½ teaspoon salt
- ½ cup unsalted butter, at room temperature
- 2 cups sugar
- 4 eggs, separated, at room temperature
- 2 cups milk
- 2 tablespoons vanilla extract

Vanilla Buttercream Icing:
- 6 tablespoons unsalted butter, at room temperature
- 2 teaspoons vanilla extract
- ⅛ teaspoon salt
- 1 pound confectioners' sugar
- ¼ cup milk

WHAT'S COOKING TIP: BAKING LAYERS

If you are baking several layers of a cake separately in the oven, do not place the pans directly over each other—stagger them to allow better heat circulation, but do not get too close to the oven sides, where the heat tends to be uneven. A distance of at least 2 inches between pans and away from the walls is recommended.

1 Preheat the oven to 350° F. Lightly grease and flour three 8-inch round cake pans.

2 To make the cake, in a bowl sift together the dry ingredients.

3 In the bowl of an electric mixer cream the butter with the sugar until light and fluffy, about 5 minutes. One at a time, add the egg yolks, beating for 1 minute after each yolk is added.

4 One cup at a time, add the dry ingredients to the mixer, alternating with the milk. Beat in the vanilla until the batter is smooth.

5 In another bowl beat the egg whites until they form stiff but not dry peaks. They should be the same consistency as shaving cream. Fold the beaten egg whites into the batter.

6 Divide the batter among the prepared cake pans. Bake for 35 to 45 minutes, or until a wooden toothpick inserted in the center of each cake comes out clean. Cool the cakes on a wire rack.

7 To make the icing, in the bowl of an electric mixer cream together the butter, vanilla, and salt until smooth. Gradually beat in the sugar and milk. Continue beating on medium speed until the icing becomes fluffy and smooth. If necessary, add more milk to thin the icing.

8 When the cakes are cool, invert the pans and remove the cake layers. Spread the vanilla buttercream icing between the layers and over the top and sides of the cake.

MAKES 12 SERVINGS

Triple Chocolate Mocha Layer Cake

1 Preheat the oven to 350° F. Butter three 9-inch round layer cake pans. Line the bottom of each with a round of buttered wax paper.

2 To make the cake, sift the flour, cocoa, baking powder, baking soda, and salt onto a sheet of wax paper.

3 In a bowl of an electric mixer beat together the sugar, shortening, and eggs until the mixture is light and fluffy, about 3 minutes.

4 With the mixer running at low speed, add the dry ingredients alternately with the water, beginning and ending with the flour, and scraping the bowl frequently. Stir in the vanilla.

5 Divide the batter among the prepared pans. Bake for 30 to 35 minutes, or until the center of the cake springs back when lightly pressed.

6 Cool the layers in the pans on wire racks for 10 minutes. Loosen the cakes around the edges with a knife, and carefully turn the layers out onto wire racks to cool completely.

7 To make the frosting, in the bowl of an electric mixer beat the butter at medium speed until fluffy. Beat in the cocoa on low speed. Add the confectioners' sugar, a cup at a time, alternately with the coffee, beating until smooth and of a spreadable consistency. If needed, add more sugar gradually. Stir in the vanilla and mix well.

8 Fill and frost the cake and garnish with pecan halves, if desired.

MAKES 12 SERVINGS

Cake:
- 3 cups sifted cake flour
- 2/3 cup unsweetened cocoa powder
- 1/2 teaspoon baking powder
- 2 teaspoons baking soda
- 1/2 teaspoon salt
- 2 cups sugar
- 1 cup vegetable shortening
- 4 large eggs
- 2 cups water
- 2 teaspoons vanilla extract

Mocha Frosting:
- 3/4 cup softened unsalted butter
- 2 tablespoons unsweetened cocoa powder
- 6–7 cups confectioners' sugar (about 1 3/4 pounds)
- 1/2 cup cold strong coffee
- 1 teaspoon vanilla extract

- Pecan halves as garnish (optional)

WHAT'S COOKING TIP: SIFTING FLOUR

Most baking recipes call for sifting flour before it is measured. Sifted flour will give you airier and lighter baked goods. It is usually a good idea to sift your flour and all the other dry ingredients together at the same time. The sifting will give a more even distribution of the ingredients.

Flourless Chocolate Cake

10 ounces semisweet chocolate
7 tablespoons unsalted butter
7 eggs, separated
⅓ cup granulated sugar
Confectioners' sugar

1 Preheat the oven to 275° F. Butter and flour a 10-inch springform pan or line the bottom of a deep cake pan with parchment paper.

2 In the top of a double boiler over simmering water melt the chocolate and butter until smooth. Remove from the heat.

3 In a mixing bowl beat the egg whites until slightly stiff. Add the granulated sugar and beat for 30 seconds, until stiff.

4 Whisk the egg yolks into the slightly cooled chocolate mixture.

5 Gently fold the chocolate mixture into the beaten egg whites, mixing only until no white streaks remain.

6 Pour the cake batter into the pan and bake for 30 to 40 minutes.

7 If you are using a springform pan, gently release the sides of the pan and let the cake cool on a wire rack. If not, carefully place a sheet of parchment paper on a baking sheet and place the baking sheet, parchment paper facing down, over the cake. Invert the pan to release the cake and set the cake pan aside. Remove the parchment paper used to line the bottom of the pan if it has held fast to the bottom of the cake. Set a wire rack over the cake and invert again so that the top side is up. Allow to cool for 1 hour.

8 Dust lightly with confectioners' sugar.

MAKES 8 SERVINGS

WHAT'S COOKING TIPS: STORING CHOCOLATE

1. The ideal temperature for storing chocolate and cocoa powder is between 55° and 60° F. If chocolate is stored in a place where the temperature is about 80 degrees, the surface will develop a white powder called a "bloom." It is harmless and the chocolate is still safe to eat or use in baking.

2. Cocoa powder is sensitive to humidity. If there is more than 50 percent relative humidity the powder can lose some of its rich color and texture.

3. Both chocolate and cocoa powder are very sensitive to odors, and absorb them quickly. The ideal way to store chocolate and cocoa powder is to place them in airtight containers, avoid humidity, and keep them in a temperature range of 55° to 60° F. A food storage cabinet away from the stove is a good spot.

4. Keeping chocolate in the refrigerator is not recommended, but if you must, double wrap it first. Keep in mind that cold makes the chocolate harder and diminishes its sweet and delicate taste. The lower the temperature, the more difficult it is to get true chocolate taste. So be sure to remove chocolate from the refrigerator about 20 minutes before you plan to use it, and let it come to room temperature.

Carrot Cake with Cream Cheese Icing

Carrot Cake:
- 2 cups sugar
- 1½ cups vegetable oil
- 4 eggs, lightly beaten
- 2 cups all-purpose flour
- 1 teaspoon salt
- 2 teaspoons baking soda
- 2 teaspoons ground cinnamon
- ½ teaspoon grated nutmeg
- ½ teaspoon ground allspice
- 3 cups finely shredded carrots (6–8 carrots)
- ½ cup chopped walnuts

Cream Cheese Icing:
- ½ cup unsalted butter, at room temperature
- 1 8-ounce package cream cheese, at room temperature
- 2 cups confectioners' sugar
- 2 teaspoons vanilla extract

1 Preheat the oven to 325° F. Butter a 13- × 9- × 2-inch baking pan.

2 In an electric mixer or by hand thoroughly mix together the sugar, oil, and eggs.

3 Sift together the flour, salt, baking soda, and spices. Gradually add the flour mixture to the egg mixture, blending well before adding more.

4 Fold in the carrots and walnuts. Pour the batter into the prepared pan and bake for 1 hour to 1 hour and 10 minutes, or until a wooden toothpick inserted into the center comes out clean. Remove to a rack to cool to room temperature.

5 To make the icing, in a bowl cream the butter until light and fluffy. Mash the cream cheese with a fork and work it into the butter. Add the confectioners' sugar and vanilla and beat vigorously, until blended.

6 When the cake is cool, spread with the cream cheese icing.

MAKES 12 SERVINGS

Glazed Applesauce Cake

1 Preheat the oven to 350° F. Butter and flour a 9-inch springform pan.

2 To make the cake, in a mixing bowl cream the butter and gradually add the sugar. Beat until light and fluffy. Beat in the egg and blend in the applesauce.

3 In another bowl sift together the dry ingredients. Fold the mixture into the cake batter. Add the pecans and diced apple.

4 Pour the mixture into the prepared pan and arrange the apple slices decoratively on top. Bake for 1¼ hours. Remove to a rack and allow to cool. Release the sides of the pan.

5 To prepare the glaze, in a small saucepan combine the apricot jam, honey, and water over low heat. Stir until melted and smooth.

6 Brush the top of the cooled cake with the glaze.

MAKES 8 SERVINGS

Cake:
- ½ cup unsalted butter
- 1¼ cups sugar
- 1 egg
- 2 cups sweetened or unsweetened applesauce
- 2¼ cups all-purpose flour
- 1 teaspoon ground cinnamon
- ½ teaspoon grated nutmeg
- ⅛ teaspoon ground cloves
- ¼ teaspoon salt
- 2 teaspoons baking soda
- ½ cup pecan halves
- 1 apple, peeled, cored, and finely diced
- 1 apple, thinly sliced

Glaze:
- 1 cup apricot jam
- ¼ cup honey
- 1 tablespoon water

ABOUT CLOVES

The spice we know as clove is the unopened flower bud of the clove tree, *Eugenia carophyllata*. Cloves are native to the tiny island of Amboina, one of the true spice islands of the Dutch West Indies, near Australia. Fortunes and wars have been won and lost over control of the trading in cloves, along with nutmeg, pepper, and cinnamon. Many of the cloves we use today are grown from transplanted trees in Zanzibar and the West Indies.

In cooking, the truest clove flavor comes from using the whole clove bud. It is common to see a baked ham studded with cloves. An onion stuck with 2 or 3 cloves is a classic ingredient in French soups and stews. It is best to remove any whole clove buds when serving food, but ground clove blends right in. Clove and clove oil are used as a toothache pain-killer and in making perfume.

Scripture Cake

Cake:
   1 cup unsalted butter
   2 cups sugar
   6 eggs
   6 tablespoons honey
3½ cups all-purpose flour
   4 teaspoons baking powder
   1 teaspoon ground cinnamon
   1 teaspoon ground allspice
   ½ teaspoon freshly grated
      nutmeg
   ½ teaspoon salt
      Pinch of ground cloves
   ¾ cup milk
   1 cup raisins
   1 cup pitted and chopped
      dates
   ½ cup sliced toasted almonds

Glaze:
   1 cup sugar
   ¼ cup milk
   1 tablespoon light corn syrup
   ¼ cup honey

1 Preheat the oven to 325° F. Butter and flour a 10-inch tubed pan.

2 To make the cake, in a large bowl cream together the butter and sugar until light and thoroughly mixed. Add the eggs, one at a time, beating well after adding each egg. Mix in the honey.

3 In another bowl sift together all of the dry ingredients. Add one-third of the dry ingredients, then half of the milk and continue alternating, mixing each one in completely, but without overbeating. Mix in the raisins, dates, and almonds.

4 Pour the batter into the prepared pan and tap to settle the batter. Bake for 55 to 60 minutes, or until a wooden toothpick inserted in the center comes out clean. Cool the cake on a rack.

5 To make the glaze, in a small saucepan mix together all of the ingredients. Bring just to a boil, making sure the sugar is melted.

6 Pour the glaze immediately over the cooled cake.

MAKES 12 SERVINGS

ABOUT ALLSPICE

Allspice is not a combination of spices ground together. It is a round berry, about the size of a peppercorn, that comes from the pimiento tree that grows in Jamaica. Allspice has the fragrance and overtones of clove and cinnamon but it also has a dark richness of its own.

Besides being used in pies and cakes, allspice is used as the primary flavoring of the Jamaican smoked meat barbecue that is called jerked pork. The meat is marinated in ground allspice, then smoked over a fire made with the wood and leaves of the allspice tree.

Chocolate Silk Pie

1 To prepare the crust, put the chocolate wafers in a food processor or blender and process until finely crushed. Mix the crumbs with the melted butter. Evenly press the mixture into the bottom and sides of an 8-inch pie pan.

2 To prepare the filling, in the top of a double boiler set over simmering water, melt the chocolate. Set aside to cool slightly.

3 In a large bowl beat the butter and sugar together with an electric mixer at high speed until the mixture is light and fluffy, about 10 minutes.

4 Blend in the cooled chocolate and the vanilla. One at a time, add the eggs, beating thoroughly after each addition.

5 Pour the filling into the piecrust and refrigerate for at least 3 hours.

6 Serve with sweetened whipped cream.

MAKES 8 SERVINGS

Crust:
1 8½-ounce box chocolate wafers
6 tablespoons melted unsalted butter

Filling:
7 ounces bittersweet chocolate, grated or finely chopped
1 cup unsalted butter
1½ cups sugar
2 teaspoons vanilla extract
4 eggs

Heavy cream, sweetened and whipped

Old-Fashioned Strawberry Shortcakes

Traditionally, Old-fashioned Strawberry Shortcake was served with heavy unwhipped cream simply poured over it. Nowadays, it's usually topped with whipped cream.

Shortcakes:
- 4 cups all-purpose flour
- ¼ cup plus 2 tablespoons sugar
- 1 tablespoon plus 2 teaspoons baking powder
- 1 teaspoon salt
- ¾ cup unsalted butter, chilled and cut into bits
- 1½ cups heavy cream
- 2 tablespoons unsalted butter, melted and cooled

Topping:
- 2 pints fresh ripe strawberries, washed and stemmed
- 2 tablespoons sugar, or to taste
  Heavy cream, sweetened and whipped

1 Preheat the oven to 425° F. Lightly butter a large baking sheet.

2 To make the shortcakes, in a large bowl mix together the dry ingredients. Add the butter pieces, and with a pastry blender or fingertips, rub the butter into the dry ingredients until the mixture resembles coarse meal.

3 Add the cream and mix thoroughly until a soft dough forms.

4 Gather the dough into a compact disk and place on a lightly floured board or work surface. Knead the dough for about 1 minute, folding it end to end and pressing down and pushing forward several times with the heel of your hand.

5 Roll out the dough into a ½-inch-thick circle. With a 3-inch cookie cutter, cut out 9 rounds. With a 2½-inch cookie cutter, cut the remaining dough into 9 rounds. (If there isn't enough dough, gather the scraps, knead briefly, and roll out again.) Arrange the 3-inch rounds on the prepared baking sheet. Brush each with melted butter and top with a 2½-inch round.

6 Bake in the center of the oven for 15 minutes, until firm to the touch and golden brown. Remove to a rack to cool.

7 To make the topping, coarsely chop half the strawberries, reserving the most attractive ones for the top.

8 Pull the smaller tops away from the bottoms of the shortcakes. Spread a layer of chopped strawberries on the bottom halves, sprinkle each with sugar, and gently cover with the top halves. Garnish with whipped cream and whole strawberries.

MAKES 8 SERVINGS

Pecan Pie

Shell:
- 1 cup all-purpose flour, sifted twice
- ½ teaspoon salt
- ⅓ cup vegetable shortening
- 3 tablespoons ice water

Filling:
- 6 eggs
- ¾ cup firmly packed dark brown sugar
- ¾ cup white granulated sugar
- 1½ cups dark corn syrup
- 1½ tablespoons all-purpose flour
- ¼ cup unsalted butter, melted
- 1 tablespoon vanilla extract
- 1½ cups pecan pieces (6 ounces)

Heavy cream, sweetened and whipped, or vanilla ice cream

1 To prepare the shell, in a large bowl sift together the flour and salt. Cut in the vegetable shortening until the mixture resembles coarse meal. Sprinkle on the ice water and toss with 2 forks until the dough pulls together into a ball. Do not handle.

2 Shape the dough into a flat disk. Wrap in plastic wrap and refrigerate for at least 1 hour.

3 Preheat the oven to 350° F.

4 On a well-floured surface, roll out the dough to a thickness of ⅛ inch. Press the dough into a 10-inch pie pan and flute the edges. Set the pie pan on a baking sheet.

5 To prepare the filling, in a bowl, beat the eggs and stir in the sugars, corn syrup, flour, butter, and vanilla. Mix until well blended. Add the pecans and mix again.

6 Pour the filling into the prepared shell (the pecans will rise to the top) and bake for 40 minutes, or until the back of a spoon pressed in the center of the filling feels solid and no liquid comes to the surface. Remove to a rack to cool.

7 Serve with sweetened whipped cream or vanilla ice cream.

MAKES 8 SERVINGS

ABOUT VEGETABLE SHORTENING

Vegetable shortening is a thickened vegetable oil substitution for animal shortenings, lard, and butter. Vegetable shortening is lower in saturated fat than butter or lard. The shortening was developed by the Procter & Gamble Company in 1911 and is known by the marketing name Crisco. Vegetable oil, usually soybean oil, is made thick and white by the process known as hydrogenation.

The other advantages of vegetable shortening is that it is almost completely tasteless and odorless when used in cooking, and it can be kept for long periods of time.

Lemon Tart

Tart Shell:
1⅓ cups sifted all-purpose flour
¼ teaspoon salt
½ cup vegetable shortening
¼ cup cold water

Filling:
5 eggs
1 cup superfine sugar
7 tablespoons unsalted butter, clarified (see sidebar), cooled
½ cup fresh lemon juice
Zest of 1 orange, finely grated

Confectioners' sugar
(optional)

1 Preheat the oven to 400° F.

2 To make the shell, in a mixing bowl combine the flour and salt. Add the shortening. Combine with a pastry blender or 2 knives, or rub between your fingers until the mixture is fairly coarse.

3 Mixing with a fork, sprinkle with 1 tablespoon water at a time. Gather the dough and knead for 30 seconds until smooth.

4 On a lightly floured surface, press the dough into a flat circle. Roll the dough to a circle about 1½ inches larger than the tart or pie pan. Gently transfer the dough to the pan.

5 For a tart pan, trim the excess dough. For a pie pan, leave ½ inch of dough beyond the edge of the pan. Fold the edge back under to make a double thickness of the dough around the rim and flute the edge with your fingers or a fork.

6 Bake for 10 to 15 minutes, or until lightly golden. Remove from heat, still on a baking sheet. Reduce oven to 325° F.

7 To make the filling, with a whisk beat together in a bowl the eggs and sugar. Gradually add the clarified butter and blend well. Stir in the lemon juice and orange zest.

8 Place the baking sheet with the tart pan on top into the oven. Pour the egg and lemon mixture into the shell. Bake for 25 minutes, or until the liquid has set. (The batter-filled shell spills easily; putting it in the oven first saves a tricky move.)

9 Remove to a rack to cool to room temperature. Dust lightly with confectioners' sugar before serving.

MAKES 8 SERVINGS

THE DIFFERENCE BETWEEN A PIE AND A TART

The difference between a pie and a tart is that a pie is generally made with a crust on the top as well as on the bottom, while a tart has only a bottom crust. In France, pies are always made with the crust on the bottom and always called tarts. But in England, a pie is anything baked in a baking dish with a crust on top. They don't always use a crust on the bottom. Shepherd's pie is crusted with mashed potatoes. A pork pie is meat and gravy wrapped in pastry dough and baked. It is called a turnover in America. Pies in fourteenth-century England were called coffins because they were baked in long rectangular tins rather than round pie pans.

An English tart has a pastry crust on the bottom with a fruit filling on top. Anything baked in a pie pan is called a pie in America; pumpkin and pecan pies, among others, do not have top crusts but they are still called pies. The term tart is used to describe a miniature pie.

WHAT'S COOKING TIP: HOW TO MAKE CLARIFIED BUTTER

Clarified butter is regular butter from which some solids have been removed. It can be heated to a much higher temperature than whole butter, without burning. It also stores better.

1. To make clarified butter, cut regular unsalted butter into small pieces. Put them into a heatproof measuring cup. Put the cup into an oven that's set to its lowest temperature.

2. When the butter is melted, there will be three distinct layers. Skim off and discard the top foamy layer. Carefully pour off the middle layer, which is the clarified butter. Leave the bottom layer behind and discard.

Apple Tarts with Almonds

Dough:
¾ cup all-purpose flour
7 tablespoons unsalted butter,
   at room temperature
2 tablespoons ice water

Filling:
4 medium Golden Delicious
   apples, peeled, cored, and
   thinly sliced
1 cup sliced almonds
3 tablespoons granulated sugar

¼ cup confectioners' sugar

1 Preheat the oven to 450° F. Line 2 baking sheets with parchment paper.

2 To make the dough, in a large mixing bowl pinch together the flour and 4 tablespoons butter with your fingers. After a few moments, add the ice water and shape the dough into a disk. Wrap in plastic and refrigerate for at least 30 minutes.

3 Divide the dough into 4 pieces. Roll out each piece into a 5-inch circle. Place the circles on the prepared sheets.

4 Arrange the apple slices in an overlapping circular pattern on each disk of dough. Melt the remaining 3 tablespoons butter and brush onto the apples. Sprinkle with the almonds and the granulated sugar and bake for 12 to 15 minutes. Allow to cool.

5 Just before serving, sprinkle the tarts with confectioners' sugar.

MAKES 4 TARTS

ABOUT ALMONDS

Almonds come from the kernel of a fruit that is similar to an apricot. They are sold with the skins on, blanched or toasted, or untoasted with the skins off, whole, sliced, or slivered. The almond is low in fat compared to other nuts, but a cup of almonds still contains 850 calories.

Almonds keep best in their shells, stored in a tightly closed glass jar in the refrigerator or freezer. Limit their contact with light, heat, moisture, and air. As a general rule, 1 pound unshelled nuts will yield ½ pound shelled nuts.

Scottish Shortbread

1 Preheat the oven to 325° F.

2 In a mixing bowl combine the butter and the sugar. Knead in the flour and add the water, 1 tablespoon at a time, to make a smooth dough.

3 Divide the dough in half. Roll out each half into an 8-inch disk, about ½ inch thick. (You can press down the bottom edge of an 8-inch pot lid to give you a clean cut.) Use the rim of a glass to cut a 2- to 3-inch circle in the center of the dough. Cut the 8-inch circle into 8 equal wedges. Repeat the procedure with the remaining piece of dough.

4 Transfer the wedges and the circles to a baking sheet. Prick the shortbread all over with the tines of a fork. Bake for 25 minutes.

5 When the shortbread is baked, reassemble it into the original shape with the circular disk in the center.

1 cup unsalted butter
½ cup sugar
3 cups all-purpose flour
3 tablespoons cold water

MAKES 2 SHORTBREADS OR 16 WEDGES AND 2 CIRCLES

ABOUT SHORTCAKE, SHORTBREAD, AND SHORTNIN' BREAD

To make something "short" was to mix lard or butter into flour to make it brittle, or flaky, rather than smooth. Shortcake, most often referred to in combination with strawberries, is a basic American biscuit dough that has been "shortened" with butter and sweetened with sugar. Often it is also made with double sifted ingredients to make it lighter than ordinary biscuits.

Shortbread is a thick Scottish cookie that is made with equal amounts of butter and flour.

Southern shortnin' bread is a derivative of the Scottish shortbread and is a cross between a cake and a cookie. Shortbread and shortnin' bread are both much heavier and sweeter than shortcake. Scots and Scotch-Irish were the dominant colonist population in the South before the Civil War and they probably brought their shortbread with them to America.

Apple Torte

2 large apples
2 tablespoons melted butter
⅔ cup sugar
1 sheet (½ package) frozen
   puff pastry, thawed, or 1
   unbaked piecrust
   Vanilla ice cream (optional)

1 Preheat the oven to 425° F.

2 Peel, core, and cut each apple into 10 wedges.

3 Coat the bottom of an 8-inch ovenproof skillet with 1 tablespoon melted butter. Sprinkle on ⅓ cup sugar. Arrange the apple wedges like the spokes of a wheel over the bottom of the pan. Top with the remaining 1 tablespoon butter and ⅓ cup sugar.

4 Cover the skillet with foil and bake for 30 minutes.

5 Remove the foil and place the pan over medium heat. Cook for 6 to 8 minutes, shaking the pan often, until the sugar is syrupy and light golden.

6 Cut the pastry into a disk just large enough to fit inside the rim of the skillet. Cover the apples with the pastry. Return the skillet to the oven and bake for 12 minutes, or until the pastry is golden.

7 Invert the torte onto a plate. Serve apple side up with vanilla ice cream on top.

MAKES 4 TO 6 SERVINGS

APPLES IN HISTORY

The apple is a member of the rose family, and is often used as the symbol of all fruits. Many times in the past when a new fruit was discovered, it was called an apple until a more appropriate name was found. The list of foods that were once called apples includes the avocado, cashew, date, eggplant, lemon, melon, orange, peach, pineapple, and potato.

Contrary to popular belief, there is no mention of the apple in the Genesis chapter of the Bible. The story of Adam and Eve says only that Eve tempted Adam to eat the fruit of the tree of knowledge. It was an artist who needed a more specific image to paint and came up with the apple.

A falling apple inspired Newton to come up with his theory of universal gravitation in 1666. The apple tree was in his own orchard at Woolsthorpe, England. The remains of this tree are still preserved.

John Chapman, better known as Johnny Appleseed, did not, as legend has it, wander the countryside sprinkling apple seeds randomly in the hopes of growing more apples. He was a sophisticated seedsman and established a series of apple seedling nurseries extending from Pennsylvania to Ohio. His favorite type of apple was the Rambo.

Many of the apples in the United States come from the Pacific Northwest, which saw its first apple seeds in 1824, when a British sea captain made a gift of them to a young girl.

Ricciarelli (Siena) Cookies

2¼ cups blanched almonds
   (about 12 ounces)
1¾ cups sugar
 2 egg whites
1½ teaspoons vanilla extract
3–4 tablespoons confectioners'
   sugar

WHAT'S COOKING TIPS: BAKING COOKIES

The name cookie is probably derived from the Dutch *koejke*. Its origins go back to the ancient Persians. Whether you call them *biscotti*, biscuits, *keks,* or *galletas* there are a few basic tips that can make your cookie making easier.

1. Accurate measuring is the key to success in all baking. Don't depend on regular table utensils, such as tablespoons. Use spoons and cups made for measuring.

2. Cookies bake quickly, so it is important to regulate the baking carefully. Check the accuracy of your oven's thermostat with an oven thermometer, and adjust the thermostat to get the exact temperature called for.

3. Cool your baking sheet before you put the dough on it. A warm sheet will melt the butter and cause the cookies to spread too much.

1 Preheat the oven to 350° F. Line 2 baking sheets with parchment paper.

2 Put the almonds and sugar into a food processor and blend until you have the consistency of flour. Pass through a medium-mesh strainer. Return the larger chunks of the mixture to the food processor and process again until the mixture is uniform.

3 Transfer to a mixing bowl. Add the egg whites and vanilla and beat until the mixture becomes a smooth paste. Gather into a flat disk.

4 Sprinkle a work surface with confectioners' sugar. Roll out the dough into a continuous rope about 1½ inches in diameter. Cut the rope into ¾-inch lengths. Coat the palm of your hand with confectioners' sugar and pat the pieces into even flat disks.

5 Place the cookies about 1 inch apart on the prepared baking sheets. Bake for 8 to 10 minutes, or until just lightly colored. Let cool before removing from the parchment paper.

MAKES 2½ DOZEN COOKIES

Kirsch Cherry-Walnut Drops with Kirsch Glaze

1 In a small bowl soak the cherries in the kirsch for 1 hour. Do not drain.

2 Preheat the oven to 375° F.

3 In the bowl of an electric mixer cream the butter with the sugar until light and fluffy, 3 to 5 minutes. Add the eggs, one at a time, and the vanilla; blend well.

4 In another bowl sift together the flour, baking powder, and the salt. Stir into the butter mixture and mix well. Fold in the soaked cherries, soaking liquid, and nuts.

5 Drop the cookies by level tablespoonfuls about 2 inches apart onto ungreased baking sheets. Bake for 8 to 10 minutes, until the edges are light brown and the tops spring back when lightly touched with a finger. Transfer to a wire rack to cool.

6 To make the glaze, in a small bowl whisk together all the ingredients until smooth.

7 Dip the tops of the warm cookies into the glaze. Let the cookies cool completely on the rack.

MAKES 3½ TO 4 DOZEN COOKIES

⅓ cup chopped candied cherries
3 tablespoons kirsch
¼ cup unsalted butter, softened
1 cup sugar
2 eggs, at room temperature
½ teaspoon vanilla extract
1½ cups all-purpose flour
½ teaspoon baking powder
¼ teaspoon salt
⅓ cup chopped walnuts

Glaze:
¾ cup sifted confectioners' sugar
2 tablespoons kirsch
1 tablespoon water

ABOUT KIRSCH OR KIRSCHWASSER

Kirschwasser is German for "cherry water." It is a clear fruit brandy that is a member of the eaux de vie (water of life) family. Kirschwasser is an important flavor for Swiss fondue and is used extensively in cake, candy, and cookie making.

Praline Cookies

2 tablespoons all-purpose flour
7 ounces hazelnuts, ground
1 cup sugar
6 egg whites

1 Preheat the oven to 350° F. Generously butter 2 baking sheets.

2 In a mixing bowl blend together all of the ingredients.

3 Spoon tablespoonfuls of the batter onto the prepared baking sheet and smooth into thin rounds with the back of a spoon.

4 Bake for 5 minutes. Let the cookies cool for 5 minutes on the baking sheet. Return the sheet to the oven and bake for 5 to 7 minutes more, until golden brown and set.

5 Remove the baking sheet from the oven. Place the still-warm cookies over a rolling pin to give them a curved shape. If the cookies harden while molding, return them to the oven for a minute, until they are flexible again. As soon as they are cool in the curved shape, they are ready to serve.

MAKES 2 DOZEN COOKIES

ALL ABOUT FLOUR

Flour is the powder that comes from grinding grain. It is used to make bread, pastry, pasta, rolls, and cakes. It is also used as a thickener for sauces and in various other cooking methods.

Flour has been used since the dawn of agriculture. It was the logical first step as soon as somebody figured out that they could get a different result from grain if they ground it with a rock. From ancient times to the middle of the nineteenth century, farmers took their grain to the miller, where it was ground on water-, wind-, or ox-driven stone rollers. The windmills of Holland and Don Quixote's in Spain were used for grinding grain into flour.

Most Americans use bleached all-purpose flour. It is a blend of soft and hard wheat flour that is good for both bread and cake. The wheat has been ground, the brain and the germ removed, the flour bleached and fortified with vitamins.

Whole-wheat flour, or graham flour, named after the eighteenth-century New England temperance leader Sylvester Graham, is wheat that has been ground with the bran and the germ left in. True whole-wheat flour should be refrigerated because wheat germ contains oil that will spoil. Bread flour, also known as hard-wheat flour, is preferred for bread because of its high gluten content, which helps bread to rise.

Dried pasta is made with hard wheat, also known as durum wheat.

Cake flour, or soft-wheat flour, is low in gluten and preferred for the delicate soft doughs used in baking cakes and pastries. Rye flour is ground from rye grain, barley flour from barley grain, and corn flour from corn kernels. All of these lack significant amounts of gluten, so they are usually blended with wheat flour for bread or used in the making of batter bread leavened with baking powder. *Semolina* is the Italian word for wheat.

The best flour is made in grinders that produce the least amount of heat. Heat kills the germ of the grain and destroys the aromatic flavor of the flour. All grinding processes produce heat, but the local small-scale mills produce the best flour.

Triple Chocolate Chunk Nut Cookies

6 ounces semisweet chocolate
2 ounces bittersweet chocolate
6 tablespoons unsalted butter
2 eggs
1 tablespoon powdered instant espresso coffee
2 teaspoons vanilla extract
¾ cup sugar
⅓ cup al!-purpose flour
1 teaspoon baking powder
¼ teaspoon salt
1 cup walnut pieces
1 cup pecan pieces
6 ounces milk chocolate, cut into small bits

1 Preheat the oven to 325° F. Lightly butter a baking sheet and line it with wax or parchment paper.

2 In the top of a double boiler combine the semisweet chocolate, bittersweet chocolate, and butter over simmering water. Melt, stirring from time to time, until smooth. Set aside to cool.

3 In a bowl, with an electric mixer mix the eggs, espresso, and vanilla on low speed. At high speed, gradually add the sugar and beat until the mixture is thick and light.

4 In another bowl mix the flour, baking powder, and salt together. Set aside.

5 Add the melted chocolate mixture to the egg mixture. Beat on low speed until well blended. Gradually add the flour mixture and beat on low speed. Stir in the nuts and milk chocolate bits and mix well.

6 Drop the cookies by heaping tablespoonfuls onto the prepared baking sheet, 2 inches apart. Bake for 15 to 20 minutes.

MAKES ABOUT 15 COOKIES

Oatmeal-Raisin Cookies

1 Preheat the oven to 375° F. Lightly butter a baking sheet.

2 In a bowl with an electric mixer cream the butter and white sugar at high speed until light and fluffy, 3 to 5 minutes. Gradually add the brown sugar. One at a time, add the eggs, and the vanilla; blend well.

3 In a bowl sift together the flour, cinnamon, baking soda, and salt. A small amount at a time, add to the butter mixture, mixing well after each addition. Fold in the oats and raisins.

4 Drop the cookies by heaping teaspoonfuls onto the baking sheet, about 2 inches apart. Bake for 10 to 12 minutes.

MAKES ABOUT 5 DOZEN COOKIES

½ cup unsalted butter, at room temperature
¾ cup white granulated sugar
¾ cup brown sugar
2 eggs
1 teaspoon vanilla extract
1¾ cups all-purpose flour
1 teaspoon ground cinnamon
1 teaspoon baking soda
½ teaspoon salt
2 cups rolled oats (not the "quick-cooking" type)
1 cup raisins

Peanut Butter Peanut Cookies

1 cup unsalted butter, at room
temperature

¾ cup white granulated sugar

¾ cup firmly packed brown
sugar

2 eggs

2¼ cups all-purpose flour

½ teaspoon salt

1 teaspoon baking soda

1½ cups peanut butter

1 teaspoon vanilla extract

1 cup chopped unsalted
peanuts

1 Preheat the oven to 375° F. Lightly butter a
large baking sheet.

2 In a large bowl, with an electric mixer beat
together the butter and sugars at high speed
until the mixture is light and fluffy.

3 One at a time, add the eggs, mixing well after
each addition.

4 In another bowl sift together the flour, salt,
and baking soda. Gradually add to the butter
mixture, mixing well after each addition.

5 Mix in the peanut butter, vanilla, and peanuts. Drop the cookies by teaspoonfuls onto
the prepared baking sheet, about 2 inches
apart. Bake for 10 to 12 minutes.

MAKES ABOUT 6¼ DOZEN COOKIES

Great American Brownies

The brownie first received national attention when it was featured in an 1897 Sears catalogue. Recent variations made with white chocolate chunks rather than dark chocolate are called blondies.

1 Preheat the oven to 325° F. Lightly butter a 9-inch square baking pan.

2 In the top of a double boiler set over simmering water melt the chocolate and butter. Set aside to cool slightly.

3 With an electric mixer beat the eggs at high speed and gradually add the sugar. Beat until the mixture is pale yellow and the sugar is dissolved, about 5 minutes.

4 Add the melted chocolate mixture and the vanilla. Stir in the flour, salt, and nuts.

5 Pour the batter into the prepared pan and bake for 40 to 45 minutes, or until a wooden toothpick inserted in the center comes out clean.

6 Remove to a rack to cool before cutting the brownies into squares.

MAKES 1⅓ DOZEN BROWNIES

¼ pound unsweetened chocolate
½ cup unsalted butter, at room temperature
4 eggs
2 cups sugar
1 teaspoon vanilla extract
1 cup all-purpose flour
½ teaspoon salt
1½ cups chopped walnuts

Chocolate Truffles

Chocolate truffles are rich bite-size confections that get their name because they look like the extremely expensive underground fungi. Classic chocolate truffles have a chocolate and heavy cream center called a ganache, surrounded by a pure chocolate shell. Then the whole truffle is rolled in cocoa powder or powdered sugar. It is this final step that gives them their charm—the cocoa is like the soil clinging to their namesakes.

⅓ cup heavy cream
2 tablespoons unsalted butter
6 ounces semisweet chocolate, grated, coarsely chopped, or broken into small pieces
Unsweetened cocoa powder
Chopped nuts
Confectioners' sugar

1 In a small saucepan over moderate heat or in the top of a double boiler over simmering water heat the cream and butter, stirring until the butter is melted and the cream just starts to come to a boil; do not let the cream boil.

2 Remove from the heat, add the chocolate, and stir until completely melted.

3 Cover and chill in the refrigerator for at least 2 hours, stirring occasionally, until the mixture is firm.

4 Using a pastry bag or a spoon, make small balls of the chocolate mixture. Roll each ball in cocoa powder, chopped nuts, and confectioners' sugar, or leave as is.

5 Refrigerate in an airtight container until needed. If you have the willpower, let the truffles come to room temperature before serving.

MAKES ABOUT 2 DOZEN TRUFFLES

ABOUT CANDY

Candy is the name given to a large body of bite-size sweets that are usually eaten as a snack but sometimes as a dessert. The ancient Egyptians dipped fruits and nuts in honey. Middle Eastern halvah cut into small pieces has been a popular candy for centuries. Sugar boiled in water and then cooled is known as hard candy or rock candy. Hot maple syrup tossed in the snow is a favorite candy in New England. Almonds and sugar ground into a sweet paste is known as marzipan.

Sugar candies like jawbreakers, peppermint sticks, horehound drops, and lollipops were the everyday candy in England and the United States until the Great Exhibition was held in London in 1851. French cream-filled candies were introduced there and candy took on new meaning. Soon hundreds of fresh candy shops opened in the United States, run mostly by German and French immigrants.

Chocolate-Covered Orange Slices

These orange slices need at least 2 weeks to marinate before they are dipped in chocolate, so remember to allow the time.

3 large navel oranges
3½ cups sugar
1½ cups cold water
⅓ cup dark rum
½ cup confectioners' sugar
2 7-ounce packages almond paste or marzipan
9 ounces semisweet or bittersweet chocolate, finely chopped
1 tablespoon unsalted butter

1 Wash and dry the oranges. Slice the oranges crosswise into ¼-inch-thick disks. Select the 10 largest slices. (Save the remaining slices for another purpose or discard.)

2 In a wide saucepan over medium-high heat bring the sugar and cold water to a boil, swirling the pan until the liquid is clear. Boil the syrup until it reaches 238° F on a candy thermometer (soft-ball stage), about 5 minutes. Reduce the heat to low and add the orange slices. Poach the orange slices gently, stirring occasionally, for 30 minutes, or until the peel is tender and slightly translucent. Gently stir in the rum. Transfer the oranges and their cooking syrup to a dish or bowl. Cover and refrigerate for 2 weeks to 3 months.

3 The day before you plan to finish them, arrange the orange slices on a wire rack placed over a baking sheet. Set aside to drain, uncovered, overnight.

4 Lightly dust a work surface with confectioners' sugar. Knead the almond paste on the work surface until smooth and pliable. Dust the work surface, once again, and a rolling pin with additional confectioners' sugar. Roll out the almond paste to a thickness of ¼ inch.

5 Using the orange slices as your guide, cut out 2 circles of the almond paste to the size of each of the orange slices. Brush one side of each round with a little water. Place each orange slice between the moistened sides of 2 rounds of almond paste. Using a sharp knife, cut each "sandwich" into quarters.

6 In the top of a double boiler melt the chocolate with the butter over barely simmering water. One at a time, drop a sandwich quarter into the chocolate to coat completely. Use a fork to retrieve the candy. Hold the candy on the fork above the pot and allow the excess chocolate to drain off. With a second fork, slide the candy off the first fork onto a wax paper-lined baking sheet. Repeat with the remaining quarters. Place the baking sheet in the refrigerator until set, about 1 hour.

MAKES 3⅓ DOZEN PIECES

ABOUT MARZIPAN

When made correctly, marzipan is a putty that can be shaped into tiny candies that look like anything from bananas to BMWs. Marzipan is made by boiling and rolling the brown skins off almonds, which are then ground and cooked with sugar to get the malleable paste. It is then blended with sugar and egg whites.

Marzipan can be traced back to classical Rome, although some authorities credit the ancient Arabs with introducing this candy. It was popular among the Elizabethan English, who called it "St. Mark's pain" from the French word *pain,* which means "bread." Arabs were very fond of almonds and they planted hundreds of thousands of almond trees in Spain when they ruled there in the Middle Ages. Some of the best marzipan in the world is made in Spain, in the royal city of Toledo. Good marzipan is also made in German-speaking Switzerland and Germany. German marzipan makers, like Niederegger's in the northern city of Lubeck, shape marzipan into figures and symbols to match the different holiday seasons.

Creole Praline Candies

A praline is a candy made from caramelized sugar and almonds or pecans. American Creoles imported the dish from France, where it was invented by the chef of the French diplomat Cesar du Plessis Praslin, who believed that sugar and nuts aided digestion. He may not have been right about that, but pralines are delicious, and are still extremely popular in New Orleans.

1 cup white granulated sugar
1 cup packed light brown sugar
½ cup heavy cream
2 tablespoons unsalted butter
1 cup pecan pieces

1 In a large heavy saucepan combine the sugars, heavy cream, and butter. Cook, uncovered, over medium heat until the mixture boils and registers 238° F on a candy thermometer, or until a sample of the mixture forms a soft ball in cold water.

2 Take the pot off the heat and stir in the pecans. Beat for about 3 minutes or until creamy and somewhat cooled.

3 Drop the mixture by tablespoonfuls onto a double thickness of wax paper. The pralines will harden in about 15 minutes and be ready to eat.

MAKES ABOUT 2 DOZEN CANDIES

Chocolate, Nut, and Raisin Clusters

1 In the top of a double boiler over barely simmering water, melt the chocolate.

2 Stir in the condensed milk.

3 Blend in the almonds and raisins.

4 Drop the mixture by tablespoonfuls onto aluminum foil or parchment paper. Cool until hardened.

MAKES ABOUT 2½ DOZEN CLUSTERS

½ pound semisweet chocolate
⅔ cup sweetened condensed milk
½ cup blanched slivered almonds
½ cup raisins

Breads and Pancakes

Irish Oat and Whole-Wheat Soda Bread

Soda bread, also known as Irish soda bread, is so called because bicarbonate of soda is added to the dough instead of yeast to make the bread rise. Raisins, sultanas, and currants are often added as well as a pinch of sugar and butter.

2½ cups whole-wheat flour
1 cup all-purpose flour
½ cup Irish oatmeal (not the "quick-cooking" type)
½ teaspoon salt
1 teaspoon baking soda
¾ teaspoon baking powder
1½ cups buttermilk

1 Preheat the oven to 375° F. Generously grease a baking sheet.

2 In a bowl combine the dry ingredients. Stir to mix well. Stir in the buttermilk.

3 On a lightly floured surface knead the dough for about 1 minute, until smooth. Shape into an 8-inch round.

4 Place the loaf on the prepared baking sheet. Cut an X about ¾-inch deep into the top with a sharp knife. Bake for 40 minutes. Insert and remove a toothpick to center of loaf. If it comes out clean and dry, the bread is done. Cool on a rack.

MAKES 1 LOAF

ABOUT BAKING SODA AND BAKING POWDER

Baking soda, bicarbonate of soda, and baking powder give off carbon dioxide gas, which fizzes, creates bubbles, and helps baking mixtures rise and get lighter. Baking powder is made of a combination of ingredients and it can be used in more recipes than baking soda. Both baking soda and baking powder should be added to the liquid in the recipe quickly and at the last minute and popped right into the oven or onto the griddle.

Don't substitute baking soda for baking powder indiscriminately; some recipes call for both.

If you run out of baking powder you can substitute as follows:
1 teaspoon baking powder = ½ teaspoon cream of tartar, ½ teaspoon bicarbonate of soda, and ⅛ teaspoon salt.

ABOUT OATS

Oats are the berries of a cultivated grass native to central Europe that was grown as early as the Bronze Age (1500–500 B.C.). Several strains of oats have been developed since then and they grow best in cool, wet climates. Oats are most popular in northern England, Wales, Scotland, Ireland, and North America. Most of the oats we eat are grown in the Dakotas and Minnesota, but 95 percent of all oats are used in animal food.

Oats are the staff of life in Scotland, where they are made into oat porridge, a coarser version of American oatmeal, and used in soups, sausages, and cakes. Haggis, the national dish of Scotland, is oatmeal, organ meats, suet, and herbs stuffed in a sheep's stomach and boiled.

The Irish prefer an oatmeal of dehusked and cracked whole-grain oats. It takes longer to cook and has a nutty taste and chewy texture. John McCann's Irish Oatmeal in the distinctive metal can is an excellent oatmeal. For baking or making cakes in American recipes, use regular Quaker rolled oats.

Cranberry-Orange Bread

2 cups all-purpose flour
1 cup sugar
1 teaspoon baking powder
1 teaspoon salt
½ teaspoon baking soda
1¼ cups coarsely chopped cranberries
1 teaspoon grated orange zest
1 egg
¾ cup fresh orange juice
3 tablespoons vegetable oil

1 Preheat the oven to 350° F. Lightly butter and flour a 9-inch loaf pan.

2 In a large bowl sift together the dry ingredients. Stir in the cranberries and orange zest.

3 In another bowl combine the egg, orange juice, and vegetable oil. Add the flour mixture and stir until completely blended.

4 Pour the batter into the prepared pan. Bake for 1 hour, or until a wooden toothpick inserted into the center of the bread comes out clean.

5 Cool on a rack. Serve slightly warm or at room temperature.

MAKES 1 LOAF

ABOUT BREAD

Bread is the staff of life for many of the world's cultures. It is a primary source of complex carbohydrates, fiber, and B vitamins in Europe, the Middle East, and the Americas. Asian countries rely on rice the way the West relies on bread.

The first bread was probably made of coarsely ground wheat berries that were mixed with a little water, formed into flat cakes, and baked on a rock near a Stone Age cave fire. Early breads were unleavened; these breads are still very popular—matzoh, Scandinavian flatbread, East Indian chapati and roti, Mexican tortillas, and American Indian cakes are all unleavened breads.

Leavened bread can be made out of almost any type of grain flour except corn. Corn lacks gluten and must be mixed with wheat to make bread. Wheat flour, both refined white and whole wheat, is by far the favorite bread flour. Rye flour is popular in Scandinavian and eastern European countries.

LOAVES AND WISHES

Wheat grain was first cultivated in the Nile Valley, where the first yeast was probably discovered and put to use. Yeast occurs naturally in the air and some of it probably fell on a piece of unleavened bread and caused it to rise. Besides being of nutritional value, bread is also associated with the spiritual and reproductive elements of human culture. In ancient Greece, the goddess Demeter and her daughter Persephone were the gods of the harvest, grain, and bread. Some brides find pieces of bread in their shoes to ensure a fruitful marriage. In some cultures, bread-baking is synonymous with bearing children.

The use of bread in religion is extensive. Jesus broke bread and fed it to his disciples at the Last Supper, a ritual that exists today as communion. The Jewish sabbath bread challah is a symbol of a ladder to God. Hot cross buns are baked at Easter, and a loaf of round bread signifies the continuity of life.

ABOUT CRANBERRIES

Cranberries are tart red berries and were harvested in the bogs of eastern Massachusetts and Cape Cod by the Pequot and Narragansett Indians long before the colonists touched land at Provincetown.

The Dutch gave cranberries their name after the word *kranbeere*. Commercial cultivation of cranberries began on Cape Cod in 1816. New Jersey, Wisconsin, and Oregon are also major producers. Cranberries are harvested between Labor Day and Halloween, and although there is no proof, the Indians probably brought cranberries to the first Thanksgiving.

Nutritionally, cranberries are a very good source of vitamin C and fiber. They are low in calories, but because they are commonly cooked in sugar to compensate for their tart nature, most preparations end up fairly high in calories.

Banana Bread

The rich banana flavor that is the hallmark of this bread is a result of the long baking at a relatively low oven temperature.

3½ cups all-purpose flour
2 tablespoons baking soda
¼ teaspoon salt
5 very ripe medium bananas, peeled and sliced
2½ cups sugar
4 eggs
½ cup vegetable oil
1 cup buttermilk

1 Preheat the oven to 275° F. Place an oven rack in the center of the oven. Lightly butter and flour two 9- ×5- ×3-inch loaf pans.

2 On a sheet of wax paper stir together the flour, baking soda, and salt.

3 In a food processor or blender combine the bananas, sugar, eggs, oil, and buttermilk until well blended. Stir in the dry ingredients.

4 Divide the mixture between the prepared pans and bake for 2½ hours. Insert a toothpick to center of loaf; if it comes out clean, the bread is done. Turn out onto a rack and slice to serve.

MAKES 2 LOAVES

ABOUT BANANAS

The banana is originally from India and southeast Asia and is one of the oldest fruits harvested and cultivated by man. In many parts of the tropics, banana is a staple starch crop and it is eaten in place of rice or bread. Banana plants were brought to North Africa, the Canary Islands, the West Indies, and the Americas in the fifteenth and sixteenth centuries. Honduras, Guatemala, and Costa Rica are the main banana exporters to the United States.

There is often confusion about bananas because they are also known as plantains. For American purposes, bananas are sweet yellow-skinned fruits (they are actually berries). Plantains are the nonsweet green-skinned fruits that are part of West Indian and Hispanic cuisine. Plantains are larger than yellow bananas, and they should be cooked, either boiled or fried. An extremely sweet and creamy variety of banana is that of the Spanish Canary Islands off the coast of Morocco. These are sometimes no larger than a thumb.

Jalapeño Corn Bread

1 Preheat the oven to 375° F. Butter a 9-inch square baking pan and set aside.

2 In a mixing bowl whisk the eggs with the milk until well blended. Stir in the corn, onion, peppers, and cornmeal. Add 1½ cups Cheddar cheese, along with the oil and salt. Add the flour and baking powder and mix until well combined.

3 Scrape the mixture into the prepared pan and smooth the top. Sprinkle with the remaining ½ cup cheese. Bake for 45 minutes, until cooked through. Cook on a rack before serving.

MAKES 8 SERVINGS

NOTE: The very best corn bread is made in a hot, greased cast-iron skillet. Preheat the oven. Put the oil in the skillet and put the skillet in the oven for 15 minutes. Add the batter and bake. The corn bread will be crunchy and brown on the outside and perfectly done in the center.

3 eggs
1 cup milk
2 cups chopped cooked corn (fresh, canned, or frozen)
1 medium onion, grated
1 red bell pepper, seeded and diced
1 or 2 jalapeño peppers, chopped
1 cup yellow cornmeal
2 cups shredded sharp Cheddar cheese
⅓ cup corn oil
1½ teaspoons salt
1 cup all-purpose flour
2 teaspoons baking powder

ABOUT CORN BREAD

Corn bread, sometimes known as corn pone, is made from the ground dried kernels of sweet corn plants that are specially hybridized for cornmeal. The kind of corn bread we eat now always has some wheat flour in it because cornmeal doesn't rise well.

The earliest corn bread was made by American Indians hundreds of years before Columbus sailed to the New World. Early corn bread was made by mixing crudely ground corn with water and baking it on a flat rock by the fire. This method of making corn cakes was picked up by New Englanders and is still practiced in Connecticut and Rhode Island.

In general, white corn is preferred by Southerners and Rhode Islanders. Yellow corn is preferred by other New Englanders, Midwesterners, and Texans. Boston brown bread has a high proportion of yellow cornmeal.

Bran Muffins

2 eggs
¼ cup packed light brown sugar
1 cup milk
¼ cup vegetable oil
1½ cups bran cereal (such as Bran Buds)
½ cup unprocessed bran
1 cup all-purpose flour
2 teaspoons baking powder
½ cup raisins (optional)

1 Preheat the oven to 375° F. Grease 12 muffin cups, or use foil baking cups or paper baking cups sprayed with nonstick cooking spray.

2 In a medium bowl beat the eggs and brown sugar until smooth. Whisk in the milk and oil. Stir in the bran cereal. Set aside to soak for 2 minutes.

3 Fold in the unprocessed bran, flour, baking powder, and raisins, if desired.

4 Divide the batter among the muffin cups. Bake for 20 to 25 minutes, or until the muffins are brown and firm. Cool on a wire rack.

MAKES 1 DOZEN MUFFINS

ABOUT BRAN

Bran is the rough outer hull of the whole wheat berry. Whole-wheat flour is brown because it contains the bran of the wheat; white flour has had the bran removed.

Bran is high in B vitamins and minerals. But it is most highly prized because of its high fiber content. Bran has for a long time been used as "roughage" or "bulk" because it helps keep people's digestive tracts regular. Scientists now see that a diet high in bran and dietary fiber is effective in helping to lower blood cholesterol levels and lower the risk of heart attack.

Yorkshire Pudding

Classic Yorkshire pudding is a kind of English soufflé made with the pan juices of the traditional Sunday roast beef; in fact, it is a closer culinary relative to a popover. After the roast—which the English call a joint—is cooked and removed from the pan, a wheat flour, egg, and milk batter is dropped directly into the pan on top of the hot beef fat and juices. The pan is returned quickly to the oven and the Yorkshire pudding is baked until it is puffed and browned. The pudding is cut into squares and served along with the beef, potatoes, and other trimmings.

1 Preheat the oven to 400° F.

2 In a bowl whisk together the flour, salt, and eggs until smooth. Slowly whisk in the milk to make a smooth batter.

3 Coat 10 standard-size muffin cups each with ½ teaspoon vegetable oil. Place the muffin tin in the oven to preheat for 10 minutes.

4 Remove the tin from the oven and divide the batter among the oiled cups, filling each about three-quarters of the way full.

5 Bake in the center of the oven for about 25 minutes, or until each pudding is puffed and browned.

MAKES 10 SERVINGS

1 cup all-purpose flour
Pinch of salt
2 eggs
1 cup milk
5 teaspoons vegetable oil

Whole-Wheat Applesauce Muffins

2 cups whole-wheat flour
2 teaspoons baking powder
1 teaspoon ground cinnamon
¼ teaspoon salt
2 eggs
½ cup dark brown sugar
1½ cups unsweetened
   applesauce (see sidebar)
¼ cup vegetable oil

1 Preheat the oven to 375° F. Grease 12 muffin cups, or use foil baking cups or paper baking cups sprayed with nonstick cooking spray.

2 In a large bowl thoroughly mix the dry ingredients.

3 In another bowl combine the eggs, sugar, applesauce, and oil. Whisk until well blended. Pour over the dry ingredients and fold in just until moistened.

4 Divide the batter among the muffin cups. Bake for 20 to 25 minutes, or until brown and springy when touched in the center. Turn out on a rack to cool.

MAKES 1 DOZEN MUFFINS

WHAT'S COOKING TIPS: MAKING MUFFINS

There are a few things to remember for successful American muffin making.

1. The liquid ingredients and the dry ingredients need to be mixed in separate bowls and then combined at the last minute.
2. The combined ingredients should be quickly beaten, no more than 15 to 20 strokes. Overbeaten muffins will be hard; underbeaten will be too crumbly.
3. The muffins must be placed in the oven as soon as possible because the action of the baking powder has a limited life span.
4. Muffins should be allowed to cool in their pans before being removed for serving.

EASY APPLESAUCE

Applesauce is a cooked puree of fresh apples, usually flavored with cinnamon, cloves, nutmeg, or other sweet spices. A type of applesauce was first noted in a recipe book that was compiled in 1390 by the chefs of England's King Richard II. Later, applesauce was made in huge kettles by the American colonists and preserved as an important food source through the winter.

The flavor of applesauce can be varied not only by the spices that are added but also by the types of apples used to make the sauce. Sweet Golden Delicious apples produce a pale sweet sauce that needs no sugar to cut the tang. It is easy to make applesauce at home with fresh apples. You'll end up with a fresh and individualized sauce made just to your taste.

To make applesauce, simply core the apples, chop them coarsely, and cook them over low heat with a little water added for 20 minutes or until they are soft. Puree them in a food processor. Sweeten and season as you like.

Oatmeal-Raisin Sunflower Seed Muffins

1 cup all-purpose flour
1 cup old-fashioned rolled oats (not the "quick-cooking" type)
¾ cup raisins
½ cup sunflower seeds
½ cup light brown sugar
2 teaspoons baking powder
½ teaspoon salt
½ cup milk
1 egg, lightly beaten
2 tablespoons unsalted butter or margarine, melted and cooled
2 tablespoons vegetable oil
2 teaspoons vanilla extract

1 Preheat the oven to 375° F. Grease 10 muffin cups, or use foil baking cups or paper baking cups sprayed with nonstick cooking spray.

2 In a large bowl combine the flour, oats, raisins, sunflower seeds, sugar, baking powder, and salt.

3 In another bowl mix the milk, egg, butter or margarine, oil, and vanilla until blended.

4 Make a well in the center of the dry ingredients. Add the milk mixture and stir just to combine.

5 Spoon the batter into the prepared muffin cups. Bake for 15 to 20 minutes, or until a wooden toothpick inserted in the center of a muffin comes out clean.

6 Cool the muffin tin on a wire rack for 5 minutes before removing the muffins.

MAKES 10 MUFFINS

ABOUT SUNFLOWER SEEDS

Sunflower seeds are dried seeds that grow on the big yellow flower of a sunflower plant. Anybody who has driven through Kansas in August knows what a sunflower is. Fields of sunflowers are grown there the way corn is grown in Iowa. The seeds in their shells are packed tightly in the face of the sunflower. The harvesting machines chop down the dried and mature sunflower plants and separate the seeds from the stems.

Sunflower seeds are very high in polyunsaturated oil that is squeezed out and bottled as sunflower oil. It is a fine, mild-tasting vegetable oil that is good for salads or cooking. Sunflower seeds are a good source of protein and if they are unsalted they are low in sodium.

ABOUT OAT NUTRITION

Researchers say that eating oatmeal can lower your cholesterol level and help prevent heart disease. Researchers at Northwestern University in Chicago tested over 200 men and women. They found that by feeding the group just 2 ounces of oatmeal or oat bran per day, cholesterol levels dropped by almost 5 percent in a matter of weeks.

Two cups of hot oatmeal or 2 oat muffins contain about 2 ounces of oat fiber and it is the fiber in the oats that seems to lower the cholesterol level. Soluble fiber forms a gel as it moves through the body, and it is this gel that seems to affect cholesterol. Oats are one of the best sources of soluble fiber in the American diet.

Cheddar Cheese Crackers

2 cups all-purpose flour
1 cup unsalted butter, softened
1 pound Cheddar cheese, finely shredded
1½ teaspoons salt
¼ teaspoon cayenne pepper

1 In the bowl of an electric mixer cream together all of the ingredients to make a well-mixed dough.

2 Divide the dough in half and roll each half into a 12- to 15-inch-long tube, about 1½ inches in diameter. Wrap each roll in aluminum foil and place on a baking sheet. Refrigerate for 3 hours or longer.

3 Preheat the oven to 350° F. Lightly butter and flour 2 baking sheets.

4 Unwrap the chilled dough and cut each tube into ¼-inch-thick disks. Place the disks on the sheets and bake for 15 to 18 minutes, or until golden brown. Transfer to racks to cool.

MAKES 8 DOZEN CRACKERS

NOTE: These Cheddar cheese crackers will keep for a week in an airtight container. Or, the dough can be made 3 to 4 days ahead, wrapped tightly, and chilled until you are ready to bake them.

Sour Cream Waffles

1 In a medium bowl whisk together the eggs, sugar, and vanilla. Whisk in the sour cream, milk, and melted butter.

2 In a second bowl stir together the flour, baking powder, and salt. Add to the whisked mixture and blend to make a smooth batter.

3 Preheat a waffle iron. If the iron does not have a nonstick surface, oil it lightly. Pour in about ½ cup of batter for each waffle and cook according to the manufacturer's directions, until golden brown on both sides. Serve with jam and/or sour cream.

MAKES 8 SERVINGS

3 eggs
3 tablespoons sugar
1 teaspoon vanilla extract
1½ cups sour cream
½ cup milk
½ cup unsalted butter, melted
1½ cups all-purpose flour
1½ teaspoons baking powder
    Pinch of salt
    Jam and/or sour cream

Low-Fat, High-Fiber Pancakes

2 egg whites
¼ cup unbleached white flour
¾ cup whole-wheat flour
¼ teaspoon baking powder
1 cup skim milk

1 In a bowl beat the egg whites until stiff.
2 In another bowl combine the flours and baking powder. Add the milk and stir with a fork to make a smooth batter.
3 Gently fold the egg whites into the batter.
4 Preheat a nonstick skillet. Spoon the batter by ¼ cupfuls onto the skillet. Cook until bubbles form on the pancakes or the edges turn brown, then flip the pancakes over and cook for 1 minute more.

MAKES 8 PANCAKES

ABOUT FIBER

Fiber is indigestible vegetable cellulose that is also known as roughage or bulk. Bran, the outer husk of wheat berries, is a well-known fiber; fresh vegetables, whole grains, fruits, nuts, and seeds are other good sources. Meat, eggs, cheese, and milk are poor sources of fiber. In general, the more refined your diet is, the less fiber you get. The American low-fiber diet is one reason why scientists think we have a high incidence of colon and rectal cancers. The digestive system is just not getting enough fiber to keep digested food moving through the body.

Index

Page numbers in boldface refer to recipes.